THE TOM REPORT

Road Dog Publications was formed in 2010 as an imprint dedicated to publishing the best in books on motorcycling and adventure travel. Visit us at www.roaddogpub.com.

No part of this book may be reproduced by any means, nor transmitted, nor translated into a machine language, without the written permission of the publishers.

Editors: Lynn Reuter and Mike Fitterling

ISBN 978-1-890623-82-1
Library of Congress Control Number: 2022930403

An Imprint of Lost Classics Book Company
This book also available in eBook format at online booksellers. ISBN 978-1-890623-83-8

THE TOM REPORT

SEATTLE TO SANTIAGO ON MOTORCYCLE

by

Tom Reuter

Publisher
Lake Wales, Florida

This book is dedicated to my grandmothers, Bitsey and Grandma, whose literary prowess inspired and motivated me throughout both of their lives. They will both be missed forever.

About the Author

Tom Reuter remains most proud to be a Washingtonian, an Eagle Scout, and a Zag.

He was diagnosed with multiple sclerosis shortly after returning home from this South American motorcycle adventure. Modern medicine and healthy living have kept him running, playing, and laughing every day since then. A healthy dose of perspective from nine months on the Pan-American Highway is what really got him through it. That and the love of his wife, Julia.

Tom and Julia now live near Tacoma, Washington. Having grown up in both Mexico and Alaska, Julia is the love of Tom's life. They spend their time with family, friends, and in the great outdoors almost exclusively. A barbeque, mountainside, or beach are where you will find them.

Hiking, skiing, and kiteboarding keep Tom focused on making memories and having fun to this day. His DR650 sees less action, but it's always ready for the next adventure.

CONTENTS

To Recount

My single fear at Gonzaga University's 2009 graduation ceremony was that the following four decades would only increase my workload and responsibilities until some wrung-out retirement party. My ambition for academic advancement and career growth had been sapped from straight As in high school and a 3.7 GPA in college. Like many young graduates, I had no clue where I would fit into the professional world as the ink dried on my degree. So, with the Great Recession taking its strangle hold on the job market anyway, I accepted an offer as a windsurfing instructor. Over the course of a weekend, I revamped my Subaru into a recreational vehicle and drove straight to the West Coast's windsurfing capitol in Hood River, Oregon.

Hood River was my first taste of the road as I traded my calculator and notepads for a surfboard and sandals that summer. I bathed in the river and camped on the beach for my first two weeks of employment while learning the ropes. Eventually, I called a county park home for a month and in July, I even convinced my friend to let me pitch a tent in her backyard. Every morning I would wake up with the sun, stretch in the grass over morning coffee, and report to the water for my nine-to-five in an Eagle Scout's dream come true.

That fall I returned home to Washington and signed on with Mount Baker Ski Area, outside of Bellingham, where a barrage of early season snowfall progressed my skiing talents to the point of savagery until January, when I was diagnosed with a sports hernia. Ski season was all but over by the time I recovered from subsequent surgery, at which point I was broke, out of shape, and bored with a minimum wage anyway. I wanted to do something bigger on my next adventure, and I listened intently when my friend, Alex, pitched his idea for a motorcycle trip around the world.

Alex and I had been lifelong buddies, dating all the way back to Cub Scouts in second grade. I'd been just as close to his inseparable twin brother, Andy. Andy and Alex had always been oversized for their age, standing a foot taller than the rest of us, with an extra thirty pounds each. Their testosterone levels had been equally overpowered too, leading to many wild and outrageous memories for anyone given the opportunity to experience their endless boasting, betting, and bickering while growing up. Whether they were constructing pipe bombs in their dad's garage, mounting homemade PVC Jet Ski racks to the top of their hand-sawed topless Geo, or swan diving off ninety-foot cliffs at Banks Lake in Eastern Washington, Alex and Andy had constantly pushed each other's mental and physical limits.

One weekend in October 2008, Andy flew to a skydiving meet in Idaho with some of his friends from the local flight club, and that Sunday their Cessna Grand Caravan failed to check back in on its flight path over the stormy Cascade Mountains. Images of Andy's sobbing girlfriend plastered local and national headlines the following day when the aircraft's fuselage was found with one hundred percent confirmed casualty rate. Although this was my first experience with death, I was shielded from its darkest valleys at the time, due to Gonzaga's distance from home and the distraction of my new college environment. It was Alex who was forced to confront the finality that followed in wake. Grieving his best friend and only brother at an unknowable level, Alex took a year off from college at Western Washington University to travel across the USA in a van and then backpack across Peru. He returned to school in Bellingham, Washington, in 2010, and it was there, during my surgical recovery, that he and I reconnected meaningfully for the first time since Andy's death.

Talk of the motorcycle trip started over drinks on some dreary February evening when Alex and I met up in Bellingham during his final quarter at WWU. Not nearly done globe-trotting yet, Al swore up and down that his coupe de grâce would be to ride all the way around the world on a dual-sport motorcycle with his girlfriend, Kristi, after graduation. He planned to start in 2012 with a loop to Alaska, then ride through Central and South America to Buenos Aires, freight to Cape Town, and continue up through Africa to Eurasia and Australia. Al never stated explicitly that his determination was tied to Andy, but I understood it regardless, as he explained the itinerary over and over again.

His urgency found a captive audience in me as we connected more frequently, and I began to understand his seriousness. Al's proposal harnessed both my keen disrespect for the future and my meticulous enthusiasm for hard work and planning. Additionally, his $50,000 savings target was a welcome alternative to my previous year without purpose or direction. Getting behind Al's idea would allow me to apply myself again, while still disregarding the chains of life. Plus, it was just pleasant to be hanging out with one of the twins again. The more Alex talked, the more I was enthralled.

Fifty grand was admittedly a lot of money for two broke college graduates, but Alex had a solution for that too. He had been working for a local third-party contract delivery outfit during college, and that spring he got me hired to the Bellingham Office Depot commercial route. We each saved aggressively and bought Suzuki DR650s as our trip built momentum. I had never ridden a motorcycle before, but I took to the raw power quickly in the North Cascades' logging roads that summer. My commitment to ride to the ends of the Earth cemented completely in August as my bank account rolled to five digits for the first time in my life.

Our boss had two types of contracts. There were stable local routes like Office Depot, and there were the coveted two-person Home Depot Rapid Response positions, which popped up randomly around the country whenever long-term drivers were fired. The lucrative Rapid Response scab contracts required a CDL, which Alex had earned already. Alex transferred to Rapid Response in Juneau, Alaska, for higher pay right after his graduation. The route required an assistant, and he contracted Kristi to help him from August to September, allowing the two of them to save double for their increased expenses. I was given orders to replace her on October first, when Kristi flew home for her junior year of undergrad.

My new position as Alex's assistant was effective immediately according to our boss, who had waited until the last minute to notify me of the backfill plan. I packed up my life again over the course of a weekend and flew north that Sunday for six-day work weeks delivering appliances and materials on the last frontier.

I adapted well and learned fast in Juneau. I trained on-the-job, learned Shito Ryu karate, and earned my own CDL over the next eight weeks. All the while, Alex and I each banked $1,200 a week, which stoked enthusiasm morning, noon, and night for our adventure. The collaboration lasted until December first, at which point I was promoted to my own Home Depot contract in Fairbanks, just a day after my CDL certification. On Friday I learned of the reassignment, on Saturday I packed, and on Sunday I flew further north—yet again over the course of a weekend.

My greatest test ever lay ahead in Fairbanks, where I trained three different assistants while tolerating a spitefully cranky coordinator amidst -30F degree average Arctic temperatures. Crunching across the tundra day after day, I never wore less than five layers and seldom felt all my toes or fingers for the next two months. The Alaskan winter was so cold that my exposed skin would break into frozen blood blisters upon the touch of metal (which was an abundant element in both driving trucks and delivering appliances). My nostrils would freeze with ice, my pee would shatter at my feet, and my twenty-three-year-old joints ached throughout the day.

Confined to the indoors while off the clock, on account of such conditions, I encountered unimaginable states of boredom and obsession in Fairbanks. The sun peaked barely a sliver over the southern horizon and only for twenty minutes during, literally, my darkest night at winter equinox. It was the furthest I'd ever felt from home.

Dad told me I'd built character when I returned home for a brief vacation at the end of January after four months of hard Alaskan labor, but all I cared about was the money. I'd exceeded my own savings goals in hoarding ninety percent of my income that winter. I relished the progress as I hit the slopes and tinkered on my bike at home, but everything turned upside down when my boss announced that all present and future jobs were canceled indefinitely due to contract dispute.

Alex was sent home from Juneau ten days later, and we both went feverishly to our spreadsheets in his parents' basement to regroup as soon as he deplaned. We looked at each other nervously with a half-empty bottle of tequila between us after crunching the numbers that night.

Our 'round the world budgets had been based off our $1,200 a week Rapid Response incomes for the next eighteen months. Neither of us could make that kind of money anywhere else in such short time. Meanwhile, Kristi still had well over a year until her graduation. When the bottle hit empty at midnight, we came to the only realistic decision—

Al and I would leave early for México with the savings that we had, and Kristi would fly down during her summer break.

"This is the opportunity we've been waiting for, regardless of how we planned it," Alex confirmed that night over the last of our drinks. "Kristi knows that it really is the best that we can do."

We set our start date for my twenty-fourth birthday, April second, and prepared fanatically for the subsequent month until Saturday, at which point I sat alone on Camano Island's Madrona Beach and stared questioningly into a Puget Sound sunset with less than a week until departure.

I had $20,000 in the bank, my schedule was wiped indefinitely, and my motorcycle waited in the garage, but the precipice of my destiny overwhelmed me, regardless, as dusk consumed the horizon. I'd been on the road for so long since that first taste of freedom back in Hood River—non-stop for two years seeking adrenaline, cash, or character across Oregon, Washington, and Alaska. I'd had one hell of a ride already. I had to wonder.

"Why not just hang up the cleats for a season? Maybe meet a girl and build my career for a bit? $20,000 could go a long way at home too," I mused aloud on the beach.

Then as the sun's deep orange radiance slipped behind the Olympic Range, I closed my eyes and found myself suddenly at peace. The familiar twilight left behind was a goodbye from the land I loved, and an open invitation to come home when ready. I was prepared to live completely in the moment from that point forward. The extreme solitude of Alaska had taught me that I had a lot to live for in Washington with my loving family, dynamic friends, and all the comforts of the most beautiful place on Earth. Why was I leaving willfully?

Well, Mom had always said that I'd watched one too many *Indiana Jones* movies as a kid, and she was right! This was my chance to follow a childhood dream. Not many people grew up to be who they wanted, but here I was staring down Harrison Ford in the mirror, and it was time to pick up the whip.

GEAR

Lake Stevens, Washington
Thursday, March 31st, 2011

"We're going to be unstoppable," Alex and I agreed after final bike modifications in Dad's garage on Wednesday. We'd chosen Suzuki DR650s because they were simple, reliable, and strong, with carbureted thumpers pushing fifty horsepower and ground clearance equal to most pickups. Their design was so durable and adaptable that Suzuki hadn't altered it since 1996, which was why adventurers worldwide revered the DR as "the perfect overland machine". My 2008 like-new DR650 was ready for any conceivable obstacle, given the alterations that we'd completed. Since purchasing her for $3,500 in Boise the prior year, I'd amassed quite a few farkles:

4.9-gallon gas tank
Corbin seat
Engine guard
Raised handlebars
Lowered foot pegs
Front and rear suspension springs
Heated handgrips

Hand guards
Windscreen
Aluminum panniers with steel racks
Pelican rear case with quick release
Shinko dirt tires with heavy-duty tubes
Extended fuel mixture screw
Upgraded air filter and secondary breather
Auxiliary lights

I'd modified everything but the engine itself to make my bike fit better and ride harder. Raised bars, lowered pegs, and an upgraded saddle allowed my 6'2" frame to sit securely in an upright riding position. Hand guards, heated grips, and the windscreen permitted long-haul comfort. Additional front and rear spring upgrades kept the suspension firm and high under the oversized tank and aftermarket luggage. With everything installed that afternoon, all she needed was a name.

"Thirio," I said to Alex as we wiped the grease off our hands. "I'm going to call her Thirio for The Horse I Rode In On."

"Whatever man," Alex replied. "Let's load them up."

Part of riding a motorcycle was maintaining it, and Alex and I knew we would not get far without the right tools. Our personal kits included an assortment of spanners, sockets, and Allen wrenches. We also had vice grips, pliers, screwdrivers, three tire irons, a tire pump, and tube repair supplies. For spares we had amassed an extra quart of oil, several filters, four spark plugs, a front sprocket, a master chain link, various gaskets, two tubes, and a can of chain wax each.

"Throw in the stock Suzuki toolkits and we have everything short the Jaws of Life!" Al exclaimed as we piled it all into our panniers.

He and I packed for a glorified Boy Scout expedition with the rest of our limited space. We expected to camp frequently, so a tent, sleeping bag, sleeping pad, pillow, sit pad, and cooking pot was stowed in one of my side boxes (Alex had the stove). My backpack, ten essentials, toiletries, towel, trowel, netbook, and iPod fit snugly in the other atop the tools. Minimal day-to-day clothing suited for all climates, seasons, and elevations rounded out the last of my worldly possessions in the Pelican case on Thirio's tail. After loading everything at once for the first time, Alex and I were ready to test the bikes at full hilt.

We slipped into our premium Rev'It Cayenne Pro riding suits. My high thirst for adventure came with a low tolerance for risk, and personal protection was paramount. Completely armored, three-layer waterproofed, and zipper-connected, my brand-new motorcycle jacket and pants would be warm down to freezing when fully lined and wearable up to 100F degrees when emptied and vented. I had two sets of riding gloves and calf-high logging boots for my fingers and toes. Last, but not least of course, was my Shoei Hornet helmet.

"All the gear, all the time" was our motto regarding these outfits.

Alex and I confirmed it to each other again after a successful test ride that evening before separating to our parents' homes with just three days until departure.

"See you Saturday morning."

On Thursday, I battened down my final hatches. On Friday, I said goodbye to Mom, Dad, and my sister, Lynn, over dinner. Everything was settled nicely when my head hit the pillow that evening at T-minus ten hours before takeoff. After several tosses and turns in bed, though, I acknowledged one last unresolved issue.

I wouldn't have been able to tell a sprocket from a gasket without Alex's help and guidance over the past twelve months, but now thanks to him I understood gear ratios, combustible engines, and complex mechanics. Alex was the backbone to our trip's successful launch.

He and I had earned Eagle Scout, graduated high school, and become Alaskan together through the years, but that didn't mean that we always got along. Al's mathematically inclined long-windedness could put even the best listener in a bad mood on the wrong day. Meanwhile, his aggression in arguments grew often unreasonable. Al did not like to be overlooked either, and plus, he still had thirty pounds on me at 6'6".

I figured it best to set the record straight with one simple Facebook post that night and give him credit where it was due. It ended neatly with the following statement:

"You're the expert Alex, and I'm just the one guy crazy enough to trust you."

POSSE IN EFFECT

Glendale, California
Tuesday, April 5th, 2011

I couldn't help but cry as I pulled out of the driveway with Mom, Dad, and Lynn waving goodbye. Then after meeting at his house, Alex and I hit the road excitedly to eight hours of onset drizzle on Saturday.

"Not bad for Day One," Al remarked when we arrived in Eugene, Oregon. "At least our waterproof liners held dry and our bikes got over forty mpg as expected."

We spent that night with Dad's childhood friend from Wisconsin, who was also named Tom. Despite our best intentions to go to bed on time, we woke up extra groggy after partying with Tom until midnight. Alex and I reminisced of the wild night on Sunday evening as we set out tents in the woods of Big Sur.

Hoping that Highway 101 would continue to deliver pleasant coastal S-curves across fields of American dreams like it had in the north, I was disappointed to encounter three hundred and fifty miles of freeway traffic south of the San Francisco. I felt the miles when we arrived in Glendale, California, on Tuesday, wincing with every movement from sunburn, sore back, and tired neck as I peeled off my armor.

"That's alright mate; there'll be plenty more aches and pains along the way. You're just getting started!" our new acquaintance, Charlie, jested from across the dinner table that evening.

Charlie was the reason we'd stopped in Glendale. He was an Australian rider who'd happened to be starting his own motorcycle adventure for Argentina at the same time. Charlie and Alex had met online via the ADVrider forums, and the three of us hit it off splendidly over a round of pitchers.

"Gentlemen, seeing how you two speak Spanish, and I'm 16,000 kilometers from home, what do you say we cross into México together?" Charlie proposed as we paid our checks.

With our common ambition for southbound international motorcycling, it was natural to band together. Everyone raised his drink and clinked in the center to form a motorcycle posse. New friendships and unexpected opportunities were unfolding after just four days on the road, and already I could sense the same excitement that I'd first encountered in Hood River. This was the freedom that I'd worked so hard to recapture.

BORDER CROSSINGS AND BEER

Ensenada, México
Friday, April 8th, 2011

"I reckon traffic will be shit at this hour," Charlie remarked as we mounted up Wednesday, "but don't worry, that's why you Yanks invented lane splitting."

Lane splitting is when a motorcycle passes between side-by-side cars on the freeway over the dotted white line. Insane in its own right, the maneuver's difficulty is only compounded with two huge panniers. Nevertheless, Alex and I managed to follow Charlie's confident lead as he threaded Southern California's gauntlet that afternoon.

Charlie's brand-new Yamaha Teneré 660 was a true head turner on account of its not being available on the American market. Meanwhile, the twenty-eight-year-old Aussie turned out to be charismatically assertive, mechanically inclined, and mentally tough. He was a cheeky bastard too—always quick with a dirty joke or an Australian colloquialism.

"Ten years of industrial mining has given me a lot of good material," he joked on Thursday morning as we packed for México.

Charlie had the self-assured demeanor of a terrier and the quick-witted cadence of Ricky Gervais. He was young enough to remain on our level, and old enough to remain one step ahead too.

"Alright mates, the first of us to score with a Mexican girl gets free drinks for a week."

"That's not fair!" Alex rejected. "I got a girlfriend homie; you got to make this interesting for me."

"Too bad, Alex. It appears a lot of this trip will be less interesting for you then," Charlie laughed as we pulled away.

Half an hour later, Charlie, Alex, and I slowed in the far left lane as we approached the border on southbound I-5. Over a single speed bump we hopped gingerly into the chaotic streets of Tijuana without stopping.

"Don't you Yanks tout that as the most secure border in the world?" Charlie yelled over the bikes as we integrated into the swirl of foreign traffic ahead.

I soon learned that Mexicans liked to honk horns and change lanes at random through a mile of flurried congestion. Mexican traffic was like nothing I'd experienced.

"See, Tom, all that lane splitting was just a crash course!" Alex gasped on the shoulder at our first chance to regroup after a series of three-lane roundabouts. "Now where the hell do we get our immigration papers?"

Charlie, Alex, and I had anticipated an aggressive proof of entry process to obtain proper documentation at the border, and the last thing we wanted was to start in our first new country with screwy paperwork (there would be plenty of opportunity for that down the road). The only solution that we could agree upon was to return to the border and try again.

"We'll ask American customs what to do."

Contrasting to the wide-open freeway leaving the United States, the line out of México was a half-mile long when we arrived at its end, and a swarm of insistent vendors surrounded us immediately as we parked. Uninterested in their solicitation, Charlie, Alex, and I circled up to ignore their advertisements initially, but we opened up quickly when it became clear that the street salesmen were not actually pushing merchandise.

Instead they were ushering us forward through the traffic, parting the cars ahead to clear the way so that all we had to do was hop a curb, cross fifty feet of donkey path, and duck a guard rope to be next in line for customs.

"Apparently, there are benefits to motorcycling in México," the three of us agreed as we waved goodbye to them from the front after the commotion. "As there should be, considering the way they drive so recklessly around us!"

The light turned green at our booth ahead.

"That was a short stay gentlemen," our US Customs agent chuckled upon hearing our dilemma. "Just take the right-hand lane for Mexican Customs on your next pass. Until then, welcome back!"

Charlie, Alex, and I looped around and stamped as legal aliens into México on our second entry. We headed sixty miles south along the Baja coast to Ensenada with our affairs in order. Ensenada was a natural choice for our first night abroad, considering the port's constant cruise ship tourism. It was also where we'd planned to meet with another motorcyclist named Megan, whom Alex had encountered online like he had Charlie just days prior. We found her there in the hotel lot as expected.

"I bet we had you worried at how late we are, but you should have seen the Tijuana border," Alex greeted Megan upon our arrival as she looked up casually from beside her Yamaha XT225 that evening.

"Nah, I know how it goes. I crossed two weeks ago on my way to San Felipe. Welcome to México!" she replied. "Go ahead and stow your valuables in the room, and then let's go get tacos."

Megan fit in cordially as the four of us got acquainted over delicious one-dollar tacos. A twenty-six year old Colorado native, she absorbed our male mentality, language, and odors surprisingly well too—especially considering our tight quarters. Thursday's hotel packed two beds, a bathroom, and a kitchen into its hundred square foot area. On top of that, the beds were lumpy, the air conditioner didn't work, and my pillow was actually a couch cushion with a case. I was in too much of a taco coma to notice any of those creature discomforts when my head hit the pillow that night, though, at least until 3AM when I awoke to the sound of Moctezuma's Revenge in the bathroom next to me.

"For the sake of God!" Charlie's muffled voice murmured forlornly between explosions from behind the door.

For the better part of the next hour, I had the pleasure of hearing the expulsion of his remaining inner demons.

"All yours mate," he whimpered finally at 3:45AM, emerging with a wry grin. "But you might want to give it a couple minutes."

I rolled to my other side to find Alex's bed just inches away and his ass in my face. It was safe to say that we were getting to know each other quickly on the road. Surprisingly, Megan had not cut and run by the following morning.

THE GOD-KING BLEEDS

Rosario, México
Sunday, April 10, 2011

Alex got a hair up his ass to cook some beans from the Rosario mercado atop his brand-new camp stove on Sunday. Feeling cocky, he also ignored everyone's vocal suggestions to cook outside, pour a bucket of water, or even place an aluminum pan under the diesel-fueled apparatus. Instead, Al insisted on testing his Whisperlight MSR for the first time right on the Turista Hotel bathroom counter.

"Don't worry. I know what I'm doing," he argued.

With the flick of his lighter, the entire device went up in flames due to too much fuel being pumped into its reservoir basin. Alex dove onto the not-so-proverbial grenade by lifting the flaming fuel canister and sprinting immediately out the door, at which point I was the closest bystander to deal with the residual inferno that had leaked onto the counter. Grabbing the closest object in sight, I brandished a hotel towel against three-foot indoor flames until they were extinguished.

The room still smelled like gasoline when the smoke eventually cleared, but in the end, it was Al's ego that ended up most severely burnt that day. It wasn't just the fire that had bruised his image, either, because that same afternoon Alex had also walked away from a fifty mile per hour low-side motorcycle crash, which, too, had been completely of his own undoing.

"You should have seen it, man! I was mobbin' through these tractor ruts off-road when all of the sudden . . . BAM, I'm on my ass!" he'd explained at the scene of the accident earlier that day, still pumping with adrenaline. "Check out the damage, dude!"

His bike's right pannier rack had cracked from hitting a stump.

"I'll find a welder to fix it in Rosario. Alright, follow me there!"

Al's hubris had remained unshaken as he'd launched onto the road in the lead afterward—on his way to set Turista Hotel ablaze over a spat of beans in the hours to come. There was a reason I'd always called him the God-King. Since the day I'd met Alex, his confidence had proven both his greatest strength and weakness.

THE LIVESTOCK AMBULANCE

Rosario, México
Tuesday, April 12th, 2011

"The son of a bitch just flew off my handlebars," Charlie stamped as he and I pulled over to recover a piece of his mirror that had broken loose in the wind on Monday.

We were eight miles south of Catanina, where we'd just filled our tanks from a mechanic's jerry can. Alex and Megan had been there with us, and I wondered why they hadn't caught up yet as we scoured the shoulder for the mirror, until an American in a 4Runner pulled up and rolled down his window.

"You the guys with the other two riders? Yeah, your buddy crashed on that big curve outside of town two miles back. He's up and talking, but his bike looks totaled man."

"Twice in two days? Impossible!" Charlie exclaimed.

We scrapped the mirror salvage and headed north toward the incident. I'd hoped to find Alex ramped on adrenaline recounting his epic crash from every possible angle, again, as we approached the scene, but the shape of his bike in the distance indicated immediately that Monday would be different. The motorcycle was upright on its kickstand with pretzeled tires, bent forks, and only one Pelican case remaining. Alex was slumped over a nearby rock with Megan standing beside him.

"Megan, what day is it? How long have I known you?" he mumbled as I dismounted. "Tom, where are we?"

With his riding gear beside him, Al was developing cuts and developing bruises across his body. His helmet lay discarded in the dirt, pelted with chips and scratches. He was neither exuberant nor gallant like normal. He was mellow, dazed, and confused. The gravity set in further when Megan pulled Charlie and me aside.

"We need a doctor immediately," she stressed gravely. "We don't know how hard he hit his head."

Megan explained that Alex had been facedown and motionless when she'd found him. She'd thought he was dead.

"Tom, you speak the best Spanish. Head back into town and fetch help," Charlie commanded.

I surveyed the crash site to memorize its location before I departed. The road banked slightly downhill to the left with a high dirt berm on its inside edge. A ten-foot drop into a rock garden, a patch of sand, and a field of cacti were opposite on the outside. Alex had shot off the right-hand shoulder, bounced across the boulders, and rag dolled into the sand with his bike. There was a crater where he'd impacted.

I shuddered at the thought of such trauma as I blasted to Catanina. Without a clue where to find a hospital, I came to a skidding stop in front of the first person I saw there. Struggling to explain my situation in broken Spanish, I managed to make two themes clear to the lady named Rosa behind the nearest taco stand: there had been an accident, and we needed a doctor.

"Vamos! I have a first-aid kit in my car," Rosa exclaimed in response, waving toward her Lumina with the keys.

Rosa took control immediately upon arriving at the scene fifteen minutes later. She checked Al's vitals methodically and immobilized him in a neck brace.

"Don't worry. I am one of Catanina's volunteer first responders," she tempered confidently with her stethoscope. "He should be OK, but he needs to see a doctor."

Lying in the shade under a cactus with his feet elevated, Alex was making more sense now (he at least understood that we were in México), but his bruising had worsened and his skin was cold to the touch. Rosa blanketed him in the 85F heat as he continued to babble in Spanglish.

A livestock pickup with a whole family inside crested the highway dune from the south and pulled onto the shoulder. Another carful came next, and then five more vehicles after that. For a city with no gas station within a hundred and fifty miles, Catanina's emergency response burgeoned instantaneously. Rosa commissioned the livestock truck's driver to haul Alex back to the nearest clinic in Rosario. She directed him and his personal items onto a stretcher and into position at the back of the makeshift ambulance.

"Some days you haul pigs, some days you haul gringos... no difference really," Charlie grunted as we lifted Alex to the bed and closed the tailgate behind him. "Go with him. We'll see you back in Rosario at the hotel tonight, mate—the same one that Alex nearly razed last night. Megan and I will clean up the mess here."

I thanked Rosa and looked over to the truck driver, Hector, who nodded toward the road. Dressed like a cowboy, with skin more leathery than his boots, Hector was the oldest Mexican I had ever seen. In fact, his drooping frame appeared to be moving in slow motion as he slid back behind the wheel for departure. That didn't stop Hector from driving like Mario Andretti through the tortuous roads ahead though. Forget lane splitting—Hector used whichever lane he wanted all the way back to Rosario, dropping below fifty miles per hour only three times the whole way and only to urinate on each occasion. It was 6PM by the time we arrived at the clinic, where two paramedics hauled Alex away as I thanked Hector and paid him. I trudged in behind them to hear the on-duty physician's diagnosis.

"You likely suffered a concussion and possibly broken bones," the doctor explained inside. "I'm going to call a real ambulance to take you to San Quintin for X-rays."

He was a jovial practitioner, joking about Alex's accident with a "boys will be boys" attitude. I laughed along with him too, venting my fried nerves as I assembled Alex's cash, documents, and necessities onto his stretcher. When the ambulance arrived, I shook Al's hand, shut the door behind him, and watched the flashing lights dip below the northern horizon into dusk. Suddenly, it was a calm Mexican evening with a warm desert breeze blowing. A couple of quads roared by, their drivers without helmets. Exhausted, I turned back for Turista Motel down the road.

"We hired another rig to carry his shit for a hundred dollars after you left. It seemed like a good deal considering that we were spending Alex's money," Charlie explained proudly when I arrived to find Al's bike and luggage in the hotel lot already. "As far as we know, we recovered all of his gear too, which is incredible, given the way it had fanned in every direction from ground zero."

That evening our hotel owner, Doña Betty, was so horrified by the day's events that she offered to haul Alex's bike to San Quintin on her normal Tuesday errand run to help. Charlie, Megan, and I loaded the crumpled motorcycle into the bed of her Chevy and followed in pursuit as Doña Betty drove straight to San Quintin's local motorcycle mechanic the next morning. Tato, the owner, walked out from his office to pick over Al's damage when we arrived. I expected Tato to dismiss the wreckage as a total loss, given his stern face during initial inspection. After full examination, he jotted into his notebook and nodded.

"I'll have it running in two weeks," Tato asserted confidently, to my surprise. "Never underestimate a Mexican mechanic. Now, did the rider survive?"

Charlie and Megan negotiated pricing with Tato while I rode with Doña Betty to the hospital, where Alex was waiting on his gurney.

"No serious injuries, dude, not even a broken bone!" Al smiled proudly when we arrived.

Doña Betty nearly cried at the sight of him. Only after talking to Al's doctor would she agree to leave him to continue her day, and furthermore, she had a stipulation for me.

"Promise me you will ride safely back to Rosario," she demanded solemnly.

It took the rest of the afternoon to check Alex out of the hospital, due to an endless process of paperwork, during which I enjoyed the irony of smoking a cigarette with the head doctor as he drove me to withdraw Al's money. In the end, Alex paid only $250 for a night in the hospital, three IVs, and constant medical supervision.

"You were right in our arguments back in Alaska, Tom. This would have cost thousands at home. Maybe the American healthcare system does need a change," Al admitted as he looked over the bill on our way out.

"You'll have plenty of time to dwell on that on your own over the next several days, Alex. I think we've upheld our end of the bargain plenty on this accident," Charlie replied, flicking a hotel key to Al from the parking lot. "Since you did so insist."

Back in Ensenada, Alex had come up with the idea that our posse would leave behind anyone who was delayed on account of his or her own undoing. He'd even reiterated the consensus again to us on Sunday after his first accident in the mud.

"If this happens again, you guys can leave my ass at the next town over," he'd exclaimed.

"Got it," we'd replied then, and now two days later, we were executing his wishes without remorse.

To his credit, Alex didn't complain once as we shuttled him to the hotel afterward for exile. Instead, he thanked everyone for salvaging his belongings and bought us all tacos.

"Tato says he can get my bike running for less than $1,000. I'm going to try to help out around his shop for trade value," Al grinned in relief as we said goodbye. "Tell Doña Betty thanks for rescuing me, and the people of Catanina too. See you guys soon. I'll be right on your tail."

MILES AWAY FROM ORDINARY

Charlie, Megan, and I pulled into Mulege and headed straight through downtown to Baja's eastern coastline on Thursday after our second attempt at riding south from Rosario. At a beachside tiki bar on the Sea of Cortez, we parked excitedly to unwind with the trauma of Al and his accident now four hundred miles in the rearview mirror.

"Tres cervesas, por favor!" Charlie yelped from his bike before even dismounting.

We grabbed the nearest table in the shade of some palms to watch the waves through the lens of a Corona commercial.

"Welcome to paradise," the Minnesotan bar manager, Tim, twinkled as he served up our first round. "What brings you here?"

He was somehow both surly and jolly, with a bearish demeanor and a Santa Clause beard.

"Well a number of things really, but mostly the opportunity to imbibe at a place as beautiful as this," Megan replied.

"Let me know if I can get you anything else," Tim smiled knowingly as we raised our glasses.

Over the course of the next hour, the tiki bar filled steadily with expat American retirees enjoying their golden years. The mid-seventies clientele made for interesting company as Charlie, Megan, and I doubled down on our buzz and ordered more beers.

"These are on the house," Tim remarked, dropping a bucket off. "Bottoms up!"

At midnight, when the tides rose and the snowbirds dispersed, Charlie, Megan, and I moved to the bar to consult with Tim on where to pitch our tents in Mulege.

"Don't worry; you can camp on our beach," he gleamed, popping three more beers out of the cooler. "Now, tell me why you're really here."

Tim smiled in admiration as we explained our adventurous aspirations there at the bar. Before any of us finished our beers, he handed out another round. Tim was ready to talk; and with an open bar, a warm sea breeze, and no place to be that night anyway—so were we. Tim's cheeks glowed rosier and the empties piled higher as the four of us delved unwaveringly into one of the most amazing dialogues of my life over the next several hours.

Our topics covered every subject under the stars, but focused most thoroughly on politics, religion, morality, the 1960s, and Australian army theatrics (as regaled to us by Charlie, with one Aussie war victory after another). Everyone's unique upbringings, representing several different generations and two distinct hemispheres, came together to view the world harmoniously from all angles through the wee hours of the morning under the clarity of liquid courage. The philosophic experience turned us from chance acquaintances into true friends in the end, and by the sixth round of house beers, we understood two things for certain that night: our common bond in humanity and our mutual thirst for alcohol.

"You kids are on one hell of a trip," Tim concluded when I finally stopped him from reaching back into the ice chest again at 4AM. "Don't ever forget the moments like tonight.

They are all that life is worth living for. Now on a serious note, make sure you take the roads slow down south. They are completely unpredictable."

I thanked Tim for his hospitality and found a flat patch of sand out front to pitch my tent. I was inside with my mummy bag by the time Charlie stumbled out, finally, after one last drink. I knew to expect trouble too as he kicked sand drunkenly onto the side of the tent on approach. He lined his ass against the zipped mesh door and tipped straight backwards to flatten the entire structure across me.

"Sorry to crash your after-party mate," Charlie giggled as he untangled on hands and knees.

He sardined into the tent until a seven o'clock sunrise woke us with jarring hangovers.

"Tato already straightened my forks and my frame, dude," Alex exclaimed over Skype as Charlie and I nursed Bloody Marys back at the bar with Tim that morning. "He says he needs three more days, so I'll catch up to you guys next week if I ride five hundred miles every day!"

Al's enthusiasm was encouraging, but we stressed Tim's advice to him.

"You missed out last night, Al, but it was no anomaly. We'll have plenty more "find your beach" moments along the way so don't rush," Charlie and I both reiterated. "We're continuing to head south on Saturday. Give us a call when you're on the road, and we'll come up with a rendezvous."

Tim opened his ice chest again after Charlie and I closed our laptops. We both handed back our empties for a refill to continue our morning.

CHIVALROUS SHITS

Loreto, México
Sunday, April 17th, 2011

"To think I was starting to like this place!" Charlie muttered from inside Mulege's thrift store on Saturday.

Unbeknownst to us until that morning, his five hundred dollar Shoei Hornet helmet had been stolen outside the tiki bar on Thursday night. He was understandably fuming.

"Too bad there are no real lids here, because I can guarantee you that this piece of shit will be good for piss-all in a high-speed accident on the bitumen," he complained, holding a quarter-inch-thick skateboard helmet dourly.

He latched the plastic buckle tightly around his chin and purchased it nevertheless.

"Best we get on with it anyway. I'll find a something better in Loreto."

Charlie, Megan, and I headed south on Highway 1 to find peek-a-boo pocket lagoons around every corner of the beautiful Bahia de Concepción coastline. We stopped to take in the view at noon along a particularly perfect stretch, where the yellow sand and turquoise water tested our continuity immediately.

"Sure, it looks like paradise, but I wouldn't take an eye off my belongings for one second at a tourist trap like this," Charlie scoffed, still aggravated about his helmet.

I agreed that we should keep riding, but for completely different reasons. First, I wanted to put some distance between the American border and myself after our past week of delays in northern Baja. Second, and more importantly, my guts were on edge and the only toilet in sight was a hole in the sand.

"You guys go ahead then," Megan replied. "This place is too beautiful to be in a hurry. I'm going to take it slow today."

"You're not much one for the herd mentality are you Megan?" Charlie cautioned back.

"No, I can take care of myself."

"Right, then. I suppose separation is inevitable amongst a group of adventurers seeking their own definition of self-enlightenment, especially considering that we all planned trips separately. Meet us at Loreto, Megan. We'll be parked outside town."

Several hours later, Charlie and I pulled into the outskirts of Loreto and parked our bikes predominantly at the first taco stand as planned. A Mexican pimp tried to sell us his prostitutes while we smashed fifteen tacos with our eyes glued to the highway for Megan. After a brief period of digestion, I had to scramble for our communal roll of toilet paper.

"Do NOT go in there!" I exclaimed as I stepped down from the outhouse afterward to find a 6'6" gringo waiting next in line to enter.

"What up?" Alex beamed enthusiastically for a high five.

I hit him square in the palm and pulled him in for a solid bro hug (chests in, chins back, hips out with extra force to knock the other off balance). Despite still being bruised from his left knee to his right elbow, Al's condition had improved significantly since I'd last seen him. He pushed past me immediately before we could catch up any further.

"Now, let me past. I haven't seen a toilet in two days."

"Mate, you got balls getting back on this machine," Charlie marveled over Al's bike when he returned from the toilet. "How'd she ride?"

"Like brand new," Alex replied exuberantly. "Tato was a boss. He worked so fast that I had to hit the road without telling you guys on Friday. I left at noon and rode ten hours straight. I camped in the desert and woke up at 6AM this morning to keep going. I hauled ass again all day today. So good thing the three of you rode so slow this week! Wait, where's Megan?"

"Funny you should ask," I muttered.

Charlie and I had been scouring the main drag for the past two hours without seeing Megan. Meanwhile, Alex had approached from the north without passing her, which was troublesome, considering that Highway 1 was Baja's predominant north-south route from Tijuana to Cabo.

"I don't know mate, but something tells me it's our job to find her," Charlie answered reluctantly.

We rose and paid our bills.

Every sixty miles there were Mexican army outposts erected along Baja's lone Highway 1, where the soldiers had waved us through without issue since the American border (except when they'd been feeling bored or lucky, in which case they'd searched us first). Charlie, Alex, and I returned to the last one we'd passed to find six army helmets shaking their heads back at us an hour later when asked whether they'd seen Megan. The description of a white girl on a motorcycle wearing a bright yellow jacket should have triggered some memories, we figured, which meant Megan had to be further north. Naturally, I asked the commander if he could radio ahead to the next checkpoint.

"No, this radio is for official use only," he said with both hands on his assault rifle.

In light of the boring conversation anyway, we continued north, asking every construction worker, farmer, and vendor from there, until a roadside bartender recognized Megan's description thirty miles further.

"Your friend seemed happy and alert," the bartender explained. "She was just thirsty. I sold her a bottle of water, and then she kept going the direction you just came from."

"Where in the hell is she?" Charlie, Alex, and I asked each other as we slugged our own iced waters there in the evening heat.

No one wanted the misadventure of an innocent gringa on his conscience that evening, but the sun was going down, and I was still liable to cake my pants with a second round of diarrhea. We headed back south and skidded to a stop, again back at Loreto, an hour later. Then a collective sigh of relief was followed by a loud outburst of frustration when we found Wi-Fi and connected.

"Women!" we exclaimed with a range of Australian and American profanities as we read an online update that Megan was safe.

"I ended up following the advice of some locals to take the scenic route into town along the water," she greeted us that evening with a case of beer at her hotel. "I appreciate your efforts to find me guys, but next time you got to remember that I am an independent woman. You said it best, Charlie, I planned this trip separately, and I intend to ride according to my own pace."

Charlie, Alex, and I acknowledged Megan's independence. Rather than point any fingers at anyone, we instead pointed the beers down our throats until the case was gone and our heads hit the pillows that night. Normally, after a six-hour ride and a quarter-case of beer, I'd have slept like a rock, but Saturday night had a perfect storm of deafening culture and biological unrest in store for me. The nightmare started when a Mexican wedding reception kicked off across the street at 9PM. It intensified turbulently with the returning throes of acute intestinal cramping that night.

"Tacos and beer—what was I thinking?"

I winced into the toilet to the trance of a mariachi bass line off and on until 5AM, when the party finally ended. Just when I was finally dozing off, the Sunday morning farmer's market opened down the street at 6:30AM with a marketing truck driving in circles around my block blaring onion prices through a pair of rooftop tower speakers. It wasn't until the afternoon that I eventually found the strength to waddle out of my room to find Charlie and Alex working light bike maintenance in the hotel lot. Megan had gone out to explore town.

"Don't worry, Tom, we weren't going to leave you on your own here, like we did Alex," Charlie jabbed from underneath his bike.

"Well, maybe we'd have left Megan, considering that she's only part of the group when she wants to be," Alex shrugged.

I nodded back knowingly.

"Yeah, I guess four's a crowd."

EAGLE SCOOTIN'

La Paz, México
Tuesday, April 19th, 2011

A loud SNAP rang out as Thirio's clutch lever released tension all at once in the middle of my downshift on Monday south of Loreto. She lurched instantly back into fourth gear and jolted the drive chain through the tires. With a tight turn ahead, I cut the throttle and steered into a gap on the opposite shoulder as she started to gargle. I killed her engine under full brakes with a bucking stop in the dust. Then I cussed grandpa-style at the top of my lungs and signaled to Alex and Megan as they passed from behind.

"Your clutch cable just broke, dude. Megan, you should keep going and tell Charlie what happened. I'll stay to help Tom," Alex instructed as he and I dug into our tool kits.

A broken clutch cable was a setback, but Alex and I were prepared. Proud Eagle Scouts, we'd packed spare cables and screw clamps for this very situation. What we hadn't done, however, was any research on how to actually employ the important essentials. We spent a half hour attempting to "patch" the original cable by feeding its broken ends into our screw clamps with the spare, but failed ultimately, due to relentless slippage at the metallic pinch points.

We wiped our brows and looked out across Baja's surrounding orange dunes while we gulped the last of our water. There was not a tree or building in sight.

"Time for a new approach, or we're going to roast out here," Alex and I agreed, as drips of our perspiration fell from our foreheads and sizzled onto Thirio's block.

Next, we detached the entire clutch cable assembly from Thirio's frame, removed the snapped line from its housing, and worked our spare cable back through its original sheath to create a complete replacement cable. The new approach delivered one solid line from start to finish, which was our goal. There was just one additional setback, which we encountered while routing it back onto the bike.

Thirio's OE cable had come with cylindrical end-points that locked perfectly into the clutch lever and actuator slots, and our spare cable had not. So, Alex and I used Boy Scout knots to wrap the new cable through each slot and spread the tension across multiple half-hitch loops. Grease, sweat, and blood abound everywhere, but the Eagle Scout fix held another hundred and ten miles to La Paz after that. Alex and I stood proudly as we showed Charlie in town.

"Marvelous work mates!" Charlie exclaimed, as he inspected our handiwork that evening. "Boy Scouts clearly paid off. You blokes are almost as ingenious as Australians."

MEXICAN SOLUTION

La Paz, México
Wednesday, April 20th 2011

Neither Alex nor I had seen the police cruiser across the intersection during our illegal red light U-turn on Wednesday while we shopped La Paz for a replacement clutch cable, but he'd certainly seen us. The sirens and lights ignited before I could even hit second gear in the opposite direction.

I'd always known the day would come, but regardless, I was nervous to see Mexican Federales in my mirrors as Alex and I pulled over and turned off our bikes. Two officers stepped out of the squad car and approached, while two more watched from the back seat. They introduced themselves, gave our legal documents a congressional review, and detailed our violation with a paper infraction table, which listed our fines at a hundred dollars each.

"You got to be kidding, amigos!" Alex refuted. "Is this a joke? You got the wrong guys."

Alex had read about outsmarting foreign police during his preparation for the trip, and he was eager to try his hand. His strategy: tell off-color jokes, deny the incident entirely, and interrupt the officers incessantly (basically be an American pain in the ass). I watched the chief grow tired of Alex's slapdash attitude.

"Gentlemen, all jokes aside, this is a serious matter with grave consequences. Technically, I can take you to the station for this offense," he warned with a new demeanor.

Alex stepped back and reiterated our virtue with a more respectful tone.

"Señor, please, we are innocent. There must be a solution," Al proposed.

The police looked at each other and squared up against us.

"Solution? We can find a solution," the chief replied.

Negotiations started in the ballpark of sixty dollars. Thirty seconds later, I caved like a house of cards as soon as Alex argued them to fifty.

"It's a deal!" I exclaimed nervously, extending my hand toward the officers with the cash in my palm.

The chief looked up at me disconcertingly without taking the money. For a moment I thought I'd just written my own life sentence for attempted bribery until he finally opened his notebook and pointed to its center with a nod.

"Thank you for your cooperation, gentlemen," the chief replied as I deposited the 1,000 pesos discretely. "Enjoy your stay in México."

The officers straightened their hats and retreated in unison.

"Dude, I totally had them!" Alex complained. "We could have gotten off way cheaper."

"You can bail yourself out of jail next time," I argued back.

Unlike Al, I had not trained myself to argue with cops. I remained shaken by the incident until we arrived at La Paz's Suzuki dealership afterward, where the parts counter clerk confirmed Alex's notion indisputably as we inquired for a replacement.

"You could have gotten away for only twenty dollars, amigos. Remember, waste the cop's time enough, and he will cave. He doesn't actually want to take you down to the station—that's a lot of real police work. Good luck with your cable repair."

I thanked him with a sense of relief as we left. The clerk's best clutch cable option had been a glorified version of what Alex and I had rigged already, just with a smaller gauge and one cylindrical end that fit into my actuator slot. I'd install it that afternoon.

"It's a step in the right direction," Al reassured as we tied the other end again. "But you'll still need to find an OE replacement soon. Until then, the Mexican solution will have to do."

I looked back and smiled.

"Well, if I've learned anything in the past three weeks, Al, it's that the Mexican solution works just fine."

VACATION FROM VACATION

La Paz, México
Wednesday, April 20th, 2011

Aside from motorcycling, there were two sports that I truly loved: skiing and windsurfing. I didn't expect to find much snow in Central America, but wind was a different story. Over the past three weeks of inquiries, I'd learned that a little town called La Ventana was home to Baja's best breeze. La Ventana was just an hour south of La Paz, and I was determined to see the famed windsurfing beach. On Thursday morning, I enticed Charlie and Alex to come along too, with the promise of athletic girls in bikinis. Meanwhile, Megan opted instead for her normal rogue agenda.

"You guys go on your own. I've been reading about some beaches here in La Paz that I'd rather go see," she replied without looking up to a collective male shrug.

An hour later, Charlie, Alex, and I rode into La Ventana to discover gold sand and clear water as far as the eye could see.

"Something tells me Megan's beach is paling in comparison to this right now," we snickered to each other as we parked along the dusty main strip.

La Ventana's shoreline was the best we'd seen in Baja, but I was disheartened, regardless, by the distinct lack of wind in my hair. I wandered to the nearest surf shack for an explanation, while the boys found a bar for drinks.

"You're a week too late. The wind here is shut down for the season. We are actually closing up shop today until August," the Mexican-French-Quebecker kite instructor, Lucy, explained to me down the street.

I was crushed by the news, but I pivoted quickly to cut my losses, asking Lucy instead whether she'd be around for the weekend.

"I am heading to the Pacific coast to kiteboard, but there are no windsurf rentals there. I recommend that you stay here to celebrate Semana Santa in La Ventana. Then come back in August and I'll teach you to kite."

Lucy returned to her work as I stared out at the placid beach. Windsurfing was known to be a heartbreaking sport, due to its utter dependence on fickle wind, and Lucy's tanned skin and skimpy bikini only added insult to injury as she walked away. Eventually, I accepted my losses and returned to the bar.

"You can't win 'em all mate, and sometimes you can't win any of them," Charlie consoled me at the bar. "But this journey hasn't been a complete bust. You see, I was talking to locals while you were getting your heart broken, and it turns out that this weekend is México's Semana Santa holiday. It's their Easter, and everyone reckons it's bigger than Jesus himself around here. I went ahead and booked us the last room in town at my new mate's joint. So your consolation prize is to drink at the beach and lick motorcycle adventure wounds for the next few days. That ought to ease the disappointment about your girl and your surfing. Admit it, mate—you could use a vacation, eh?"

EASTER BOUNTY

La Ventana, México
Monday, April 25th, 2011

Mexican Easter weekend was a three-day fiesta of uncontrolled bonfires, drunken police, and chaotic Salsa along La Ventana's sandy beach until sunrise on Sunday. Then after seventy-two hours of continuous mayhem, the hundreds of campers cleared the beach by 8AM and vacated piously for Mass. Alex and I rented a pair of snorkels, a mesh bag buoy, and the Devil's Tail tool when they left. With the coastline clear for the first time in days, we waded into the ocean to hunt scallops like the locals had shown us.

Scallops are giant mollusks that filter nutrients from passing currents offshore. They bury all but one inch of themselves in the sand to camouflage as rocks. La Ventana's Semana Santa campers had decimated the local population already though. The scallops proved consequently elusive at first as Alex and I searched in the shallows, until Al spotted one along a rock bed seaweed garden.

Clutching the Devil's Tail, Alex dove down and hovered above it in the water's muted tranquility. The scallop's open slot mouth was liable to clamp closed and suck into the sand at the first sign of danger, but that's why the T-shaped Devil's Tail had a flat barb at its metal spike end.

Al arched his arm back with the Devil's Tail glistening from the sunlight above, and then he shoved the tool lengthwise into the scallop's mouth as far as he savagely could. The shell closed instinctively and squirted back into the sand as expected, but Alex turned the Devil's Tail ninety-degrees to stop its retreat. He flipped himself underwater with the Devil's Tail as his anchor and snatched the ten-inch catch out of the seafloor through a cloud of dark sand.

"Dinner's on, dude!" he smiled triumphantly on the surface as we tossed the catch into our buoy bag. "Look at the size of this thing! It's the width of my hand."

A complete slaughter unfolded afterward when we figured out how to spot more scallops in the rocks below. Alex and I took turns amassing an additional sixteen shells to fill our bag that afternoon. Back on shore, Charlie waved merrily as we crawled out of the ocean. He had a beer in his hand and an assortment of meats over the grill.

"Easter tradition in Australia mates . . . there'll be plenty to go around! Toss those vermin on the barby," he hollered from over the coals.

La Ventana was not my typical Easter, but this had not been my typical April either.

MAINLAND

Mazatlán, México
Thursday, April 28th, 2011

I realized during Semana Santa that I'd burned too much money with too few miles to show for my first month on the road. So, I was excited for mainland México when Charlie, Alex, Megan, and I booked passage to Topolobampo on Tuesday. As a Washington native, I'd been privy to the posh Puget Sound ferry fleet growing up. That made the Baja Ferries' *California Star* an eye-opening experience outside of La Paz. The deckhands waved us urgently into the six-story behemoth along a frenzied succession of slick metal ramps and eye-level girders to the bottom of the hull.

"Not to say I don't trust her seaworthiness, but I think I'll be spending most of this voyage on deck with Eddy and Lizzie just in case," Charlie joked as the *California Star* creaked loudly overhead while we lashed our bikes to available floor mounts.

Eddy and Lizzie were two mid-twenties Australians who had booked voyage with us as foot passengers after becoming our acquaintances in La Paz. The five-hour ferry ride was our first opportunity to get to know them as we cracked beers on the deck that afternoon. Backpackers with 'round the world flights and year-long aspirations, Eddy and Lizzie had started their trip in Hawaii back in January before traveling down the Pacific Coast from Seattle. They were currently bussing to Buenos Aires, and ultimately, they would fly to Italy and overland home.

"Somehow, I'm jealous of you, given my limitation to just two continents with the bike," I admired in awe as they explained the itinerary.

"Ay, you blokes got it figured out," Eddy scoffed back. "Those motorbikes are your freedom!"

"Eddy, if you get any more freedom, I'm not sure I could date you," Lizzie interjected.

He smiled back sheepishly from under his matted surf hair and gave her a bear hug.

Eddy was a personal trainer with biceps bigger than my quads (he'd packed his duffel half-full of protein powder when he'd left the States just to get through Central America). Lizzie was his dainty blonde girlfriend, completely independent and yet always within reach. The two of them were perfect for each other as they continued to interact on Tuesday, but that didn't mean Eddy wasn't ready for a little locker room banter when Lizzie got out of earshot. Visibly contented to be in the company of men, Eddy had to admit to us what had been on his mind since crossing the border.

"Boys, I love Lizzie," Eddy pondered aloud. "But these Mexican girls are driving me insane. They're just so bloody stunning!"

Charlie and I nodded back with grins.

We'd discussed that very topic at length since Tijuana, actually, and we agreed that there was something about the long black hair and disproportionate curves that caught the eye, to say the least. Then as an entire flock of Latinas walked past us toward the bar, we rose on a silent count to follow.

Even with the help of Eddy and Alex as our wingmen, the only digits that Charlie or I could amass were those of our bar tab totals during the rest of the voyage. I struggled to communicate even basic courtesies with the mainland girls at the bar. I descended the stairs empty-handed and disappointed as we came to port that evening.

Five years prior, I'd studied for six weeks in México with a host family, during which time I'd become completely engrossed in Spanish language and Mexican culture. My mack with the señoritas had been excellent on that trip, and for the final three weeks of it, I'd even dated a schoolteacher there named Cintia. The prevalence of English-speaking expats had reaffirmed my sense of Mexican assimilation falsely throughout Baja until Tuesday. My strikeout on the *California Star* was an unexpected punch to the gut.

"Well Tom, your Spanish game may be a little rusty, but you're still heaps ahead of me," Charlie encouraged back in the hull as we mounted up to disembark.

He flipped open his visor and grinned devilishly.

"Don't let it get you down, though. One afternoon of shortcoming is nothing to worry about. We're still in México after all. So watch this!"

Charlie dropped his clutch into a wheelie toward the surface as the deckhands clapped jubilantly through the trail of smoke.

"I'm assimilating just fine!"

SEMANA DE LA MOTO

Mazatlán, México
Saturday, April 30th, 2011

Eddy and Lizzie headed south from Topolobampo via tour bus to Mazatlán, while Charlie, Alex, Megan, and I followed along two hundred and fifty miles of farmland scenery on Thursday. The rich scents of manure, corn husk, and tractor fuel were sensational after Baja's 1,500 miles of desert, as was the novelty of a seventy mile per hour divided freeway.

"I was beginning to wonder what that fifth gear was for after four weeks on Highway 1," I jabbed that night.

After checking into a hotel, we learned that Mazatlán was hosting México's biggest motorcycle rally of the year over the weekend, and that there would be a parade on Saturday of over 14,000 bikes!

"I'll be damned if I'm not staying for that," Charlie exclaimed, booking his room until Monday.

Charlie, Alex, and I kicked off the festival the next morning at the main convention lot, where Alex and I balked immediately at the forty dollar tickets.

"That's a day's budget for us. You go ahead, Charlie," Al and I reasoned cheaply. "We'll meet up with you afterward."

Charlie wanted handlebar risers though, and there were aftermarket dealers by the dozens inside the fencing ahead.

"Well, considering my Spanish, there's no point in me going in without you two cheapskates," he replied eventually.

Then like a boss, he handed over an extra 1,500 pesos to pay our entire entry. Alex and I already knew better than to argue when Charlie intended to spend his money. Charlie had a bigger budget than we did, and he enjoyed retail therapy. With that in mind, we accepted our convention T-shirts and followed him graciously.

"You can buy me a beer," he sneered with a smile as we entered together.

Typical of American auto conventions, Mazatlán's chain-link lot was lined with vendor tents and gearheads along its outer edges; but unlike anything I'd seen before, its open central area was total chaos. Tire burnouts, rev-limiters, and wheelies erupted through clouds of exhaust in every direction as young riders tried to one-up each other's showmanship for the surrounding crowd of spectators. There were neither barriers nor helmets to protect the pedestrians or the exhibitionists, and the premises reeked of alcohol.

"Looks like we're a few drinks behind the rest of this nitro circus, mates," Charlie joked as we parked outside the beer tent.

He pointed toward a BMW R1200 GS ahead of us in the lot.

"Hey, those plates look like yours, don't they?"

Sure enough, Washington's iconic Mt. Rainier was stamped on the tail of the bike ahead, and towering next to it in the crowd was 6'5" Jim, who introduced himself excitedly with a firm handshake.

"What a cool adventure, guys!" Jim exclaimed as we explained our stories over beers.

Jim had just returned to Mazatlán on Thursday from his own multi-month motorcycle adventure to Panama and back, but he was still envious of our itinerary.

"You should come spend the afternoon at my condo, and we can talk motorcycles all day ... well, maybe I should clear that with my wife first," he continued.

He called her and left a message.

"I'll have to get back to you on that, but regardless, we should meet tomorrow afternoon for Saturday's parade. It's a can't-miss event, and I can help you through the madness."

The next morning, Jim's massive structure, personality, and motorcycle were easy to locate in the line of 14,000 bikes before the parade. When the engines started firing around us, he offered one final statement of advice.

"Get ready," Jim warned, "this is going to get loco."

I soon found myself locked into a streaming current of motorcycles lined four across in fluid formation as the procession started. The parade intertwined through a crowd of spectators lined ten-deep along Mazatlán's entire shoreline until a mosh pit of motorcycles, G-strings, and farkles unfolded at the end.

I spat out into downtown Mazatlán on my own eventually after losing the boys, and it was then that I finally realized I was, in fact, fitting in just fine with Mexican locals—at least from atop my motorcycle. As dictated by the cacophony of Mexican traffic and infrastructure, I weaved between pedestrians, busses, and donkeys alike while riding the shoulder frequently and opposite lane equally back to the apartment that afternoon. Such was the role of motorcyclists in México, and I was happy to join their ranks.

FORK IN THE ROAD

Mazatlán, México
Sunday, April 31st, 2011

Alex and I had originally imagined a nine-month round-trip to Tierra del Fuego when we started our motorcycle adventure in Seattle, but on Saturday we had to acknowledge the truth. We were hardly on pace for Argentina by October.

"It's safe to say we're taking our time, but I could care less about riding back through Baja, let alone the entire Western Hemisphere," I remarked that afternoon as we plotted on our map.

"I agree. By the bottom of the world I'll have bigger goals than to ride it all over again. We can figure out what to do with the bikes later," Alex replied with a nod. "Still, we need to start taking some bigger chunks out of México if we want to get there. Not only are we running late, but we're over budget too."

Alex and I had spent double what we'd anticipated as of Saturday due to northern México's modern prices.

"What do you say we cover some ground this week?" he asked.

"Perfect, because my ex-girlfriend, Cintia, is over 1,200 miles away in Cuernavaca, and she's confirmed that she'll be free next weekend."

Although I'd lost touch with my host family, I'd kept in certain contact with twenty-nine-year-old Cintia since my Spanish immersion program. I'd been twenty when we'd met, and she'd been twenty-five. We'd sizzled together that summer and left on open-ended terms. Finances were driving Al's urgency, and something far more powerful was driving mine.

In stark contrast to Baja's 1,500-mile stretch of solitary Highway 1, there were a variety of routes south from Mazatlán. That evening, Alex and I pitched the coastal highway via Puerta Vallarta to everyone else, since it was the most direct for Cuernavaca. The unexpected consequence of the mainland's bountiful options became clear immediately in everyone's responses though. Eddy and Lizzie were set for Guadalajara, while Charlie and Megan were eyeing Durango. Thus, the posse agreed to split for the very first time since we'd banded.

"We'll stay in touch and reach out after we're through with Guadalajara," Eddy and Lizzie promised that night over our final drinks.

"Cheers, mates. Megan and I will head to Durango together and see what happens next," Charlie agreed. "It sounds like she and I might not share the same timeline after that. Let's face it—we all know how Megan enjoys her own pace."

"Yeah, we'll see," Megan smirked back.

"Don't worry, this won't be the last we'll all see each other," Alex finished. "We're all funneling the same direction toward Panama's same narrow isthmus, although I can't promise that any of you will be able to keep up with me!"

I smiled and raised my glass.

"Until then, I'll miss the camaraderie."

JIM AND CINDY

Mazatlán, México
Monday, May 2nd, 2011

México was known because of its laid-back culture and sedating heat as "la tierra de manana" (the land of tomorrow), and Alex and I exemplified that on Sunday when we decided to shack up with our new friends, Jim and Cindy, instead of departing Mazatlán like we'd planned. Although our introduction to him had been brief in the motorcycle convention lot on Friday, Jim had actually gone home and gotten approval that night from his wife, Cindy, to host two dirty motorcyclists for the weekend. Alex had traded contact information with him during the parade, and on Sunday morning, Cindy answered the phone gleefully.

"Well, come on over!"

Jim was an Alaskan fisherman from Seattle who spent five months a year up north at sea. Meanwhile, Cindy managed a restaurant in Seattle's popular Ballard neighborhood. Together they frequented Mazatlán for vacation every spring to relax on the beach and to look after the pair of condos that they owned there. Jim and Cindy saved one of the two-story, two-bedroom, two-bathroom units for themselves and rented the other year-round. As luck would have it, the spare was available on Sunday. Alex and I moved into our first private rooms in over a month with elation.

Eight-foot waves broke into a warm yellow beach at the base of the unit's stairs, where we skirmished in the break for hours while Jim and Cindy were running errands. Alex and I joined them at the condo's community patio to socialize with their gaggle of snowbird neighbors that evening. The real entertainment started when Jim pulled Alex and me upstairs for shots of tequila.

"Bottoms up, boys," he said raising his glass. "You two are smart to do this young. I'm envious. It's just not the same at my age. Live it well. Cheers!"

Jim's tequila went down smooth, and he refilled my glass as soon as I set it down. On his nod, we all slugged the second round, with barely enough time to recover from the first.

"This tequila is good, huh?" Jim asked rhetorically.

Alex and I held our hands out for another as he nodded again with a smile. The three of us remained on the balcony for the next two hours until the sun disappeared, and not once in that stretch did we wait longer than ten minutes between subsequent shots.

"Jim, what are you doing to these boys?" Cindy exclaimed when she walked in to find the three of us melted into her furniture around the empty two-liter.

"Celebrating!" Jim awoke, beaming to his feet. "They're on the adventure of a lifetime, and I'm cashing in for one night of it!"

Cindy smiled back.

"Well it looks like you three are going to be hungry soon," she said as she opened the fridge.

I vaguely remembered devouring a plateful of delicious tacos and starting into Jim's second bottle of tequila after that. Things got fuzzy from there, until midnight, when I came to with the second bottle empty in my hand, chanting, "Rot in pieces," at the top of my lungs to the newsbreak of Osama bin

Laden's assassination (tequila had apparently brought out the patriot in me). After a rollicking round of high fives, I finally became dizzyingly aware that I was too drunk. I stumbled downstairs, took a spew off the rental balcony, and passed out over the couch.

On Monday, it hit me like an icepick through the temple that I'd partied a little too hard while I scrubbed my vomitus from the outside railing. In fact, Jim and Alex were also so brutally hung-over that nobody left his lounge chair even once that afternoon. It wasn't until after dinner that we finally sat down with Jim's maps to plan Tuesday's ride.

"You're right that Puerta Vallarta is more direct, but I've ridden all the roads around here, and I recommend you head east toward Durango, if you're headed to Cuernavaca," Jim explained. "The route over the mountains is so much of an adventure in itself that it's known as the Devil's Backbone. You can head inland to the south on wide open highways afterward."

Gazing across the map of México, I was suddenly humbled by how much of the country we were going to miss. Already we'd passed the legendary Copper Canyon, said to be four times larger and a thousand feet deeper than the Grand Canyon. There were scores of other attractions out of range to the north too.

"Adventure isn't about where you stood and where you didn't anyway. It's about who you met and what you ate. We can nitpick and stress over the things we're missing, but we're better off just celebrating the experiences we do get," Alex and I reasoned as we agreed to follow Jim's route. "People like Jim and Cindy give us a reason to come back anyway. Who cares if we've only known them two days—they're our two best friends in the world at the moment."

THE DEVIL'S BACKBONE

Durango, México
Tuesday, May 3, 2011

The one road connecting Mazatlán's heavy port traffic to inland Durango over the Sierra Madre range was known ominously as the Devil's Backbone. Jim had warned all weekend long about its treacherous corners and frequent accidents. Therefore, Alex and I rode cautiously on Tuesday as our highway meandered away from the tropical coast and ascended into a mountainous forest toward the legendary pass. As the palms faded away to evergreens, the curves intensified into increasingly technical switchbacks. The Devil's Backbone's steep pitches and hairpin coils validated its notorious reputation completely as Al and I pressed onward, but its ruthless onslaught of truck drivers proved even more hazardous overall.

Engineered before Mazatlán's current era of international freight, the Devil's Backbone's corners were, in fact, so sharp that semi combinations could not round their apexes without encroaching into our oncoming lane. The semis didn't slow down for oncoming traffic either—they held their dangerous speeds right through each turn and forced everyone else into the downhill shoulders.

Trucks rolled frequently as a result, which was evidenced disturbingly when Alex and I passed two Kenworths on their sides in our first twenty kilometers. Such imagery violated everything that we knew from our own CDL experience, and so did the driver's nonchalant attitude beside the second rig with his cell phone in one hand, a cigarette in the other, and diesel spilling out around him. Alex and I pulled over just beyond him to shake our heads.

"They'd never let semis on this road at home," we agreed, lighting our own smokes.

Jim had explained to us that the Mexican government was aware of the route's dangers, which was why a much safer and much straighter freeway was being erected overtop of it. Construction of the new road was being funded principally by Chinese business investment as a means to reduce transportation costs on exported goods, since crossing mainland México on a modern freeway would be much cheaper than paying the monopolized passage fees at the Panama Canal. Scheduled to open in 2012, the new superstructure would host the world's second-highest bridge (taller than the Empire State Building), among many other civil engineering marvels. Alex and I could see bits and pieces of the new infrastructure from where we stood on the shoulder, but we were far too early to take any advantage of it.

"That new road will definitely help, dude. In the meantime, at least this one can't get much worse, right?" Alex quipped as we both extinguished our butts.

Two more semis rounded into the straightaway ahead at full speed toward us as we buckled our helmets. There were only three hundred yards between them and the upcoming turn by the rollover, but still their engines pressed as the second truck downshifted into the oncoming lane to pass. Al and I stepped back cautiously as they thundered past us side-by-side, the overtaking truck barely a bumper length ahead. With a rock wall to the inside, a cliff ledge opposite, and two trailers fishtailing in tow, both semis held their positions right into the blind arc and out of sight in a trail of exhaust. In the silence left behind I hardly could react. My fists were clenched white knuckled. Even the driver of the rollover threw up his arms in the distance as Alex and I lit a second set of cigarettes in disbelief.

"Jim was right." Alex remarked. "Let's get the hell off this mountain range alive."

Cresting the Sierra Madre incident-free an hour later, we discovered the Devil's Backbone's clear and convincing namesake in the spine of rock pinnacles above the pass. We stopped there at the top for a well-deserved taco break, where the only other vehicle in the lot was an R1200 GS. Naturally, the BMW's owner, Sergio, introduced himself as soon as we sat down.

"Good to meet you both. I am the photographer, writer, and editor of my own quarterly magazine, in which I document everything from my personal motorcycle adventures to promote northern México's hidden local gems," Sergio continued, "Why don't you guys pose in front of the mountaintop? I'll feature you in my next issue."

After the photos, Sergio offered to guide us the rest of the way to Durango, which we, of course, agreed to immediately. I was completely caught up in the idea of Sergio's never-ending ride as we descended east. Sergio had made a career out of my dreams. For miles and miles and miles and miles I followed his lead in a state of bliss, until that fantasy ended suddenly at the toll outside Durango when Alex sped off alone, while Sergio and I paid at the gate.

"I'm low on gas, so I'll find you in town!" Al waved as Sergio and I stood with our helmets in hand.

Sergio looked at me perplexedly as we fastened them for pursuit.

"Does he know how big Durango is?" he asked.

"Apparently not," I laughed.

"Stay on my tail," Sergio instructed as we passed through the toll. "You don't want to get lost in Durango."

So, with that, I'd lost my wingman in one of México's most dangerous cities (more on that to follow), and I now clung to a journalist for survival (don't tell my mother). For a 6'6" gringo, Alex proved surprising difficult to locate as Sergio and I searched at gas stations and plazas alike for over two hours throughout Durango. We connected finally via Facebook at Sergio's hotel.

"I guess I kind of blew the buddy system there," Al admitted bashfully as he walked into the lobby that evening. "For some reason, I got a hair up my ass that I'd run empty if I waited around."

"The important thing is that you guys conquered the Devil's Backbone successfully today," Sergio reminded us. "It's too late for you to continue south. Go into town and find a hotel. Enjoy Durango, but keep your wits about you. You can get into just as much trouble here in town as anywhere on the Devil's Backbone."

Regarded as a cultural mecca singular to the rest of México, Durango hosted an enticing nightlife, but unfortunately, the city was also notorious for its strong cartel presence. The police were currently exhuming a mass cartel grave, where the latest body count was a hundred and four souls. Additionally, the municipal and federal police were known to break out in gunfights against each other. Regardless of Durango's heavy constabulary presence downtown, Alex and I agreed that we did not need a late night. Charlie and Megan were gone already, anyway, and we still had fourteen hours of highway before Cuernavaca.

"I don't want to be the one that explains to your girlfriend, Kristi, how you died in a Mexican standoff," I explained to Al that evening from the safety of our balcony. "More importantly, I can't let another hangover get between me and my hot date with Cintia on Friday."

FLAT TIRED

Alex and I planned to camp in the desert on Wednesday night, which meant we would ride until dusk, due to inland México's 90F temperatures and limited vegetation. Our 7AM to 8PM aspirations were cut short that afternoon when I started experiencing severe signs of heat exhaustion, however. My turns were out of sync, my toes were missing their levers, and my head was unable to focus. Feeling as if I could just slip off Thirio at any moment, I pulled over and killed the engine as Alex sped ahead without noticing.

The empty desert ambiance was quiet in all directions as I staggered off the bike, but still my ears rang with alarm like I'd just been punched in the nose. I doused myself with half a Nalgene and drank the rest in one gulp. I applied sunscreen, draped a bandana over my head, and slumped down against a rock with no shade in sight. Alex found me in fifteen minutes later, unmoved.

"Come on, man," he said, handing down his spare water. "There's a taco stand a few miles from here in Lagos de Moreno. Let's rehydrate and find some air conditioning."

I still felt wasted after five tacos and two Gatorades, and the owner could tell when we explained our plans to camp.

"Are you kidding? You two are clearly finished," he said with a laugh when he brought back the bill. "You'll roast out there in the sun. Why don't you go to the hotel down the street? You could have air conditioning in five minutes. Better than waiting four more hours for sunset."

Alex and I did not need convincing.

"You don't have to tell us twice!" we waved as we left.

We should have asked for the directions again at least once more, though, because Al and I found ourselves back in the sun and disoriented anew only three turns later.

"Didn't he say derecho, derecho, derecho?" Al recalled when we pulled over at a dilapidated corner to recount our steps.

"Correct, take a right, a right, and a right," I agreed confidently.

"Yeah, but isn't that a circle?"

A young vagabond across the street assured us that we were just ten minutes away. Then as we pulled off the curb at his direction, Thirio fishtailed off the line underneath me.

"Flat tire dude—you're not going anywhere," Alex confirmed with one look. "Routine maintenance was starting to get boring anyway."

A flat tire seemed poignant, considering that Thirio's odometer had just passed the 10,000-mile-mark that morning. Al and I hopped off our bikes with gusto to find that a sharp piece of steel had somehow folded in half and punctured both ends into Thirio's tube.

"Son of a bitch. We're patching two holes today."

The vagabond watched us in a trance from across the street, but I paid no attention as Alex and I removed the wheel and laid it on its side to break the bead. After separating the tire and the rim using our tire irons, we removed the tube and repaired it. The tire's pressure leveled off at 10 psi after reconstruction.

"Probably a third puncture," Alex said. "I guess we're patching more than two."

An hour had passed since we'd started the operation, and the sun was hanging lower. The vagabond had found a friend, so now two strangers watched as Alex and I filleted the tire again and patched the third puncture. In our hurried reassembly, we pinched the tube while stretching the tire back over the rim.

"Shit! It's a common mistake," Al admitted. "But we have to patch again. We should have practiced this at home in a garage."

We repeated the dissection, patched the pinch, and pumped the tire a third time as the sun hit the horizon slowly. The gauge read 33 psi at first check and 32.5 psi several minutes later, which seemed a reasonable margin for error. I reinstalled Thirio's wheel and loaded my tools. Covered in sweat, grease, and mosquitoes, I finally threw my leg over the saddle to find Thirio unpromisingly low between my butt cheeks. The tire had folded lifelessly flat again in the twenty minutes since I'd measured it. As the sun disappeared behind the horizon, I slammed my toolkit back onto the sidewalk and sat down for a smoke.

"Dude, it's getting dark, and we need a place to stay," Alex reasoned as I fumed. "Let me run to the hotel and book us a room while you disassemble again."

I grunted an affirmative with my head in my hands before he hit his ignition and left. After sulking for several minutes, I looked back up to discover that the pair of vagabonds had grown to a crowd of seven. They faced me from across the street, leering silently with furrowed brows. I dared not make eye contact out of fear. Instead, I returned to my tire guardedly, with my imagination running wild on stories of Durango. Laboring in the dark with my tools fanned out behind me, I had never felt so exposed in my life. I swore I could feel their piercing stares plotting deviant assault. Worrying that they represented the local cartel, I even began to think that the taco stand owner had led me there as a trap.

"He probably put the hole in my tire too!" I muttered in frustration.

Alex returned before they could execute their attack.

"I got us a place. Now we just got to get your pile up and running," he encouraged in reaction to my stiff demeanor. "Why are you so tense?"

I was ninety percent through the repair and one hundred percent through my nerves. Too freaked out to explain, I shifted my eyes over to the shoulder and nodded toward the audience. There were ten of them now.

"Don't ask. Let's just hope this time I got it right," I replied sullenly.

My fourth reassembly was complete, and it was time for the moment of truth. My gauge had read 33 psi ten minutes earlier. I checked it again anxiously to find out that SUCCESS—it was holding steady at 33 psi with no margin for error. Alex raised his fists in the air and turned with a smile toward the crowd of youth, who burst enthusiastically into applause and rushed forward to congratulate us.

"They don't seem that bad to me," Al replied.

Frozen in terror as they approached, I eventually curtseyed a bow.

"We kept wanting to offer help, but we didn't want to intrude because you were so standoffish," they explained. "There's not much to do in Lagos de Mareno, so this corner is where we always meet up. You guys are big news around here. How did you end up on this block anyway?"

Al and I repeated the taco stand owner's directions to even more uproarious laughter.

"How did you even make it this far into México!" they joked back. "Remember, you should only do circles in a roundabout!"

Then it hit me. In first year Spanish I'd learned that *derecha* meant *right* and *derecho* meant *straight*, but until that moment I had only remembered *derecha*, since they were so similar. Every time a Mexican had told us to go straight for the past month, Alex and I had, instead, taken a right, which explained why we'd kept getting lost!

"You still have six hundred kilometers to go until Cuernavaca," the youth explained after we all caught our breaths. "Keep going derecho."

I knew I'd jumped to conclusions and let my nerves get the best of me as my head hit the pillow that night. Unfortunately, I was asleep too soon thereafter to know whether I'd learned any lesson or not.

ENDURANCE

Regardless how fast I rode on Thursday, 95F degree heat still felt like riding through a toaster. I took to soaking my undershirt in water at every stop to create impromptu onboard air-conditioning. The shirt stayed cool and wet until crusting inevitably back with sweat every time.

Gone were the badlands of Baja and the tropics of the Pacific. Instead, Alex and I encountered industrial and agricultural development featuring modern John Deere combines and state of the art irrigation. With factories and supermarkets sprawling at every crossroads, inland México was as contemporary a place as I'd ever known, aside from its infrastructure—which remained quite shit. Thursday's roads had neither guardrails nor road markings; their potholes were either three inches deep or two inches overfilled; their shoulders (if there were any) were actually passing lanes (or parking spots). Most heinous of all—all routes were covered in unmarked *tope* speed bumps of varying sizes placed everywhere I was inclined to go fast.

México's typical hub and spoke city layout did not make for easy navigation either. Alex and I followed signs for the free road to México City for forty-five minutes in Morelia for example—only to end up at the exact same stoplight where we'd started. I admit that the chaos was not entirely unjustified. Regardless of how easy it was to get caught in the endless loop, eventually you were bound to see signs for your destination again if you continued in circles long enough.

"All roads lead to where you want to go in México," Al and I agreed that afternoon when we finally escaped.

Outside of Toluca that evening we found a hotel for only twenty dollars that came with its own garage, a hot water shower, a king size bed, and a wide variety of adult channels (which we had not requested). The place was a palace by our standards, and more importantly, it was only two hours from Cuernavaca, where Cintia had reserved us a room for the next week. Charlie wasn't far back either, according to his most recent email update. Our grueling trek from Mazatlán was setting up for one wild reunion in the coming days!

EL ROLLO

Cuernavaca, México
Sunday, May 8th, 2011

Friday at the Cuernavaca Plaza de Armas I stood proudly beside Thirio as Cintia flittered to me in a tiptoed sprint.

"Hola, Tom! Welcome back to Cuerna!" she exclaimed with a chiquita-sized bear hug.

I'd forgotten how small she was; her petite frame felt like a feather in my grasp. Cintia's scent flashed me instantly back to my first sniff at international adventure. After greeting Alex, Cintia hopped back in her VW Golf and led us to our gated downtown studio rental, which featured a kitchen and two beds.

"So, what would you boys like to do this weekend?" Cintia asked after we changed into street clothes.

El Rollo was my immediate response. I'd been promoting México's largest water park to Alex for weeks by this point, recalling my college memories of El Rollo as an adrenaline-fueled playground with neither weight limits nor safety precautions.

"I thought you might say that," Cintia smiled back.

El Rollo had been our first date four years prior as well. Aside from the romance, I remembered one ride in particular, which I described to Alex Saturday morning as we approached the park's entrance.

"Like all water parks, El Rollo has a lazy river, which ironically for the Mexican version, is faster than a Class V rapid," I explained. "The intensity is on account of a man-made break, where water floods onto a sloped wall so people can surf on an artificial wave. Directly behind that wall is a pit for the fake wave's runoff, which flushes down an eight-foot-wide drain spout to power the river's current. And every five minutes the wave recedes, spitting its surfer into the river at the end of his or her turn. It sounds pretty standard, right?"

Al nodded back questioningly.

"Except here's where it gets crazy," I continued as we navigated through the main gates toward the site for a first look. "Between each surfer's wave, when the water is low, they let twenty guests cram into the pit behind the wall at El Rollo. Then when the next surfer starts, the swell curls back over and onto the people below like a typhoon."

Alex didn't completely understand my enthusiasm until we walked up to witness the event first-hand. After watching one round of the chaotic fight for self-preservation against the surge, the three of us hunkered down in the pit between waves, ultimately to be shot into the spout, despite our best efforts to stay put. Over twenty more attempts followed, during which we realized an unwinnable plight, as everyone always got swept at full boar, regardless of strength or positioning. It started every time with the weaklings, who would lose grip when the water reached one-foot depth. They cut down the others as they floundered until everyone was broken loose. You could catch your breath among the continuous mass of spattering bodies just for a brief moment while shooting the ramp, but a four-foot drop sucked you into the river for up to ten seconds before resurfacing. Just hold your breath, plant your feet, and grab a small child to pull yourself up. Hit the first exit out of the lazy river and run back to the start again.

Cintia, Alex and, I rode the other slides too, but the lazy river remained our favorite on Saturday as we staggered waterlogged out of El Rollo's gates at 6PM. My plan from there had been to ditch Alex and take Cintia on a date for the evening, until on the way back she revealed that she had a boyfriend waiting at home (after she'd fleeced me for several meals and a park ticket of course).

"That's what I get for leaving the country," I shook my head salaciously on the curb as she drove away after dropping us at the apartment. "The strikeouts continue here on the road."

"At least you're still getting lucky with your riding," Alex replied.

He was referencing Charlie, who had laid down his bike at sixty miles per hour over the weekend, due to a failed valve stem. Charlie had described it over Skype to us that morning.

"Ay, my tire went flat instantly. I battled as long as possible, but she high-sided me directly out in front onto the highway. As I skipped across the bitumen beside her for the next one hundred feet, all I could think about was not breaking my spine. Good enough results I guess. My shoulder and wrist are buggered, but otherwise the bike and I rode away fine. Unfortunately, mates, this all means I won't catch up so soon after all, but I'll let you know as soon as I sort this out. I've lost Megan for good now, so rest assured, I'll be free to cover ground ahead."

That left me as the last bike standing. I continued to say my prayers.

BITSEY

Sunday night, my sister Lynn notified me that our grandmother, Bitsey, had passed away. Although it was the inevitable culmination of a long and drawn-out process that had been deteriorating for years, the news didn't hurt any less to hear.

Bitsey had been filled with love and cheer her entire life, and I was grateful for every moment I'd shared with her in my twenty-four years. Despite the 2,000-mile distance from Seattle to her residence in Wisconsin, my parents had taken Lynn and me out to the Midwest to connect with our roots twice a year during our youth. My fondest childhood memories included reading stories with Bitsey, playing with her toy dogs on the floor, and relaxing on the porch at Pikewood.

A month before departure, I'd flown out to see Bitsey and my surviving grandparents, Grandma and Grandpa. I'd packed a lot into the four-day visit, but most important was the afternoon that I visited Bitsey in her nursing home. She hadn't much to say, and she'd obviously lacked strength, but the excitement in her eyes had been alive and her smile as I'd always remembered.

Bitsey's funeral was going to be too far a distance for me to overcome in the upcoming week, so those memories were all I had left of her now. Before this trip, everyone had warned that I would eventually come back changed, and that home would be the same. That may have been the case in general, but these fast times and new experiences proved suddenly less magnificent against the consequence of a missed goodbye.

At least I could take solace in the words of Grandma Reuter from that same trip to Wisconsin. She'd remarked with a knowing smile, "I think it's a fine idea to go on your motorcycle adventure, Tom."

I decided to call her that night to tell her I loved her.

MAINTENANCE

Cuernavaca, México
Monday, May 16th, 2011

For several thousand miles, Alex and I had been compiling a shopping list for the spare parts that we'd left Seattle without, and on Monday we addressed it finally at Suzuki of Cuernavaca.

"Jackpot! I told you our components would be here," Al proclaimed when we arrived at the parts counter.

He had also told me that at the last six towns, but it wasn't worth noting aloud.

Spark plugs, clutch cables, inner tubes—Suzuki had them all along with a seventy percent Mexican import tax. I balked when the cashier rang me up. I even thought briefly about holding off until Guatemala. Paying nearly double in México seemed a fitting lesson for being too cheap back home. I walked away eighty-five dollars lighter with the weight of that shopping list finally off my shoulders. Alex and I rode down the street after that to the tire vendor district, where we started a bidding war between two back-alley salesmen and ended up with two Pirelli MT-60 rears for $325 total.

"The rear tire on a motorcycle wears faster than the front

for two reasons. One—it carries the most weight, and two— it powers acceleration. Neither of us needs a new front at this point. Your rear has at least 1,000 miles left in it too, so you should carry your spare a while longer," Alex explained when we pulled back up at the apartment. "My rear is down to its final ten percent of centerline tread life. I need to change it before we leave Cuernavaca. Regardless, we're both set for another 5,000 miles with our spares."

Al and I kept the maintenance momentum rolling as we checked our valve clearances next, which took me deeper into an engine than I'd ever been before. He and I stripped our seats, gas tanks, spark plugs, and valve covers for necessary access. Our feeler gauges finished the job, measuring both bikes to within their proper tolerance without adjustment.

"Didn't I tell you the DR650 was bombproof? They didn't even need their own recommended 10,000-mile tune-ups! We shouldn't need serious maintenance until South America now."

Alex was understandably proud of his own mechanical prowess. Still, I replied flatly with a high five.

"Assuming our shocks hold out over these Mexican speed bumps."

TEPOTZLAN

"You know, it's true that for every door that closes, a window opens," I joked to Alex over the wind of our bikes on Tuesday.

Despite having had my aspirations fall short with Cintia the previous weekend, harmony had since restored itself in the form of a twenty year old Mexican girl named Olympia, who was wrapping her arms around my waist at the moment while enroute to Tepotzlan. My strikeout curse had ended!

"It's also true that motorcycles are a great way to pick up women," I continued. "Or in your case—men."

"You owe me for this one, bro," Al grumbled back with Olympia's brother, Daniel, holding onto him from behind like his sister was doing to me.

Alex and I had met the siblings at a dance club, coincidentally through Cintia. Olympia and I had gotten along intriguingly when first introduced, but we'd really hit it off after Cintia's boyfriend had been announced.

Olympia was young, trilingual, and confident in her ability to speak English, which was perfect for my broken Spanish. Her brother, Dan, spoke three languages too, and luckily for me, he didn't seem to mind my courtship of his sister. In fact, it had actually been Dan's idea that we all head northeast to Tepotzlan on Tuesday. His only stipulation had been that he got to ride along, which I'd agreed to immediately, on Al's behalf.

"This makes up for my saving your ass in Baja," I reminded Alex as we arrived at the city and parked that afternoon.

Tepotzlan's attraction was evident immediately within its first several blocks of red cobblestone streets and beige stucco buildings. Vibrant corridors bustled with commerce and flourished with foliage. Meanwhile, the ageless marketplace downtown teemed with authentic arts, crafts, and delicacies in a romantic's dream come true.

"Tepotzlan has been inhabited since 1500 BCE. There is amazing history here, but the main attraction is the pyramid. Come on, I'll take you," Olympia instructed, pointing toward vine-covered cliffs overhead to a distant temple up top.

She led us down an alley behind the flea market to an ancient trailhead shrouded by thick tree roots, dense forest jungle, and the lively buzz of tropical chatter. Each step was a foot higher than the next, leading straight into the overhead cliff.

"Apparently native Mexicans never caught on to the 'switchback' method of trail construction," I wheezed halfway up the five-hundred year old staircase of hand-laid boulders that followed.

"The manpower required to construct this trail is unfathomable, even in modern times," Olympia confirmed, to my humble amazement.

I was equally impressed at the top to lay eyes on pyramid Tepozteco's hundreds of foundational stones, which were all over twice the size of the steps we'd just ascended.

"The amount of societal determination required for such an undertaking could only have come from the ancient spirit that still thrives in the streets below."

Despite archeological intricacies spanning atop the foundation's every surface, there were neither ropes nor guards to restrict exploration up top. I scaled right to Tepozteco's highest point and sat down reverently to take in the view. Central México's greater terrain spanned ahead, with blanket farmland to the north and rolling jungle to the south. I could see the streets of Cuernavaca to the west and the haze of México City to the east.

Olympia held my hand and pointed out childhood memories for the next hour of amazement in a moment of lowered guards. I didn't know what potential we had, given the fact that she was only twenty and still in college, but that didn't stop me from scheduling dinner with her for that evening.

Those plans were dashed subsequently when a rainstorm cooled my core temperature to below tropical for the first time in weeks on the ride home. Forty-five days of adventure caught up to me immediately as my immune system crashed during the torrential ride. Heavy eyes, a sore throat, and a clogged nose were all in full swing by the time we reached Cuernavaca. With a muted goodbye to Olympia, I collapsed into bed on a rain check that evening.

The apartment's cement walls, gas stove, and underachieving ceiling fan made REM sleep all but impossible throughout the next several days of 85 F nighttime lows. Additionally, the mosquitos forced Alex and me to lock the unscreened windows and doors every night before dinner to keep from being eaten alive. My nighttime routine solidified into showering, hunting mosquitos, showering again, throwing a wet bandana around my forehead, and lying spread eagle in my underwear until morning's mercy. My recovery that weekend was a delirious blur of fevers, sweats, chills, Gatorade, Mexican soap operas, and crusty-lipped hacking.

"I know you're feeling better now, but you might not get to reschedule that date with Olympia, dude," Alex warned me eventually on Monday as he poured over our maps. "She is in school until Friday."

I understood his point solemnly. Going on two weeks in Cuernavaca now, the call of adventure was thundering back at full strength again. The taste of sedentary life had been an amusing distraction, but our fate was to ride south. Olympia had never stood a chance, and she was not going to be happy.

"So much for that open window," I replied with a heavy sigh. "At least by tomorrow I'll be able to see her face-to-face."

BMW MOA

Cuernavaca, México
Thursday, May 19th, 2011

Ever since crashing back in Baja on the first week of adventure, Alex had been tying his broken side pannier shut with a draw cord. After six weeks of fretting about leaks and thieves before every ride, he finally found a replacement on Wednesday. The new case was a white fiberglass cube, which he mounted to his tail rack after swapping his top Pelican to the side. It was also the exact same case that every Mexican pizza delivery boy used, which I reminded him of that afternoon from inside the apartment as he finished the mount.

"You're going to be the baddest Domino's driver in town dude."

"Not bad for a Leatherman and a screwdriver," he smiled back, holding up the only two tools he'd used in the operation. "Now let's hope I make this tire look just as easy. I want to try this on my own, like you did in Lagos de Moreno. I should have it done in an hour so we can get drinks."

Alex rolled his new Pirelli confidently into the afternoon heat while I turned back inside to go watch more soaps. Two hours later, I came out again to find him engrossed completely in his still-dismantled rear end. Shirtless and covered in soot, Al was going into his fourth round of pinched tubes in a match for the ages. Clearly on the ropes, he still refused to quit.

"Dude, I need one more try on my own. I know we talked about going out tonight, but I'll be too tired," he admitted, wiping his brow.

I looked back impatiently.

"Go get your drink without me—I know you need one after today with Olympia."

Al was referring to a disheartening conversation that Olympia and I had concluded that afternoon, during which I'd reminded the young girl that I would soon be leaving Cuernavaca.

"Goodbye, Tom. I'll miss you. I only wish you'd given me a real chance into your heart," she'd replied, kissing my cheek and walking gracefully out the door without looking back.

I'd been glad we hadn't taken things too far as I watched her go, because it had required all my restraint to keep from following her. I'd learned in college through a series of given and received heartbreaks that relationships relied heavily upon timing. It had taken me four months in the Arctic Circle to get over my last rejection, and now it was Olympia's turn at my unflinching dismissal.

Needless to say, I needed that drink that evening, and I split the coop immediately for the best live salsa bar I knew. Half an hour later, I sat down at an empty table and ordered four Coronitas in the Los Arcos courtyard. Centered squarely amidst Cuernavaca's vibrant downtown Plaza de Armas, Los Arcos was where I'd last kissed Cintia over four years prior and where I'd first kissed Olympia only a week earlier. It was an obvious spot for some solitary reflection as I cracked my first beer gratefully.

Being alone felt bizarre initially, but the livelihood of Los Arcos proved company enough. Soon my eyes were entranced to the dance floor, where the locals twirled with an unbridled passion for expression that simply did not exist in American culture. No other dancing was so suggestive and still so innocent as Mexican salsa, and it lightened my mood immediately.

Maybe the Coronas had something to do with it too, but it wasn't long before I started chatting with the next table over about my unlikely journey south. I started explaining my story with the Alaskan ice roads and then how I'd studied in Cuernavaca, but it wasn't until I got to the word *motocicleta* that the one quiet gentleman at the table jerked his head away from the dance floor and started listening with intent. I could see his intrigue hanging on every word as I described how I'd added Thirio's modifications and packed my adventure luggage. When I finally rolled out that I was now riding from Seattle to Buenos Aires he could not resist any longer.

"Hola, amigo!" the man finally exclaimed, hopping beer-in-hand from his chair to my table to cut off the others. "My name is Oscar, and I am part of BMW MOA. I have many questions for you."

After several adventure riding queries, Oscar revealed the elaborate network of his local BMW Motorcycle Owners of America's Cuernavaca Chapter.

"My associates can guide you all the way to Panama with information on roads, maintenance, parts, and places to stay. They'll even help arrange a motorcycle convoy to escort you across the dangerous Guatemalan border."

I hesitated initially and leaned back in my chair. Alex and I had already made it deep into México without any organized help. The last thing we wanted was big brother telling us how to have an adventure. Oscar continued with conviction, though, and by the end of my second bucket of beers, I was convinced to set up a meeting.

"They'll even mount your tire for you," was all the convincing that Alex needed to tag along when I found him defeated on the floor next to his unfinished wheel that evening at home.

The next morning, Oscar's president and other members greeted us at their garage. With tens of thousands of adventure miles between them, they mapped BMW MOA's preferred route to Oaxaca for us, which would be full of ups, downs, curves, and vistas.

"More importantly, you can still reach the Yucatán from Oaxaca. You should go to the Yucatán, ultimately for two reasons," the club members admonished with concern. "First— it is beautiful. Second and more importantly—it will allow you to drop into the top of Belize and ride the coast until Guatemala's southernmost border crossing. Then you will be just a day's ride away from the safety of Honduras, because you do not want any part of the recent cartel violence along the México-Guatemala border."

Al and I had heard similar stories already about Guatemala, and we didn't know what to think of them. We'd ask a Mexican, and he'd shudder and say Guatemala was too dangerous for travel. We'd also asked every American at home about México, and they'd all warned that our heads would end up in a box. However, when we'd asked adventurers online who'd crossed either border, they'd said that everywhere was safe, if you did your homework beforehand.

"Remember, we're Eagle Scouts. We're prepared for anything," we reminded ourselves discretely. "These guys are a resource, not the end-all."

We thanked Oscar's club and took down their information. We weren't sure how much we'd use their advice beyond the route to Oaxaca, but it certainly felt reassuring to have them on-call.

WAH-HAH-KAH

Oaxaca, México
Saturday, May 21st, 2011

BMW's three-hundred-mile epoch across the volcanic Sierra Madre range delivered a totally new tropical ambiance after México's agricultural north. The jungle south of Cuernavaca was sectioned into levels with dense ground growth under thick canopy coverage. Giant cacti sprouted contrastingly through the treetops against hazy blue skies. Wildlife thickened through the trees as Alex and I passed flocks of colorful birds and several roadside iguanas. The most memorable fauna of all was my unexpected encounter with a flurry of colossal fluttering butterflies, during which one of the bugs sprawled across both lens of my sunglasses and wrapped ultimately onto my face, up my nose, and down my mouth.

"Still better animal life than the bloated dead livestock of Baja," I quipped to Alex through my closed visor after the cleanup. "This is one wild ride."

The Earth changed too, with copper-red dirt and white-streaked silt showing through the mountainsides during our climbs and descents. Forested layers of perfectly symmetrical volcanoes faded south into purple hues ahead. In between them hung low, passable ridgelines, over which the barely distinguishable trail of our highway weaved deeper and deeper. Alex and I were officially outside of agricultural México.

"Oscar nailed it! This is exactly what I imagined back in Alaska!"

That evening Alex and I descended into Oaxaca's lush green gully and sought out BMW MOA-recommended Hostel Ponchon. We parked there in the lobby next to a F650 that night, whereupon I was too tired to encounter its owner after dinner. It wasn't until Saturday morning in the commons that I met Joe, who was already over a year into his motorcycle trip around the world. Joe had covered Africa and South America to date, and he planned to finish North America in Vancouver after looping through Alaska. An architect from England, Joe was quiet in general, but he evidenced experience confidently through his demeanor and tone. I enjoyed his advice thoroughly, and I appreciated access to his maps, but Joe's guidance to an unforgettable meal that evening was his most lasting impact.

"Alright gents, first you buy the veggies, then the meat, and then the butcher will grill it all up at the end," he instructed outside of Oaxaca's public dining hall.

The hallway was lined with butcher stands and vegetable counters serving fresh offerings sourced entirely from the surrounding Sierra Madre. Alex and I bought two kilos of assorted meats and had them fried with chilies and onions inside. We found a table at the open seating hall, where our waiter served even more fixings a-la-carte: tortillas, guacamole, pico de gallo, and limes.

The feast began when our meats arrived sizzling on a platter. My eyes seared from the poorly ventilated kitchens, and I could hardly hear my compatriots amidst the chaotic screaming of butchers as I ate. I devoured tacos gloriously for the next hour and a half, enjoying a gastronomic time capsule of culinary heritage, which was the best meal I'd eaten in my life.

Joe, Alex, and I waddled back through Oaxaca's captivating Plaza de Armas downtown that evening, where conquistador wealth was evidenced in towering cathedrals and armories. Beautiful landscaping flourished along every block, and a lively cluster of markets bustled with freshness. What made Oaxaca truly unique was its clear cultural embrace of rich indigenous heritage, which permeated colorfully to fill the city with character. Nestled at the foot of such amazing mountainous jungle, Oaxaca was as exquisite and authentic as it had to have been over three hundred years prior, in my mind. In essence, it was the complete Mexican experience I'd always wanted.

That didn't mean that Alex and I could stay long. We were still antsy to cover more miles south, and Joe's final advice convinced us that night.

"There's a reason I stayed in Oaxaca a week. If you can leave here, then you can leave anywhere," Joe explained as he closed his panniers in preparation for morning departure. "You'll get sucked in everywhere, and tomorrow's destination will be no different. How you deal with it is entirely up to you. Now remember my real recommendation about southern México—hit the road early if you want to really get a move on. Otherwise, this heat will destroy you."

THE OPEN ROAD

Chetumal, México
Wednesday, May 25th, 2011

BMW MOA's route south from Oaxaca introduced another hundred and eighty miles of Sierra Madre ridgelines on Sunday. The humid air spiked past 100F degrees at noon after a river delta run out to coastal Tehuantepec, where eighty miles per hour still felt like peering into an open oven even with all armor vents open. Despite aspirations to ride all day, Alex and I surrendered reluctantly at 1PM and retreated to the cheapest air-conditioned hotel we could find.

"Joe was right," we agreed from under the fan while watching our soaps that afternoon. "To cover ground in these temperatures we need to hit the road at sunrise."

On Monday we executed Joe's advice at 6AM accordingly, heading inland into the most derelict conditions I'd ever witnessed. Subsistence farmers toiled with their backs to the sun and their brows to the Earth throughout every village that Alex and I passed during our ascent back into the mountains. Straining their oxen and plows across rugged angled fields, the laborers hardly looked up at our otherworldly ingression, due to their unwavering obedience to the soil. Alex and I found perspective regarding our own good fortune in witnessing such poverty, but we still couldn't help but bitch about the heat during our breaks.

Temperatures dropped finally on the eastern face as we carved into fifty miles of lush unspoiled wilderness highways that hadn't seen roadside maintenance in years. The immersive jungle floor grew six feet high right up to our tarmac's edge, with vines hanging in all directions and a series of overhead cliff bands on each side that narrowed at times into ten-foot-wide corridors, through which we passed. Eventually, the mountains gave way to a winding gully with intermittent gravel until Al and I finished exhaustedly in Ciudad del Carmen at dusk.

"I can't believe I'm sweating again already," I muttered the following morning as we started our engines for our final push.

At just 7AM it was 90F degrees outside already. So, forget about soaking the undershirts for relief on Wednesday; Alex and I instead used the gas station water hoses to douse ourselves completely at each stop as we crossed the Yucatán Peninsula. Mexicans watched perplexedly, pointing with laughter as I ran water down my neck and into my boots. What they didn't know was I'd been wearing the same outfit since Cuernavaca to make sure that I'd have wardrobe options upon arrival. Those showers were as much for my stench as anything!

Finally, the 1,300 miles of epic roads, breathtaking views and evolving scenery came to an end that afternoon in Tulum, where I did get to change my shirt. My first sight of the Caribbean delivered crystal clear waters, white sand beaches, and everything else that my imaginations had portrayed as we parked along the paradisiacal coastal strip.

"It's time for a break from the open road," Alex and I agreed. "Now, where's the nearest Tiki bar?"

Roped a Couple of Sea Turtles

Tulum, México
Saturday, May 28th, 2011

Alex and I stepped into the Weary Traveler Hostel courtyard in Tulum to discover a well-stocked bar to the right, two floors of dormitories to the left, and a thirty-foot open-air roundtable between them. Then, having just finished six continuous days huddled together in constant coordination, we separated immediately, as Al bolted to the table to start talking and I bee-lined to a hammock to watch.

Alex's approach to that group of unsuspecting strangers was like Tony Montana's plunge into a desk of cocaine. At the first break in conversation he inhaled, his eyes widened, and he let all hell break loose in rapid-fire chatter. Al's cadenced stories came one after another with hardly a breath in between to his fully engrossed audience from that point forward at the head of the table. As different guests cycled in and out of his attention span, he didn't stop talking once until 4AM, at which point he'd finally strung himself out on gab and he crashed like Montana would have too.

Although antisocial in comparison from behind my hammock and headphones, I interacted plenty in getting to know our Seattleite bunkmates, Zac and Amber, on my own that night. I even agreed to tag along with them for some snorkeling the following morning.

"We're on a three-week vacation through the Yucatán, Belize, and Guatemala, so we can't just lie around like you guys," Amber joked enthusiastically at breakfast as we readied for adventure on Thursday.

She looked to Al, who'd been staring at his plate of eggs in silence since he'd risen.

"Today's destination is the reef at Akumal Bay. You should rent gear and join us too, Alex. That is if your vocal hangover can handle it."

A muted thumbs-up was all the response he mustered.

Akumal's turquoise water and white sand burgeoned brilliantly with fishermen, swimmers, and sunbathers alike as we stepped off the colectivo taxi for our first view of the bay that afternoon. I dove immediately into the 80F water with my waterproof camera, while Zac, Amber, and Alex lay down on the beach. I'd purchased the camera back in Seattle and had yet to test it in water, which explained my offshore haste. Unfortunately, that haste also caused me to jump in without any knowledge of where to find the reef. Seaweed and sand were all that swayed in the crystal clear water beneath me twenty minutes later. There was no medium at all for my feature-ridden camera as I bobbed in bewildered exhaustion.

I scanned the water's horizon for any signs of the reef but found nothing. Then just before turning back, I dipped my mask into the water to reorient along the shore and spotted a sea turtle grazing in the distance. Forgetting the reef entirely, I dove down to the creature and hung still in the currents beside him. The turtle looked up for one moment before continuing to eat. He glided elegantly to a distant patch of seaweed with three graceful strokes as I returned to the surface for air. I followed from above, rejoining the turtle on the ocean floor again to snap photos with my camera on all settings. Eventually, more turtles appeared below too, fanning me from all angles as the best subjects I could have asked for that afternoon. Our dream-like interaction went on for at least a half-hour, during which I never looked up once. Finally, in my ultimate Jack Sparrow moment, I saw the glint of the reef in the distance as the turtles began to outpace me.

From its teeming borders inward, Akumal's reef proved to be exactly as every nature program had ever portrayed. The exotic ecosystem flourished with colorful fish, vibrant coral, and stunning biodiversity. Plants, animals, and formations of unimaginable shapes and sizes were illuminated against the Caribbean's white sand through my camera's lens. Most candid of all was a lone squid pushing tirelessly along the shelf in the reef's center. His massive eyes' unflinching disregard for my presence made me contemplate momentarily which of us had more control there in the ocean. Thankfully, I did not have to dwell on that for long, because Alex, Zac, and Amber caught up to provide safety in numbers right then.

The four of us concluded our outing with a delicious dinner of guacamole, ceviche, and fried fish at a beachside grill under the warm sunset breeze that night. The meal was rich, unfiltered, and plucked fresh from the sea that day.

"What an idyllic ending to our day of ocean adventure," everyone agreed that evening.

The next morning, Zac and Amber said goodbye as their bus arrived.

"Give us a call when you guys get back to Seattle! And send us some of those pictures from the reef."

Alex and I nodded back solemnly and watched them go. It had been refreshing to spend time with Americans after two months of foreign interaction. Zac and Amber's Pacific Northwest mannerisms and personalities had been a special treat.

Alex and I didn't have to lament Zac and Amber's absence for long after their departure, because later that afternoon a Suzuki DL1000 with Colorado plates pulled into the Weary Traveler. Al and I stared wide-eyed as the rider and his passenger parked beside us. We approached for introductions before they could even dismount.

"Hi, I'm Jane," the passenger exclaimed. as she stepped down from the saddle. "This is my boyfriend. Tim. We're riding two-up from Kansas to South America—or bust!"

"Nice to meet you! Looks like we're heading the same direction. I'm jealous of your light bikes, but I like my cargo a little better than yours," Tim smiled, pointing back to his girlfriend. "How has your trip been so far?"

Just as talking to Seattleites about Washington had been such a relief, so too was discoursing on the complexities of adventure motorcycling with Tim and Jane that evening. Tim and Jane were young and spontaneous like us, but likewise more focused than our hostel brethren, on account of the bikes.

"We're only here for one night, since we have a room booked tomorrow in Playa del Carmen, but let's all cross into Guatemala as a quartette next week," Tim proposed, as we shook hands at last call when the night ended.

Tulum had delivered new friends at home and on the road in just one weekend.

NEXT STOP: BELIZE

Chetumal, México
Monday, May 30th, 2011

The Yucatán continued to impress on Saturday, as Alex and I got our first glimpse of the legendary Tulum Ruins from the local beach. The site's monolithic superstructure jutted onto the shore, with massive rock pillars protecting its expansive ceremonial center against the crashing waves like the set of a 1950s-era Hollywood human sacrifice scene (despite its very real Mayan roots). Alex and I didn't have time to enter the park for a history lesson; instead we had to primp that afternoon for a highly anticipated happy hour at a bar called 317, which had been advertising a Brazilian Bikini Party all over town.

We amassed with a large group of other international males grinning from ear to ear outside the establishment at 8PM sharp. Then after paying the ten-dollar cover charge, we flooded into the open doors to discover an otherwise empty bar. Acknowledging a gringo gimmick immediately, Alex and I were determined to get our money's worth regardless. We hit the happy hour specials aggressively that evening during a pool tournament with three Germans.

"Pull ball? You Americans have no respect for the game!" they argued, as we clashed fiercely over international rules from across the table with laughter.

Dominik, Phillip, and Kris were unmistakably German, with light hair, high cheekbones, and deep voices. Interestingly, they were not the Nazis that my childhood movies and video games had always portrayed. To my surprise, these three exhibited sound values and respectful dialogue. Alex and I disgraced ourselves in turn with American jeers from across the table. We couldn't have been too bad, though, because the Germans invited us on their excursion to Cenote Dos Ojos the following morning.

"Come on!" they encouraged at Sunday's breakfast. "Cenotes are underground caverns unique to the Yucatán. They open to the sky through collapsed roofs to create dark lagoons full of stalactites, stalagmites, and creepy-crawlies. You really have to see one."

Deep in the woods, Dos Ojos' entrance was shadowed with dense vines as we approached with our guide, José. A narrow footpath led through thick foliage to the ethereal grotto's waterside, where José passed out snorkels and waterproof flashlights. He waved us into the water, wherein we fanned out into the cool ancient waters.

José wasn't especially animated as he rushed our tour from one cavern to the next (probably because we had negotiated him down from forty dollars each to thirty), although our own boyish enthusiasm made up for it just fine as we jumped from every ledge and dove into every nook from start to finish. The meandering chasm was scant with sea creatures compared to Akumal, but that didn't mean there was no wildlife. We actually got more than we'd bargained for when José led us via underwater tunnels to a deeper cave in the back, where an entire colony of bats startled into an overhead flurry as we surfaced. For once it was us hurrying José!

"It's no wonder the pirates of the Caribbean chose these seas to pillage and plunder—all anyone seems to do here is drink rum, explore ruins, and share tales of adventure," I pondered aloud as Alex and I waved Dominik, Phillip, and Kris off on their northbound bus the next morning.

"Good thing we have that rendezvous with Tim and Jane on Tuesday, or we'd never be able to leave," Alex replied quietly. "Speaking of which, we need to change our oil tomorrow, before the road."

Al was right. Bike maintenance trumped everything on a trip around the world. On Sunday, he and I rolled across the street and purchased a five-quart bottle of 10W40 at the local mechanic's yard.

"Where are you changing this oil?" the owner asked as he rang us up.

Al and I looked back blankly. We hadn't thought that far ahead. In fact, we were likely destined to have ended up in the middle of the street under a flattening Caribbean sun covered in grease and sweat that afternoon, but the owner had different plans.

"Come with me," he motioned toward his backyard carport.

He laid out rags, a funnel, and an oil basin for us to complete the job in the shade.

"Just leave the garbage here when you're done. I'll take care of it," he said, pointing toward the black sludge that poured from our sumps. "Thank you for your business."

"Everything was free but the oil itself," Al exclaimed after we finished. "I'm going to miss this Mexican hospitality."

HOPKINS

Hopkins, Belize
Tuesday, May 31st, 2011

A national border makes a world of difference if you can just get across it, and Alex and I were determined to do so without getting swindled by Mexican Customs. We'd read about extraneous gringo fees in our research of the Chetumal crossing. We were prepared upon arrival when the agent glossed our documents and replied with one stipulation.

"Everything is in order, except you owe a $262-peso tax for staying longer than seven days."

The fake exit fee was exactly what the online forums had warned about. Therefore, I replied immediately with Plan A—that my friends, Tim and Jane, crossed the same border two days prior without paying any tax. Having rehearsed the explanation thoroughly, my Spanish was articulate and my delivery flawless. I crossed my arms smugly as I finished.

"Your friends paid this tax when they entered the country," the agent replied.

Prepared for pushback, I went to Plan B next. The Internet had taught us that the agent's paperwork lacked any official insignia. I pointed to the inconsistency, but still he refused.

"Pay the fee."

Too American to take it any longer, Alex stepped in with an improvised Plan C.

"Where is this 'tax' money going? Somebody's pockets?!"

The agent stormed out from his booth and stood chest-to-chest in an outrage of subsequent profanities.

"Discussion over!" he stammered. "No more questions and no more games. You will be forbidden to cross this border if I have to come out here again."

The agent turned and walked back without allowing a response. So, with no Plan D, Alex and I each forked over thirteen dollars to leave México.

We didn't open our mouths again until our stamps were finally dried in the quarter-mile stretch of ungoverned dirt between México and Belize called the free zone. There we finally broke down and hired a border sherpa named Edward to guide us through Belizean insurance, tire disinfection, and bike importation in just half an hour.

"You just saved us hours of processing time, Edward. Where were you on the other side?" Alex asked with the Mexican exit fee in his hand for Edward to see as we received our Belizean passport stamps. "We could have used you getting out of México."

Edward and the Belizean immigration agents burst into laughter together in response, pulling the exact same papers out of their pockets and waving them in the air.

"Phony!" they exclaimed. "But come on, you Americans are good for it."

Alex and I didn't argue (we'd done enough of that already). Instead, we acknowledged the madness and took off into Belize post-haste.

Unlike México's overgrown shoulders, Belize's Northern Highway had fresh-cut lawns fading fifty feet on both sides into wide-open grasslands and outlying forests. The tarmac was without centerline or shoulder markings too, which made for difficult lane positioning through the rolling fields, foothills, and jungles that serpentined south. Having covered over half the length of the entire new country already, Alex and I arrived at docile Hopkins to meet Tim and Jane that afternoon.

Hopkins was a city like none I'd visited. All of its buildings perched atop stilts along the beach with their floorboards spaced evenly to allow sand to slip down through the cracks into the ocean breeze. There were no fences to delineate the properties. Rather, there were countless trails leading from the town's lone thoroughfare into mango groves and out to the sea, along which the community members raked their sand instead of their yards while conversing in the evening breeze.

Alex and I found Tim and Jane up north in a hammock enjoying the shade of two idyllic palms next to our cabana rental at sunset. The shelter stood two feet off the ground and twenty yards from the shore with curtains swaying in the wind.

"Welcome to paradise. Will this do?" Jane greeted.

"Grab a beer!" Tim hollered, raising his glass. "How long did it take you to figure out the road signs?"

He was referring to Belize's refreshing use of the Imperial measurement system.

"Well, we started making better time when we realized the freeway speed limit was sixty miles per hour. Somehow I don't think the locals ever caught on," I joked back, referring to how slow everyone drove in Belize.

"Plus, we don't speak Creole, so we could hardly communicate in a country where the national language is English!" Alex added.

On that note, we cracked beers and got to know the Coloradans again over an exceptionally American evening. Tim was a slender build with full beard, and Jane was his elegant brunette girlfriend. Cross-eyed in love, they were delightful company again after two months in foreign lands with backpackers. At twenty-eight years old, Tim's extra years of mellow wisdom provided welcome perspective for Alex and me. Jane, on the other hand, was our age, and even though taken, she was a heaven-sent reminder of American girls.

"This place is going to be hard to leave tomorrow," Jane lamented Wednesday morning, as we lay in our hammocks.

She was right too, because unfortunately, the clock was ticking. I wished we'd had more time, but in just two days Alex and I had already seen more of Belize than we had seen of México in two months. With just 8,876 total square miles to the country, we really didn't have time to hang around Belize more than a week, if we wanted to remain on track.

More importantly, there was so little going on in Hopkins that I felt my very presence could disturb the natural rhythm. Hopkins's slow and relaxed nature was admirable, to say the least, and our cabana owner, Jabar, reminded me movingly when he came to collect our final night's rent. Like most locals, Jabar was jovial and approachable. He preferred Creole to English and wore no shoes for lack of need. Jabar's dedication to the Hopkins class of 2013 was what truly struck me that evening.

"I am also a teacher here for the local sixteen-year-olds," he explained to me over a pair of mangos through his thick accent on the beach. "But not like your American schools. I have taught the same class of kids every grade level going back eleven years. I am responsible for their entire education, K through twelve."

A role model and a leader, Jabar exemplified perfectly the graceful simplicity that made Belize so captivating. As much as his genuineness made me want to stay forever, I knew it far better to leave Hopkins as I found it. Plus, Jane had found some very intriguing inland lodging for Friday at a place called Barton Creek Outpost.

BARTON CREEK OUTPOST

Mountain Pine Ridge Forest Reserve, Belize
Saturday, June 4th, 2011

Access to Barton Creek Outpost was limited, due its fifteen-mile dirt driveway through the Mountain Pine Ridge Forest Reserve, where the roads were in fact so rough and rocky that only three types of transportation could venture as deep into the jungle as we did on Friday—dirt bikes, four-by-fours, and Mennonite wagons.

Surprisingly, a nineteenth century-style roadside Belizean Mennonite community flourished inside the Mountain Pine Ridge just before Barton Creek Outpost. Villagers looked up from their fields with smiles and waves as we passed. Their grand barns, quaint farmhouses, and rolling fields were a time warp through history to an age before our twenty-first century ideas. I rolled through the antiquated settlement reverently in first gear, trying my best to preserve the peace. Five miles further, we found the entrance to Barton Creek Outpost through a grassy riverside orchard.

"Welcome! You can park here on the sward by the river. Set your tents wherever you like, if you plan to stay the night," the American caretakers, Jacqueline and Jim, greeted us.

105

Jacqueline continued from behind her sun-bleached bangs. She was toned from tending the grounds, wearing scrubby jeans.

"Camping is free, and I cook three meals a day for a moderate price. You're our only guests tonight. Go ahead and get settled, then find me when you're hungry. Tonight is spaghetti!"

Jim and Jacqueline had managed Barton Creek Outpost's archeological reserve for seven years to-date, during which they had raised all three of their children from birth. The boy and two girls were homeschooled on account of their environment, having grown up with limited electricity (when the generator was running), no phones at all, and surrounded by Mennonites in the Belizean jungle—truly as close to Never Never Land as ever imagined. The children ran through the grounds climbing vines, riding horses, and playing under waterfalls as Alex, Jane, Tim, and I pitched our tents under the shade of some low palms along the river.

Before dinner, the kids guided us upstream in canoes to the site's most prominent archeological feature: Barton Creek Cave. Known by locals as the entrance to the Mayan underworld, Barton Creek Cave was a narrow, hairline opening into the far bank's tall bedrock. Along each of the entry's sides were shadowy and forlorn formations, which resembled animated ghoulish faces from our bobbing vantage point before them.

"The Mayans were right to respect this cave," I uttered quietly in the silence. "I certainly don't need to get any closer."

That evening, Tim, Jane, Alex, and I joined the host family for a delicious American-style dinner in their open-air A-frame lodge overlooking a bend in the river. The lodge featured just one room in its center for cooking and maintenance, but was surrounded by a 360-degree porch filled with hammocks and Mennonite chairs. We lit the lanterns at dusk and spent the rest of the evening listening to the jungle breathe over the lapping of currents and laughing children. The next morning,

Alex and I discussed our plans for the upcoming week with Tim and Jane over Jacqueline's five-star breakfast.

"There is an ancient Mayan city called Caracol that is forty-five miles deeper into the Mountain Pine Ridge along all dirt roads. It was discovered only recently too, and so it's still relatively untouched. You guys will love riding through the wilderness just to get there," Jacqueline revealed as she served us coffee. "Caracol dates back to around 600 AD. When fully excavated, it's expected to be even bigger than Tikal."

Alex and I nodded enthusiastically to the sound of that, while Tim and Jane wavered reluctantly.

"Sorry guys, but we're going to continue for Guatemala on our own," Tim explained at the end of the meal. "Riding two-up is risky enough in good conditions. I can't push our luck any more on this dirt with Jane on the back."

So, while Jane and Tim packed for the road, Alex and I lightened the load, removing our panniers for the bumpy ride ahead. The four of us outlined a rendezvous in Guatemala and departed in opposite directions to clear skies and dry trails.

The DR650 was built to be capable and comfortable on the street, yet sturdy and agile in the dirt, and Thirio lived up to that reputation monstrously on Saturday. Stripped of everything but the necessities, she proved perfectly powered in the Belizean backcountry, with her clutch and brakes in a constant grudge match against Earth. Those forty-five miles to Caracol were the best motorcycling of my life!

Caracol's sixty-mile off-road entry into the Belizean jungle was an admittedly tough sell for most tourists, and so Alex and I arrived to an empty parking lot at noon. We entered the vacant park to discover neither signs, nor trails, nor safety precautions along the prehistoric ruins ahead. Several minutes later, I encountered a foundation that had yet not even been unearthed entirely. I sank to my knees, lifted a rubble stone, and brushed the dirt away from around it, and in doing so, realized my dream of being a true archeological adventurer.

The further I explored, the more enchantment befell me. At the main quad, Alex and I found ourselves surrounded dauntingly by towering colossal pyramids in the center grounds. I hit the biggest one first, bounding its foot-tall stairs in a feverish race upward. A second and third staircase ascended ultimately to the top, where I found two excavated vaults. Treading lightly among intricate carvings and stonework through their catacomb hallways, I continued to conquer my childhood fantasies, all the while reaching to my waist for my whip out of habit.

In total, I spent forty minutes searching every nook and cranny until ultimately taking a break on the uppermost step. The jungle blossomed around me in every direction, with monkeys swinging through the trees and parrots soaring above. There was not a soul in sight (aside from Alex, who I had well-learned to ignore by that point). I closed my eyes, and when I opened them, I could not say how much time had passed. All I knew was that I'd never forget the heat of the sun or the chatter of the jungle or the taste of sweat dripping down my tattered bandana as time stood still and centuries meshed together.

"Hey, we can nap back in the tents!" Alex eventually interrupted from below. "Let's hit the road before it gets dark."

I started my descent back to reality.

After completing the same stretch already on our ride into the park that morning, Alex and I did not anticipate any surprises while enroute back to Barton Creek. Therefore, we were unnerved at the sight of a military-green convoy kicking a dark cloud of dust ahead, about halfway through the return journey. My gut tightened when the mysterious guerrillas came into view as we advanced cautiously from behind. Clearly soldiers, they smoked their cigarettes unflinchingly, bouncing around the beds of the trucks with painted faces and hardened expressions.

The fighters examined us through the dust off their bumpers, the same as we examined them. Both sides showed mutual respect, as neither party could determine what the hell the other was doing so deep in the Belizean jungle. Finally, after ten minutes of rolling standoff, the convoy veered onto a gated, overgrown bush trail and we parted ways with neither waves nor acknowledgement.

Back at the outpost that evening, we asked Jacqueline about the shadowy commandos over dinner, and she reckoned that they were British Special Forces on routine Mountain Pine Ridge training missions. Nevertheless, I was still going to remember them as the jungle cartel that Alex and I outran on our tomb raiding adventure that day. Barton Creek Outpost was validation that Alex and I really were experiencing something truly unique on this trip, especially after the blaring social interaction of the recent hostel scene. Tucked deep in the middle of nowhere in such ancient ambiance, I couldn't have been more satisfied there in the jungle with my tent and motorcycle.

On to the Next One

Flores, Guatemala
Monday June 6th, 2011

Alex and I met a biker after the Guatemalan border who had been on the road for two and a half years on Monday. He was exhausted with the experience and on his way to fly home from Belize.

"For a long time, I loved the ride, guys," he reminisced, as if trying to remember from the saddle of his BMW on the roadside shoulder. "But the past six months have started to chisel away at my morale. The road can't last forever . . . I need to go home."

The perspective puzzled me, as I'd never considered the mental toll of adventure.

"Well, don't worry about the border ahead. We just exported bikes, exited Belize, passed Guatemalan vehicle inspection, imported bikes, and entered Guatemala in less than an hour," Alex reassured him. "High heat and humidity are your only problems there."

The old sage tipped his helmet toward us, before soldiering east.

An hour west from there, the city of Flores was our destination. Perched atop an island no greater than a square-

111

mile in area in the middle of Lago Petén Itza, Flores was so small that Alex and I were able to find Tim and Jane's V-Strom on the western shore after just five minutes of searching across the main bridge. Flores' size did not correspond with its popularity. As the closest hub to Central America's most famous Mayan ruin, Tikal, it boomed with tourism.

"We'd better get to bed early tonight if we want to be first in line for the park's opening tomorrow," Tim reckoned that evening. "At least we have one sizable advantage over everyone else . . . unlike the rest of those rubberneckers, we brought our own rides."

I nodded back emphatically. I loved motorcycles. I didn't know what had happened to that rider on the BMW. I couldn't say I judged him either, but it would take hell or high water before I'd ever leave Thirio by choice.

CHILDHOOD BEWILDERMENT

Tikal National Park, Guatemala
Tuesday June 7th, 2011

I was accustomed to cow and deer silhouettes on the yellow signs from North American roads, but anteater, jaguar, and snake set an unprecedented tone for adventure outside Tikal on Tuesday morning. Excitement was high when Tim, Jane, Alex, and I arrived at the largest excavated Mayan ruins' parking lot. A modest man named Gustavo approached us there before the entrance.

"I offer discount student rates for entry into Tikal," Gustavo greeted from behind a whimsical pair of bifocals. "It will save you each twenty-five quetzals."

At 7.8 Guatemalan quetzals to one US dollar, the potential savings were a whopping three bucks, but we entertained Gustavo with our attention anyway.

"Friends, I require no gratuity, and your entry is guaranteed," Gustavo assured us.

"We're in!" Alex decided, as the rest of us shrugged our shoulders; Al could never pass on a deal.

Rather than head toward the ticketing booth, Gus led us to the far corner of the parking lot, out of sight from the main entrance, where he tipped a park ranger at a small perimeter guard shack and motioned us past an alligator-infested lagoon (signed accordingly with a gator silhouette). On the opposite side of the swamp, Gustavo parted a patch of thatch leaves to reveal a path into Tikal.

"Something tells me we are about to short a starving government of some much needed, legitimate cash," Tim groaned as we continued.

I turned and asked Gus if we'd be receiving actual tickets.

"Tickets?" he laughed. "*I* am your ticket!"

Gus hung back in the jungle discretely when we hit the park's outermost trail.

"Goodbye . . . there is no reentry," he saluted with a turn. "Enjoy the student discount."

The surrounding chatter of monkeys and toucans stirred the exact sensations that the road signs had foreshadowed, as we turned to face Tikal from inside. Dating back 2,500 years, the park featured six temples among its 3,000 total structures, which spread across sixteen square kilometers. I had my work cut out for me as I separated from the others right away to jog every corner of the park.

From the Grand Plaza (famous for its main quad cluster of two magnificent temples and two elaborate acropolises) to the sixty-five-meter perch atop Temple Four (where I could see into the horizon and all five other temples peeking above the canopy), I scoured Tikal as if I were the first to arrive on the dig. I certainly wasn't allowed to pull bricks out of the ground, like in Caracol, but that didn't stop me from exploring all the spiral staircases, hidden tunnels, and peek-a-boo views throughout the morning.

Finally, I caught up with Tim, Jane, and Alex at noon, and we agreed we'd seen enough. Still tired from the previous day's ride, we were excited for a quiet evening and solid rest as we exited the park and walked back through the lot, but a familiar figure appeared in the distance beside our bikes when we got there. He had a helmet in one hand and a cigarette in the other.

"G'day mates. You thought you'd lost me for good!" Charlie greeted with an uproarious round of handshakes and hugs. "Hard to believe it's been since Mazatlán, eh?"

Alex and I had known Charlie was in our neck of the Americas, but we'd been unable to coordinate a reunion, due to limited Guatemalan Wi-Fi over the past week. Nevertheless, we were back together by stroke of luck. Charlie stood tall, beaming, healthy, and smiling, despite the trauma of his high-side in México, which he brushed off casually at first mention.

"Never mind that. My mate, Patrick, and I are here for the ruins now. We won't have much time in the park, but Tikal is little more than a checked box at this point anyway," Charlie continued, with a nod toward his new friend, Patrick, who smiled amicably from atop his DR400. "What say we meet tonight back in Flores. Then we can give Patrick a proper introduction and get to know Tim and Jane too. Also Tom, I'll be curious to know how you've managed not to kill Alex yet, you patient bastard!"

"So much for our quiet evening and solid sleep!" Alex, Tim, Jane, and I laughed.

ZEPHYRLODGE

Lanquin, Guatemala
Friday, June 10th, 2011

"Now I know how the Harley riders back at home feel when they wrap their throttles down Main Street, except a hundred times more badass," Al exclaimed outside Flores.

Motorcycles didn't generally get much bigger than 250cc in Guatemala, and so our 400s, 650s, and 1000s turned a lot of heads when Charlie, Patrick, Tim, Jane, Alex, and I departed as a thunderous storm of five. That trend continued throughout the day along unmaintained highways and unsigned backroads into the southern mountains, where townspeople watched us pass from homes made of cinderblock walls, tin roofs, and dirt floors. The rural Guatemalan living conditions contrasted starkly against our intrusive state-of-the-art machinery, but still we were welcomed with tremendous community pride throughout our ascent. Friendliest of all were the kids, who spilled out of every doorway and window at the unnamed crossroads where we stopped for lunch.

"Everyone stay calm ... I got this," Charlie cautioned, as the prepubescent mob circled around us like a school of hungry piranhas.

He reached into his tank bag and grabbed a handful of toffees. Smiling, Charlie tossed the candies gingerly into the crowd. Immediately, we were all wrapped spontaneously into a sugar-infused game of tag. Kids were the same all over the world, I realized as I stepped exhaustedly back into Thirio's saddle afterward—they just wanted candy. I laughed as Charlie threw one more handful to leave them chasing us out of town.

Our destination, Lanquin, was rumored to be home to Central America's paramount hostel. I'd first heard of Zephyrlodge way back in Tulum through whispered rumors of endless parties, incredible tours, and absolute remoteness. Therefore, my expectations were high at the end of a quiet dirt road on the outskirts of town. A garden entry footpath led us down to Zephyrlodge's headquarters, where the thatch roofed main lodge sat suspended atop a ridge in the highland valley. The building was open-air and barn-like in structure with a lounge bar on its first floor and private rooms on the second. Thick, green forest covered the mountains all around us, with cattle grooming their riverside lowlands and the sun shining down throughout the valley. Additionally, there were three A-frame dormitories nestled down the arm over a winding river below. I pitched my tent just beyond them, due to limited beds that night.

"This really must be Guatemala in its full glory," Charlie commented, as we caught up with him and Patrick that evening.

Charlie was full of new stories, which were a welcome alternative to what Alex had been repeating of late, and Patrick was a refreshing character too. Patrick was a forty-seven-year-old Swede who had worked in San Francisco for the past seven years as a chemical engineer. Rumor had it that Patrick had spearheaded a breakthrough against cancer recently, but you'd have never known it in talking to him. Currently on his eighth week of a four-month tour of Central America, Patrick rarely spoke of himself, which made it that much cooler when he mentioned that he'd read our blogs.

"You know, I've been reading your reports, and you guys sounded cool on paper," he remarked over happy hour that night to Alex and me. "It's impressive to find out that you really back it up. You two young guys are the real deal."

I was certainly honored to hear him say that, and I was consequently disappointed that the camaraderie would not last beyond Thursday, since Charlie and Patrick would be continuing south ahead of us.

"Charlie is meeting his mate, Andy, in Costa Rica next week. Meanwhile, I'm meeting my girlfriend in Nicaragua," Patrick explained.

Charlie's Australian friend, Andy, had already shipped his Tenere 660 weeks prior via ocean freight for their upcoming reunion. They were going to pick it up in San José and then ride into South America for three months together. Alex and I were not ready for that type of pace, though. We were too stunned by Zephyrlodge's beauty to leave just yet.

"Cheers mates, it was great to catch up. Give us a buzz when you make it to Costa Rica," Charlie concluded on Thursday morning as he mounted up in the Zephyrlodge lot with Patrick.

He turned to address Tim and Jane next.

"You guys will be in our thoughts. Get back to the road as soon as you see fit."

Tim and Jane hugged him back with stifled tears. They were also packing to head south in a hurry that same morning, but for a terribly different reason. Tim's mother had been struggling in the hospital for the past several days with a sudden blood infection, and on Wednesday, she'd deteriorated dangerously. They were heading straight to Guatemala City behind Charlie and Patrick to catch the first available flight home.

"We'll see you guys soon," Tim confirmed with determination. "We just have to be with Mom right now."

"You've got our prayers at your backs," Alex and I saluted.

Thunder cracked throughout the distant valley as both pairs pulled away. On our own once again, Alex and I turned back to the Zephyrlodge bar.

LIFE ON MARS

Lanquin, Guatemala
Saturday, June 11th, 2011

The Zephyrlodge business model: charge dirt for rent, pour drinks down their throats until 3AM, and serve hangover recovery food the next day until the cycle starts again in a spontaneous self-fulfilling, organic liquidity that makes days pass in a blur and the nights go on forever. The guidebooks hadn't discovered Zephyrlodge yet by the time Alex and I were there, but the joint sold out nightly to a fully captive audience nonetheless.

The madness was genius too—you started a tab by handing over your passport as collateral at check-in. Beds were five dollars a night, food was cheap, and drinks were priced standard, with the caveats that your third night was free and your fourth came with all-day happy hour. Plus, guided tours departed to multiple attractions daily, and partying kicked off at 6PM with funk music cranking across the entire grounds. By eight o'clock, a roadhouse environment took hold each evening. Then came the all-night madness, complete with beer bongs, sombreros, karaoke, and of course, peeing off the deck. My college binging skills had gone dormant long ago back in Alaska, but three days at Zephyrlodge reawakened them handily!

Typical of any good party, there were girls at Zephyrlodge too, but new women weren't my concern there, because instead I was hanging onto the prospect of a southbound Kiwi girl that Charlie and I had managed to coerce to our table back in Flores.

"Seeing as the three of us are all Commonwealth, why don't you ladies take a seat for a drink?" Charlie had offered cheerfully back on Tuesday to Justine and her friend, Kelly.

They'd fit in hospitably at our table full of greasy bikers the rest of that night, and I'd even gotten Justine's email by the end.

"Hope to see you down south," she'd smiled, writing it on my cigarette pack, before saying goodnight.

I'd held onto that pack dearly for the next week in hopes of reuniting with Justine again, but then somewhere during Saturday's all-day happy hour, I'd pulled out my last smoke, lit 'er up, and crumpled that empty pack coolly into the garbage can beside me. So smooth! Justine's info was long gone by the time I realized what had happened the next morning. After digging through the garbage and leaving empty-handed, I remembered why I'd stopped binge drinking in the first place.

"That's the Zephyrlodge madness," my bartender consoled me on Sunday over a Bloody Mary. "You just got to roll with it, amigo."

I decided to shake off the mistake with a six-hour tour of Semuc Champe that morning—because if there was one thing I'd learned from the road, it was that adventure cured a broken heart.

Semuc Champe was a three-hundred-meter geologic anomaly of limestone bridging across a raging mountain river gully in the highlands above Lanquin, with a series of pristine pools lapping from one to another overtop of it. A blistering two-mile hike led to our first lookout for the attraction that afternoon, where the legendary pools hung across the canyon below us shimmering blue, green, purple, and even orange under the afternoon sun. There were heaps of the pools too, none bigger than the Olympic standard, and each trickling serenely into the next as the river churned underneath the smooth limestone foundation.

Tourists in the States would have been limited to a distant boardwalk along Semuc Champe's edge to preserve such an environment and to protect public safety. In Guatemala, our guides had instead built a trail right through the formation's best jumps and slides, which we trampled in a joyous swim through the cascades upon descent. Guatemalans understood the Earth differently than Americans, and I walked away completely fine with that, despite my initial apprehension to tread too heavily—because that intimate experience of Semuc Champe's splendor left me feeling more connected than a boardwalk ever could have, and I was rolling with it.

The Characters

Alex and I had watched enough generations of guests come and go that we were starting to feel like leathery-skinned Zephyr-vets when we finally awoke with enough sense to pack our bags. I had never felt worse saddling onto a motorcycle than I did on Wednesday, having just partied out of my tent for the past seven days. I suspect Alex felt similarly, but somehow he and I managed to stay together and pass through Guatemala City with only one U-turn that afternoon.

More importantly, we survived the impatient drivers and unhurried workers of Guatemala Shitty's highway expansion project. Traffic fines, apparently, did not double in Guatemalan construction zones, because time and again my handlebars were squeezed within inches of wreckless, onrushing motorists and jagged, roadside guardrails, as drivers passed at will with neither lane distinction nor respect for human life through the ten-mile gauntlet. Thirio's nimble frame proved advantageous, allowing me to carve the mess cleanly without shitting my pants.

Wednesday's actual pants-shitting moment had already happened anyway on the outskirts of Lanquin when I'd waved to a farmer along the road. I'd been cruising at thirty-five miles per hour, mid-gesture with only one hand on the handlebars, when Thirio's front wheel knocked upward off a rock. She'd arched forty-five degrees into a sideways wheelie atop her slipping rear tire with me in the balance. I'd gassed full throttle and braced for a high-side impact, until Thirio's staunch rear Pirelli finally took hold and pulled us back to Earth. My puckered ass had kept both hands on the bars from there, especially during the subsequent construction zone that would follow.

Wednesday's destination was Lago de Atitlán, an area known for its beautiful lake and three surrounding volcanoes, but Alex and I were still sixty miles away when the sky turned orange that evening. We stopped short to detox that night in Tenpec at a quiet hotel, where I fell into bed immediately. Even as I slipped into the sheets for my first peaceful night's rest in a week, my mind raced with Zephyrlodge.

I'd made memories with countless people representing all walks of life there, including: Loancy, the twenty-one year old Costa Rican jewelry salesman who'd left home with $180 and a rock polishing kit; Maya, the cutest former Israeli soldier ever; Thomas and Ester, the Dutch couple driving a decommissioned Texan school bus hostel to Panama; Dieter, the twenty-year-old Guatemalan bartender with a British accent; Aurelie, the French dame working the front desk seven days a week; and Joost, the Dutch mountain guide with stories of his own. Saying goodbye to each of them had been individually heartbreaking the final night, until an astonishing final statement from Chi, the Brit fashion designer born to Cambodian parents.

Taking the roach as we discussed the shame of never meeting again, Chi had looked me in the eye and remarked with his British accent:

"That's the beauty of it," he'd said with certainty, drawing on the ember. "The immediacy of the situation is what makes this experience so amazing; it's the catch in this beautiful existence that is transpiring."

I would never forget those words.

KIWI GIRLS

"This might be a longer sixty-mile ride than we expected," Alex muttered as we killed engines and coasted to a stop on Thursday.

Halfway between Tenpec and Atitlán, we'd made great time covering our first thirty miles through foggy foothills that morning, but now at the base of the third valley, our path had ended with a completely blown bridge across a whitewater cascade. The closest detour would backtrack two hours, according to our map. The gap was too big for us to jump (yes, of course, we considered it). Alex and I knew that Guatemalans were too crafty to take no for an answer. It didn't take long for us to find a faint set of tracks upstream at the river's widest point.

"Expect a lot of slippage in the rear across the rocks below. The front will bounce and sway against the current, but it will stay true if you remain balanced. If any vehicle could make the crossing, then these bikes can too," Alex instructed as we approached the water's edge.

I squared nerve-wrackingly against the shoreline, rolled steady on the gas, and powered into the chop as the smooth rocks slid like ice cubes underneath Thirio's tires in the eighteen-inch current.

After being submerged briefly to my ankles, I emerged triumphantly on the opposite side, with river water steaming off Thirio's engine from between my feet.

"The amphibious DR650!"

Twenty minutes later, our destination, Lago Atitlán, panned upward into view at the crest of our highway's next saddle. Known to be Central America's deepest lake, the landmark was so wide that we couldn't see either end of it from our vantage. Likewise, the tops of the surrounding volcanoes were invisible in overhead clouds, but their majesty was evident in the steep green mountainsides rising up from the shores. A fog hung low over the shoreline, through which Alex and I could see the faint outline of our endpoint, San Pedro, on the opposite side.

San Pedro was going to be twenty miles away, regardless of which way we rounded the lake. Eyeing rain clouds up north, Al and I chose the southern path, in hopes to stay dry. The subsequent downpour caught us along the southern shore, nonetheless, and our pavement deteriorated thereafter into a muddy hill climb reminiscent of riding a bicycle up a Slip 'N' Slide (except these bikes weighed five hundred pounds and this wasn't your parents' backyard). Alex and I slid into San Pedro two hours later, having averaged twelve miles per hour all day. Immediately, we followed tourist density levels in town to the hostel center.

A hot spot along the backpacker circuit, due to its proximity to Atitlán's volcanoes, San Pedro was a common destination for backpackers moving south. I hoped to find some Zephyrlodge buddies in the bunkhouse as I parked Thirio outside our hostel that evening. Luck did me one better, because there at the front door stood the Kiwi girl, Justine—and a chance at redemption for my cigarette case catastrophe.

"Fancy meeting you here!" Justine exclaimed as I dropped Thirio's kickstand and delivered a sopping mud hug.

She took my greeting surprisingly well, despite the requisite change of clothes afterward. Picking right back up where we'd left off in Flores, we hit it off splendidly the rest of that night. Justine was smart, sexy, and foreign, all of which drove me wild. Unlike a typical backpacker, she really could keep up.

"This is fun," she mused in my ear at the end of the night. "I have a mint idea . . . let's take a guided horseback tour tomorrow morning."

I nodded back exuberantly. Then, after a drawn-out goodbye, I hurried to get some sleep for the first plans I'd made in months.

Untitled I

San Pedro de Atitlán, Guatemala
Friday, June 17th, 2011

Friday's guided horseback ride was supposed to be a romantic cavalcade across mountainous Guatemalan jungle, through which Justine and I would ignite a torrid relationship against an untethered frontier (or so went my imagination), but instead it proved nightmarish from the moment we approached the stables.

"You think these horses are OK?" Justine probed at first sight of the stock. "Their hips are showing prominently."

She was right. They didn't look like Bitsey's horses from my childhood, but things were different in Guatemala, and skinny livestock were not out of place. Neither of us wanted to pass cultural judgment too quickly, and so we mounted cautiously. From the saddle, my horse's shoulder and neck muscles appeared dangerously malnourished. Its breathing was uneasy, and it winced under my weight. The horse stamped back and forth agitatedly until the guide came by to deliver the crack of a whip across its neck. I patted the horse calmly where it had been hit, still hoping that my uneasiness was based on American preconceptions. The truth became

133

tragically obvious half a mile later, when one of the other horses fell backward in exhaustion.

"Help! Something is wrong here!" the Canadian rider yelled, bow-legged on his feet over the wearied bag of bones after the horse's hind legs had crumpled.

He dismounted as the animal tried to stand up and fell sideways again back to Earth. Bewildered, the horse caught its breath for another minute before mustering itself ultimately back to all fours. Having watched the whole ordeal, the guide finally approached to whip it across its face as he straightened the saddle.

"Your horse is fine. Please continue," the guide commanded, waving the Canadian back to mount.

So set the tone for the rest of our ride, which was only just beginning to unravel. The horses bit each other and reached agonizingly for the scant vegetation that they could scavenge, despite continued whippings. There were several more falls too, one which required the guide to drive his cowboy boot into the horse's rib cage three times before it would rise. When asked if we could dismount and walk alongside the horses, the guide denied us.

"That would be too slow," he argued. "These horses have three more tours today. Andale!"

Hearing about animal cruelty was one thing, but being at its reins was another. In the end, all of us left the stables too upset to speak on that afternoon. Neither Justine nor I had much energy for romance that night. The last I saw of her was over a brief plantain and eggs breakfast on Saturday.

"Kelly and I are departing for Antigua today so we can stay on schedule for our dive classes in Honduras," Justine lamented from across the table that morning. "I hope you can catch up."

Alex and I weren't going to be able to keep up with the girls' zigzag pace ahead. Our only hopes of seeing them again would be to ride straight to Copán Ruinas in Honduras and meet them in a week. I hugged Justine goodbye and told her to find me there.

"I'll plan on it," she waved.

I finished my coffee and fumed as I acknowledged that plans changed often on the road and memories faded quickly. The inhumanity of those damned stable owners had cost me my Saturday evening date, and now I might never see Justine again. Moreover, they had cost me my conscience, and I needed to do something about it.

"The owners are rabid alcoholics," my server explained when I paid my bill. "We are disgraced by their operation here in San Pedro, but charitable contributions never make it to the animals—they all go straight to the bottle."

Sickened, I walked to the corner produce market and then returned to the ranch to drop two carrots apiece into each of the horse's stalls. I tossed them gingerly near my feet, as if expecting the horses to trot over and forgive me for playing a role in their hell the day prior.

The trail horses hardly looked up in response. Some declined to even approach from the opposite end of their stables for the treat. Others chewed the carrots in agonizing futility like corn on the cob, too weak to snap the vegetables in half. They were not jubilant like the horses from Bitsey's stables. Rather, they were malnourished to the point of depression and resigned completely to their fate. Mindful of my impact's meaninglessness, I left the ranch deflated. If anything, I hoped that Bitsey would appreciate the effort.

HONDURAS HO!

Jalapa, Guatemala
Monday, June 20th, 2012

San Pedro's Saturday night buzz was that some gringos across the lake were throwing a techno party—and everyone was invited. I could have thought up far better ways to kill brain cells than raving, but the novelty of Guatemalan electronica managed to pique my interest, nonetheless, as word spread through our hostel that evening. In the spirit of adventure, I decided to join the crowd.

"The ferry to the party is first come, first serve," Alex explained to me as we gathered at a creaking dock behind a mob of eager partiers.

The inebriated group packed tighter as the boat emerged from the around the shore's southernmost point. A glorified dinghy, the fiberglass outboard could have seated twenty people reasonably, but it was soon sardined with more than thirty before the captain could even tie to a cleat. Alex and I hung back, watching the hull sink deeper into the water as even more passengers boarded.

"Stop! Hold!" the captain screamed when a kid jumped onto the overhead canvas.

At the literal tipping point, the boat listed hard to port and took on water. A skirmish broke out as the crew started throwing those not seated back onto the dock. Alex jumped into the fray too, plucking people from the ferry by whatever means possible, which at the height of the excitement had him steadying a boat rail with one hand and strangling a drunkard with the other! Finally, the captain pushed off the dock with his hull barely out of the water to escape the horde.

"Gracias amigo!" he saluted to Alex. "We'll be back for you in fifteen minutes."

I still despised raves, but Saturday's party proved to be worth the wait after our safe arrival, because for five hours that night I was unaware of where my body ended and where the throngs of others began in the freedom and debauchery that only an international jungle madhouse could create. You kind of had to be there for an explanation better than that. Needless to say, Alex and I had seen enough of San Pedro by the time we awoke from our hangovers on Sunday afternoon. On Monday we headed south toward the Honduran border to rendezvous as planned with Justine and Kelly.

Al and I hoped for an uneventful ride as our hangovers lingered into rainy roads south of Atitlán, but our next jolt of adrenaline hit that afternoon anyway when a vast section of earth unseated ahead from above our highway. The mass lurched and liquefied at once before dropping immediately onto our lanes in a cloud of debris as we skidded to a stop. The air smelled rich of ancient soil as sedan-sized boulders emerged smoldering from the dust, with tree roots dangling above.

"We'd have both been buried just five seconds sooner," Alex shook his head in the drizzling silence afterward.

We gave each other a humble "OK" nod and weaved forward between the stones toward Jalapa.

Having survived the rave and then the mudslide in consecutive days, I turned my attention toward surviving another round of Moctezuma's Revenge as my guts turned to geysers that night at our hotel in Jalapa. I knew it wasn't the water or the food that had wrecked me this time around as I winced in pain and prayed for mercy. Rather, it had been the lifestyle, which Jim had explained so well back in Mazatlán.

"People get the shits in México, and they blame it on the water. The truth is they come down here, eat way too many refried beans, blackout on tequila, and stay up all night partying. That's why you get the shits!"

OVER/UNDER

La Ceiba, Honduras
Wednesday, June 22nd, 2011

Alex and I opted for a Google route that included fifty miles of stable and solid hardpack through agricultural Guatemalan jungle from Jalapa to the Honduras border. Farmers waved cheerfully from the behind their straw-hat brows, driving donkey-drawn carts of burlap sacks filled with fresh coffee bean. Artisan crafts and ancient cuisines cornered unmarked crossroads and neighborhood squares alike. The storybook route wasn't on our paper map, and not a single sign marked its path. Alex and I relied upon the friendly and jovial farmhands along the way for directions to the nearest border. We knew we were getting close when we reconnected to pavement as foretold.

"The farmers said that the nearest border crossing would be twenty minutes from here!" Alex confirmed with the imminent exhilaration of a whole new country and culture when we finally hit a highway and pulled over for gas.

"Is the frontera close?" Alex asked the cashier.

"Yes, only fifteen miles. You are almost there," he replied. "The El Salvador border!"

Astounded and alarmed, Alex and I explained immediately that we'd expected Honduras, to which the cashier shrugged casually toward the other direction.

"In that case head east. You will be at Copán in sixty miles."

Alex and I stared at each other blankly, as lost as we'd been the entire trip. Then we shrugged back just as casually, and saddled up in awe of our adventure.

Al and I stamped out of Guatemalan immigration, exported the bikes, stamped into Honduran immigration, and imported the bikes an hour later. Guatemala and Honduras shared the same Customs building, but only the Guatemalan side had electricity as we crossed. Honduras's lack of illumination was not an admirable first impression there upon entry, but its antiquated paper-based systems also did not rely upon electricity. Alex and I still arrived early for our rendezvous with Justine and Kelly south of the border that afternoon.

Copán Ruinas had abundant accommodations to choose from, and we parked proudly at the cheapest of them all to prepare for the girls upon arrival (which meant a shit, shower, and shave for me, and probably just a shit for Alex, since he had no skin in the game). We headed downtown afterward to find the girls.

"Are you sure Justine said Tuesday?" Alex asked me later as we waited for the Kiwis in the main quad.

Neither Alex or I had actually planned a specific meeting time or location with Justine or Kelly, aside from Copán Ruinas on Tuesday. We were beginning to scratch our heads on how to find them.

"Yeah, I'm sure," I replied.

Copán Ruinas had a single main plaza with one predominant tangent strip, which we had just searched. Cafés adorned every corner around us, and colorful artistic banners hung overhead in the sunset breeze.

"If the girls are anywhere, it would be here."

Alex and I ducked reluctantly into the nearest restaurant to devise a different plan. Before our first round of drinks even arrived, Justine and Kelly sat down at our table, as if right on time for a reservation.

"We got in a little late, but we had no trouble finding you," Justine explained, as Al and I stared back with astonishment. "All we did was tell a street salesman that we were looking for tall white friends, and he led us right here!"

"I guess there's a reason the Mexicans called us Los Torres Gemelos (Twin Towers)," Alex replied enthusiastically as he and I rose immediately for salutations.

The street salesman stood at the entrance with a cheerful wave. I tipped my hat and flicked him some pocket change before turning back to Justine to rekindle the fire. She was so striking there in the warm evening twilight that I never wanted that dinner to end as we reengaged and drew close anew, but both of us were stifling yawns when the check came, on account of our tiresome experiences with Honduran customs.

"I'm glad we caught up again," Justine hugged me goodnight when we retired to our separate hotels that evening. "Have you made up your mind about coming with me to Roatán? We're heading there tomorrow. Come on . . . you and me in the Caribbean for five days straight?"

I promised to see her soon as I hugged her back, and that night, back in bed, I stared into my ceiling fan to confront my indecision.

A day's ride east, Roatán Island was home to the least expensive SCUBA certifications in the world. Alex, Kelly, and Justine had already booked reservations for the upcoming week there. My plans were undecided, because I'd been emailing Campamento Wind Sports Resort down the road in Trujillo, where for fifty dollars a day I could rent windsurf rigs with unlimited board and sail changes. The thought of Justine in a bikini made me drool, but June was classified as windy season on the Caribbean coast. Plus, I had a lot of expensive hobbies already outside of diving (motorcycling and windsurfing, for example). I couldn't decide whether to be over the water or under in the week ahead.

GOING ROGUE

Trujillo, Honduras
Thursday, June 23rd, 2011

Alex and I awoke early to review each other's itineraries and complete routine bike maintenance in preparation for our first time being apart on Wednesday.

"Take care of yourself and tell Justine I can't wait to see her," I requested sheepishly as we finished just before Al's ferry to Roatán.

"Don't worry man—I'll wing your ass off out there! She'll still be single when we meet again," he smiled.

I questioned my own sanity momentarily for having opted out of a week-long stay on a Caribbean island with Justine as Alex boarded the boat ramp, but when he disappeared onto the deck, I remembered why I'd chosen to go rogue. The whole point of this entire cross-continental escapade had always been to do absolutely whatever the hell I wanted for one brief moment in my life—so I was going windsurfing!

Riding solo took some getting used to enroute to Trujillo as I ventured south. The potholes seemed deeper and the turns felt sharper without a wingman for backup. The locals spooked me, too, during my first stop for gas. I walked out of the minimart to find Thirio surrounded so tightly by admiring young Hondurans that I had to push through them just to wedge myself back into her grasp.

"650ccs! How much did you pay for this?" they asked enthusiastically.

The onlookers wore ragged, incongruous clothes and lacked any clear purpose that I could see. Thirio and her modifications valued around $6,000, which I estimated to be a significant chunk of their annual salaries. I chose to downplay the disparity of our worlds and keep the lowest profile possible.

"$1,500 American," I replied with a timid nod.

They smiled in appreciation as I gave a good crack to Thirio's throttle on my way out.

Regardless of my jitters over vulnerability, Wednesday's biggest hurdle was actually another blown bridge after the gas station. From its crumbled foundation I scanned instinctively up and down for a low spot like before, but this waterway was not a Guatemalan tributary. This was a full-bore river, complete with rushing rapids, and the only way across it was an opportunistic "ferry" made from two canoes lashed under a wooden platform with an outboard Mercury. I boarded it cautiously at the next crossing, blessing myself for safety as the rope-bound planks shifted in the current beneath me.

"This boat loads and unloads from its bow. Turn your bike around before we get there," the captain instructed when we pushed off the shore. "You have three minutes before disembarkation."

Somehow I managed to ten-point turn all of Thirio's five hundred pounds atop the ferry's listing deck of rutted 2x10s without ending up at the bottom of the river like the rest of that bridge. I kissed sweet solid ground the second I was safe on the opposite side, and half an hour later I finally arrived at Campamento Wind Sports outside Trujillo to find a locked cabana on an empty strip of beach. Campamento did not appear to be the bustling congregation of wind-worshipers that its website had purported, but at least the wind was blowing as I parked. I looked for the owner, Chad, on the grounds, but he was nowhere to be found.

"You're here for Chad? You're two days late," next-door Tranquility Bay Resort's Canadian owners, Larry and Linda, shook their heads as I walked up to their bar for an explanation. "The cabana has his windsurf equipment, but he shut down early this season . . . Chad's already home in Vermont!"

I groaned disappointedly. Windsurfing was a notoriously fickle sport, and this was a classic start. Chad had certainly seemed aloof in his emails, but he'd never indicated that his entire operation would be closed by the time I arrived.

"Talk to Dennis," Larry continued. "Dennis is one of my employees, but he works for Chad too during peak season. Maybe Chad left instructions with him. It's good wind today."

It took the rest of the afternoon for Dennis and Chad to coordinate my rental over email. Eventually, I rigged up that evening just as the wind shut down—another typical windsurfing experience. Larry approached from the Tranquility Bay beach with two drinks in his hand as I disassembled my rig on the shore, never having hit the water. He handed a drink to me and looked across the placid ocean.

"Sounds like Chad didn't really explain what you were getting yourself into out here," he said as he gazed across the water.

The sun was setting behind us, but the Caribbean evening was beautiful still.

"Say, Linda and I are from your neck of the woods—Vancouver, BC. Seeing you've come this far to windsurf, we think you should hang around to wait for the wind."

He turned and motioned toward a distant building out back of Tranquility Bay.

"It's nothing special, but for fifteen dollars a night you can bunk in our employee-housing dorm if you want. We're on winter staff, so no one is staying there now, and it even has a private bathroom."

Having gone months without a decent bath, I agreed unquestioningly with a raised glass.

"The only thing is," Larry remembered, before turning back. "Our broadband provider's competition cut our fiber optic lines last week, and the Internet is still down. That's the H-factor."

He rolled his eyes and headed to the bar, where I found him and Linda that evening.

Tranquility Bay's green, landscaped lawns featured a series of secluded bungalows basking in cool pockets of indigenous shade with the open-air bar between them under an 80F degree onshore breeze. Waves lapped at the sandy shore, just twenty yards from my vantage there as I ate and drank. The resort lived up to its name in every way imaginable, with the exception of Chimmy, who introduced himself to me at dusk, upside down, slung from the roof by his tail. I stood perfectly still as Chimmy grabbed a lock of my hair, gave it a sniff, and pressed both of his baby-sized palms against my forehead. I straightened with a pause as he hopped gingerly onto my shoulder and cooed into my ear. Never had an animal examined me with five fingers and opposable thumbs. A monkey introduction was an eerie role reversal.

"I adopted Chimmy two years ago when he was a baby," Linda explained as I held him afterward. "With my nursing background, I couldn't help but nurture him. And now he's just one of us . . . except he hasn't a clue he's his own species."

She was right. Chimmy picked bugs out of the horse's mane, guarded the lawns with the vigilant dogs, and zipped between trees with the toucans as I watched inquisitively for the rest of that night. I retired to my private quarters, still miffed about the wind but with eyes ever widened by my first day of solo adventure.

Rigged Up

Trujillo, Honduras
Friday, June 24th 2011

There are two types of windsurfing: plowing and planing.

Plowing is for beginners—you stand at center of the board, pull the sail upright, and deflect enough wind to slog slowly through the water.

Planing is for adrenaline junkies—you sink into the harness, distribute your weight down the mast, and lift the rig's nose out the water. Nimble and aggressive, you can then carve the waves, jump into the sky, or simply haul ass in a mesh of surfing and sailing, with the wind as your energy and the water as your canvas.

Campamento's wind forecast was bleak for the weekend ahead, though, and Friday's light breeze was going to be my best opportunity at planing in Trujillo. I was chomping at the bit when whitecaps appeared offshore that morning, and I waded eagerly into the warm surf with a low-wind rig. On first try I waterstarted, locked into the harness, and slipped inside the foot straps. The board heaved upward onto the surface in response, but sank in a subsequent lull. I tried again, unable to get up after that. I tried again and again, still to the same end.

In the end, I failed to achieve even one steady plane that afternoon, until finally on the day's strongest gust, I caught a single tack in perfect windsurfing form with a straight back, bent knees, and loose arms under the angled sail. I buttered from one wave to the next, with water lapping across my nose for several hundred yards until losing it all on my jibe at the Honduran jungle shore. Hair on fire lit, I resurfaced overjoyed—and satisfied absolutely of that itch I'd just scratched.

CARNIVAL

Trujillo, Honduras
Monday, June 27th, 2011

With neither wind in the forecast or Internet at T-Bay, nor Alex, Kelly, or Justine until Wednesday, I relied upon age-old Honduran culture for entertainment over the weekend in Trujillo. Saturday's Carnival filled the void splendidly with an array of spectacles that included a Latin parade, a seven-block dance party, and the Roman candle man.

The Roman candle man appeared in the main quad at dusk with a wooden A-frame strapped to his head and Roman candles pointing in all directions. Then he hunched over, lit the fuse, and ran through the streets with children chasing as his bombs launched flack into the buildings, cars, and crowds. The night only spiraled more wildly from there, and Linda could see it in my tired eyes on Sunday morning.

"Carnival is a stark contrast to the normal calm here in Trujillo. It's strange to see anything happening in town at all, given how quiet it normally is," she explained over mimosas and eggs. "You see, they say that Trujillo is the beach where Columbus first landed on mainland America. The inside joke here is that when Columbus left for home he told everyone not to do anything until his return . . . and they haven't since."

I laughed champagne and orange juice straight through my nose in response, as that explained a lot of my experience with Honduras so far.

ON THE RUN

Esteli, Nicaragua
Thursday, June 30th, 2011

Contrary to its namesake, the Pan-American Highway did not connect between Central and South America. The United States had built a canal across Panama in 1914. Yet no one had built a single road to Colombia to date, due to a hundred-mile blockade of jungle so dense that only outlaw cartels claimed its jurisdiction. Known as the Darien Gap, the stretch between Panama and Colombia was regarded as one of the few places in the world where adventure motorcyclists dared not explore. Few had ever passed all the way, and those who'd attempted had warned of infection, jaguars, and violence. So, Alex's opening salvo was a great relief on Wednesday at our reunion in La Ceiba.

"I locked down our passage to Colombia, dude," he explained coming off the ferry ramp that morning. "She's a hundred-year-old, steel-hulled, sailing vessel called the *Stahlratte*. We'll board July 28th for a four-day cruise through Las Islas San Blas to Cartagena. Charlie and his mate, Andy, are riding it too . . . and maybe Tim and Jane, if they make it back in time."

Alex clearly hadn't had enough opportunity to talk on the island, and for once, I was happy to let him keep going.

"Even Justine and Kelly are thinking about riding it, man! Speaking of which, the girls are half-a-day south of us already, but we can catch them in Nicaragua if we haul ass today. Considering that we have less than a month left on this continent, I say it's time to ride!"

Having seen plenty of Honduras and not nearly enough of Justine, I could not have agreed more with Al. We set off on a feverish full day of riding and stopped at an auto hotel in Tegucigalpa near the border that evening. Auto hotels were my favorite style of Central American highway lodging after a long day on the road. Reminiscent of storage complexes, their empty parking lots all featured walls of rolling doors, which each represented a one-car garage and overhead apartment. Parking attendants waved you into an open unit from the driveway and rolled the door down upon entry. Inside, the bellhop recorded limited information at a check-in window before handing over the room key for upstairs.

Alex and I liked to stay at auto hotels every chance we got, but there was one downside—they were used primarily for prostitution. Most of them charged by the hour, all the beds vibrated, and there was always at least one porn channel available. We drew some perplexed looks every time we rolled up to share a single queen (the cheapest option, of course). Al and I stressed repeatedly that we were just friends at check-in on Wednesday, but the idea of two guys sharing an auto hotel was clearly gay in our concierge's eyes, regardless.

"What-ever!" we laughed that night.

After sleeping on opposite sides of the bed, we crossed excitedly into Nicaragua at Las Manos the next morning.

Honduras had given some brilliant moments, but outside the confines of gringo establishments, I would primarily remember the country for its downtrodden exuberance. Columbus jokes aside, Honduras had seemed the culmination of centuries of failed policy from my vantage point. It lacked the outward civic pride that I'd loved about México and Guatemala, although I did harbor high expectations for Honduras' future. The youth there aspired to great heights as they moved into a more globalized workforce, and the elderly still cemented deep cultural roots.

South of the border, my introduction to Nicaragua started intensely that afternoon when I was pitted face to face against local police just an hour into the country for passing on double yellow. Now, before my mother has visions of a closed-casket funeral procession, let me underscore the regularity with which everyone passed illegally in Central America. The old folks did it, the semi-trucks did it, the school busses did it—everybody did it. Nicaragua's two-lane highways were so clogged with cumbersome Kenworths that you had to take every opportunity to pass if you wanted to cover any ground. I'd leaned out and gunned past three trucks in a row before noticing the police checkpoint in the distance.

Unfortunately, the cops had noticed me. Forthcoming negotiations lowered my punishment from a night in jail to just sixteen dollars cash, under the one condition that I didn't tell any other authorities about the crooked transaction. The blatant corruption proved surprisingly effective too, because I played by the rules for the remainder of the day.

"Traffic laws seem a little stricter in Nicaragua," I admitted disappointedly to Alex that evening before bed in Estelí. "Time for me to stop riding like a Mexican."

FIREWORKS

San Juan del Sur, Nicaragua
Tuesday, July 5th, 2011

Alex and I reunited with Justine and Kelly south of Estelí in Granada, the oldest city in the Americas, where Justine and I escaped immediately for a long overdue romantic dinner.

"It's about time that we ended up on the same page," she and I agreed that evening, with abundant eye contact over a delicious seafood display.

Overlooking Granada's ancient streets from the hotel balcony that night, I couldn't help but steal my first kiss goodnight.

"She's so elegant and adventurous, dude," I gushed to Alex, back in our room afterward. "I'm not sure what she sees in me."

"Probably just the motorcycle," Alex guffawed back.

Justine and I spent the rest of the weekend seeking privacy and sharing secrets in Granada's outlying grottoes and groves until Monday, by which point everyone had grown weary of the city's overbearing beggars.

"I think we have seen enough of Granada. Let's head to San Juan del Sur next," Justine recommended that morning. "*Lonely Planet* here reckons it's the surf town of Central

America. What say Kelly and I hop a chicken bus and meet you boys there?"

Alex and I snickered with a nod. A chicken bus was a decommissioned US school bus that had been covered in religious paintings and converted to Central American mass transit. Chicken buses looked ridiculous, and they often carried livestock, but they were a staple of transportation for our backpacking acquaintances. The buses were admittedly reliable too. The girls arrived in San Juan del Sur an hour after Alex and I did, just in time to celebrate Fourth of July at a beachside bungalow rental.

The Kiwis probably couldn't have cared less about Independence Day that evening, but they partied respectably to keep up with our American pride, as Al and I downed two forties each. There were no traditional pyrotechnics to celebrate afterward, but there were still plenty of fireworks that night. Justine and I lay on the beach in each others' arms under warm winds and unmarred stars for hours exploring the universe, and in truth, I had never had a more patriotic night in my life.

VOLCANO ISLAND

Ometepe, Nicaragua
Friday, July 8th, 2011

The Fourth of July gave me pause to reflect about the image that Alex and I projected as Americans on the road and how the bikes had come to define us. The backpackers called us "the Yanks doing it on motorcycle" with marveled excitement, while the locals whispered "the big bikes" in quiet appreciation. This was for good reason too, because Alex and I were not your typical tourists. Dismounting from menacing black steeds in thick armored suits, our entrance into every city center or hostel courtyard was thunderingly loud, geared to the hilt and larger than life! As a complete package, Alex and I couldn't have been more American if we'd tried as two brazen Eagle Scouts riding giant dirt bikes at age twenty-four through rain, heat, breakdowns, borders, and banditos along two continents of unsigned crumbling roads. When you factored in that we'd both saved the money by ice road trucking in Alaska, it was no wonder that we sometimes got cocky.

The state of the union may have been a little bruised of late over global politics, but Alex and I were living proof that

Americans still had it going on. That was never more evident than on Thursday when we fired up and roared out of San Juan del Sur with the whole block watching in awe (and while Justine and Kelly followed from behind on the next available chicken bus).

"We'll get to the boat about an hour ahead of the girls," Alex yelled over the engines as we accelerated onto the highway outside of town. "We'll need the extra time to book the bikes for the island. It's a passenger ferry primarily, but I read online you can pay extra for motorcycles."

Straight out of an adventure novel, Thursday's destination was the island of Ometepe, which rose out of the water with a land bridge between the two active volcanoes in the middle of inland Lago de Nicaragua. Smoke wisped ominously from Ometepe's twin, smoldering, green peaks when Al and I pulled up to our ferry's landing an hour later. The stark image set an unsettling stage for drama should either dome decide to blow, but luckily, I did not have long to dwell on the prospect of a fiery molten death as we waited.

Instead, my apprehension was shifted quickly to a shallow watery grave when the ferry arrived with no boarding ramp for the bikes along its rusted hull. The deckhands looked at each other anxiously as Alex and I parked on the docks after buying our tickets. They had hand-lifted two 125s over the water and onto the ferry's deck already, but that plan wasn't going to work for DR650s. After huddling in intense deliberation for several minutes, they emerged with their solution—a ten-foot 2x10 plank, which they laid from the dock to the deck.

"Don't worry," one of the crew quipped to me while the others came for Thirio.

He embraced my shoulder as his four friends began to push Thirio across the six-foot gap. I gritted my teeth as all of my worldly possessions hung suspended over open water atop the moving platform. One misstep would have ended life as I knew it there at the bottom of Lago Nicaragua, but

Nicaraguan ingenuity came through spendidly, with both bikes lashed safely to the deck by the time the girls arrived.

"Kelly and I are flying to the Corn Islands tomorrow. So with our limited time here on Ometepe, we want to see Santo Domingo beach. It is one of *Lonely Planet*'s top recommended attractions," Justine explained when we disembarked and entered a nearby hotel.

"I can taxi you to Santo Domingo beach tonight round-trip," our host, Yazzin, replied forthrightly at check-in. "Meet me in the lobby in an hour."

I primped myself as best I could for what was going to be my last date with Justine for the foreseeable future, and then I met the others as planned.

"Do you like Whitesnake?" Yazzin asked proudly, as Alex, Kelly, and I piled into his ancient Chinese sedan.

He slammed a cassette into the dash and started pumping his fists at full volume. Yazzin's under-engineered ride was so overloaded that Alex and I had to hop out and walk alongside it over every speed bump. The spectacle of two gringos unfolding themselves in unison and then hopping back into a car blasting "Here I Go Again" was witnessed a dozen times over by Ometepe's locals all the way to Santo Domingo that afternoon (how's that for American imagery?).

Justine, Kelly, Alex, and I watched the open-air sunset from under the shadow of both volcanoes during dinner, knocking back enough drinks to end up screaming along to Yazzin's power ballads the whole ride home—most notably Mr. Big's "To Be With You". The night's main excitement was still ahead, though. Justine and I had booked a private double bed for our final evening together, which we retired to promptly upon return. Waking up in her embrace was strangely foreign to me the next morning. I'd ignored romance for the past two years in preparing for the road, but Justine had managed to dismantle my defenses. Somehow her warmth, scent, and liveliness had me swooning beyond my better judgment. Plus, she had filled my head with Kiwi vocabulary over the past weeks too—I think to make sure I didn't forget her.

"Just when things were getting good," I regretted as she packed that morning.

"I know. It's too bad Kelly and I booked these Corn Island fares so far in advance, but we'll pick up where we left off next time," Justine smiled somberly. "I know we'll see more of each other. Perhaps in Panama or Colombia?"

I nodded back, and we left it at that. I was going to miss Justine on the road ahead. There were many traits that attracted me to her, most important of which was that somehow she'd maintained her female elegance every step of the way through our adventures. I waved to her longingly as she and Kelly boarded the ferry that afternoon.

Eventually, I turned back for Yazzin's hostel with unexpected relief. All the moving and fussing in trying to keep up with the girls had really worn Alex and me out over the past several days. Our main priorities would just be eating and sleeping for the upcoming weekend with the girls finally gone—our truest display of American colors yet.

Brash Delivery

Unknown, Costa Rica
Monday, July 11, 2011

"I can't find this town we're in on a map," Alex exclaimed from our roadside Costa Rican dinner table on Monday. "But according to the mileage markers, we are sixty miles north of San José. That should be close enough to find the Aussies there tomorrow."

His disorientation was a result of that afternoon's border crossing, which had been as cavalier as Alex or I'd ever managed. We hadn't even decided to even leave Ometepe until that same morning, when we'd received an email invitation from Charlie.

"Hey mates, Andy and I are heading south from San José in the next few days. Not sure your whereabouts, but you Yanks should come along. Drop me a line if you're in the area.— Charles"

Having just spent the preceding week working around feminine preferences and chicken bus sluggishness, Alex and I had both salivated at the opportunity for another motorcycle posse as we'd read the note aloud. Immediately, we'd confirmed to Charlie that we were on our way.

Crossing at the Costa Rican border several hours later, we'd followed signs for San Jose to our no-name town for dinner.

"There's no correspondence from Charlie or Andy today," Alex continued at the table, checking his email before returning to Google Maps.

He snapped a picture of his computer screen with his camera and examined it. With no physical map of Costa Rica yet, he and I had resorted to photographing online screenshots of our route for directions in the new country.

"Let's just ride to San José tomorrow and figure it out when we get there."

I nodded with my mouth full of food while swallowing, and that was the extent of our planning for the next twenty-four hours. Alex and I hadn't had a deadline in three months under the sun of an endless summer. Every night had lasted as long as we'd wanted on our eternal vacation. On top of that, we each still had $15,000 in the bank and enduro motorcycles in the middle of Costa Rica, with nothing remotely close to a schedule. It was no wonder that the trip was becoming more off-the-cuff every day.

ANDY THE AUSSIE

San José, Costa Rica
Tuesday, July 12th, 2011

"G'day mates! How the hell are you bastards?" Andy greeted when Alex and I pulled up to his and Charlie's hotel after connecting over Facebook.

He approached us with excited eyes and a firm handshake. Tall, loud, and one hundred percent Australian, Andy smiled wide through his red bearded jawline with a cigar between his teeth.

"You gents are right on time. My bike arrives tomorrow."

His Teneré 660 had been scheduled for delivery originally back in June, when Charlie had met him after Zephyrlodge, but it had been delayed five weeks since then, due to rerouting of its freighter.

"You can imagine we didn't get bored waiting for five weeks," Charlie chimed in, as he stood up further back in the lot from behind his glistening bike, which he'd just finished detailing. "Andy and I have toured all of Costa Rica, flown to Cuba and back, and raised absolute hell here in San José over the past month. At least those are the details I can share with you."

Charlie and Andy flashed shit-eating grins to each other, reliving their escapades again.

"Tell you what, mates—don't unpack just yet," Andy followed. "I've got a rewards program with my business back in Australia that earns points for me to spend abroad. It turns out that San José is one of the only cities in the network around here, so Charlie and I are packing up now to spend some points at the Hampton Inn and Suites. I booked you two a room."

Dumfounded, Alex and I followed excitedly with our dirty luggage and smelly gear into the Hampton lobby across town, where we were greeted with automatic sliding doors, a spotless modern interior, and an American breakfast buffet! Upstairs, our rooms had HDTVs, pillow top mattresses, and even air conditioning! Al and I groveled endlessly to Andy while donning our plush bath robes and complimentary slippers, thanking him blue in the face until finally that evening he'd heard enough.

"Alright mates, that's sufficient talk about the room," Andy implored. "Let's talk dinner. There's a renowned steakhouse across town that also accepts points, and I'm getting the tab tonight."

Tuesday's dinner at Los Ananos Grill included multiple racks of ribs, a steak each, corn, guac, beans, and bottomless scotch on the rocks. Back at the Hampton, I slept until 9AM without waking once from Central America's typical cacophony of roosters, marketers, or mufflers. That didn't mean that the wee hours had been entirely restful, because six weeks of Third World malnourishment in Guatemala, Honduras, and Nicaragua had left my gastrointestinal tract ill-prepared for Tuesday's calorie surge. Alex and I both suffered turbulent flatulence, and Charlie fared even worse, spewing from both ends into the toilet throughout the night.

Charlie was still so wrecked that I stayed at the hotel to monitor his toilet paper and electrolyte levels, while Alex went with Andy to retrieve his bike from customs on Wednesday.

After several hours of our favorite Mexican soaps in between his outbursts, Charlie waved me over eventually to make a request. I pointed over to the two rolls of toilet paper stacked atop the bathroom counter and shrugged back questioningly.

"No, not that," Charlie winced. "You need to clean your girl mate. You can't be riding a filthy pig."

He nodded toward his leftover degreaser, kerosene, and toothbrush in the corner. Charlie was tired of an audience, I realized. I stacked him an additional three rolls and headed down to Thirio in the Hampton parking lot to take the hint. Andy and Alex pulled up alongside me as I finished soaking, scrubbing, and wiping her.

"Bloody Costa Rican port paperwork went on forever!" Andy remarked as we roasted a round of his Cubans while he outfitted his own luggage in the lot.

Alex cleansed his ride too, like I'd done to mine. After the cigars, all three bikes were pristine for the next adventure.

"Ay, let's say we head for Panama now that I got my wheels?" Andy suggested in the elevator on our way back upstairs to Charlie. "A month in Costa Rica has been plenty in wait. I know Charles is ready too, assuming his colon can keep up."

Alex and I agreed resoundingly. Costa Rica had proven too Americanized for our budgets already, and the American dream was definitely not cheap—even with Andy's handouts. More importantly, we were excited to be back in the company of proper adventurers—even if one of them was still completing trips to the toilet every hour.

TROPICAL STORM TOM

Volcán, Panama
Friday, July 15th, 2011

"The plan is to meet Patrick in Panama tonight, boys. He's shipped the Mrs. back to San Francisco, and he's on his way to meet us there," Charlie remarked as we descended the Hampton elevator for the final time.

Alex and I hadn't seen Patrick since our brief introduction in Guatemala, but Charlie and Andy had caught up with him and his girlfriend in Costa Rica more recently. We were all keen for a reunion south of the border now that he was back on his own.

"First up before we get to the Pacific coast is a mountain pass," Andy warned, looking up from his GPS as clouds formed overhead.

The skies released a drizzle as we donned our waterproof layers in the Hampton valet cover. The precipitation intensified during our ascent of the 4,000-foot pass ahead, whereupon sheets of water amalgamated into my lap from down my chest and up my thighs. I blessed my Gore-Tex liners all the way to the top, as the cool pools pressed against me through the torrent. Just when the air temperature sank below 60F degrees, those waterproof membranes failed with a cool rush into my shorts and down my legs. From the inside out, my boots soaked next. Moisture crawled slowly up my undershirt to armpit level. My gloves had never stood a chance, and even my noggin was mopped from open vents in my helmet. Only my shoulders remained dry by the time we crested the pass.

Cold seeped from every direction from there upon descent, where for the first time in three months I actually felt endangered in Central America. My hands and feet turned to ice blocks, mangling Thirio's levers without feeling. My legs and arms burned in cold pain. Only by locking my jaw could I keep it from rattling. I focused solely on the heat of my core to keep Thirio upright through the icy fog vertigo that enveloped the next three hours of the coastal face. We arrived at Costa Rica's jungle Pacific coastline as prunes riding submersibles.

"Rendezvous with Patrick will have to wait until tomorrow," Charlie, Andy, Alex, and I agreed immediately at the nearest hotel that evening, still a hundred miles from the Panama border.

"We are in for another wet one, mates," Charlie groaned disappointedly the following morning at the discovery that our riding armor remained saturated, despite the wall of fans that we'd assembled to dry them overnight. "We'd be better off in neoprene at this point."

Warmer coastal rains pounded even harder as we continued south toward the border on Friday. The four of us crossed into Panama at noon and checked into our rendezvous hotel in Volcán with wet passports and waterlogged spirits.

"Patrick has been equally delayed by downpour according to his email here, but he's planning to meet us tomorrow," Charlie reported to everyone's approval that evening after checking Facebook.

"By the way, Andy, you've hit the ground running if your first ride on the continent happens to be through a storm that can slow Patrick's progress," he exhaled, closing his laptop after checking email.

"That was one hell of an introduction to Western Hemispheric riding," Andy exclaimed in reply.

Everyone laughed back in appreciation as wet gear and tired bodies sprawled across every flat surface in our dormitory with the deluge pounding overhead. Central America's rainy season had started, and the forecast was for no end in sight.

HOLDING TOGETHER

Volcán, Panama
Saturday July 16th, 2011

"Ahoy! Let me out of this rain!" Patrick yelled from outside our dormitory on Saturday morning.

Upon being let in, he poured a cup of water from each boot as he removed them at our doorstep. He looked up through matted hair as he sat down in his own puddle.

"I don't know, man. We can keep riding south if you want, but it's wet out there."

Finally dry for the first time since the Hampton, Charlie, Andy, Alex, and I all shook our heads back in unison. We had scant interest in returning to the elements on Saturday. We had a laundry list of rain-related chores to attend to anyway. So without further discussion, we booked a second night in Volcán and started our errands that morning with, well, laundry.

My nose had grown accustomed to the sweat that had crusted across my riding gear over the past ten weeks, but Panama's tropical humidity had recently changed that musty, distinguished funk to mildewed, downright putridity. The other boys' armor had fared similarly, and our hotel dorm room smelled like a gasoline-soaked compost bin. The gear was so rank that I actually apologized when dropping it at the laundromat.

"Oh, and I need this done same-day," I finished shamelessly on the way out the door that morning.

My errands continued across the street at the hardware store in the afternoon, where I purchased a thick set of bright yellow rubber coveralls to fit over my armor for the rains ahead. I didn't care if I was going to look like a fish sticks spokesperson throughout South America—I wanted to stay dry.

"OK, Charlie, what is that "thwacking" sound that just started coming from Thirio's drive train?" I asked back at the hotel carport afterward, turning my attention to overdue maintenance.

"You either got a shit sprocket or shit wheel bearings, mate," Charlie reckoned after a test ride.

I swapped both for spares, but the sound persisted.

"Check your chain too," Alex added. "That kerosene soak could have dried your O-rings in San José."

Thirio's links rejuvenated marginally after half a can of wax.

"We're both going to need new chains soon, given our mileage, anyway. Squeaks and cracks only get worse over time."

"Agreed. Something tells me that her next 10,000 miles will not be as effortless as her first, but at least I'll be dry," I replied.

Thirio was at 13,000 miles without a tune up since México and showing every bit of it.

PANAMA PAUL

Bocas del Toro, Panama
Wednesday, June 20th, 2011

Charlie, Andy, Patrick, Alex, and I came upon an adventure DR650 while enroute to Bocas del Toro on Sunday. Its rider carried no luggage and sat casually in the saddle at a four-way stop wearing jeans and a Western Washington University Vikings T-shirt. Alex killed his engine and stammered as we pulled up.

"I went to WWU! Who the hell are you, man?" Then eyeing the man's bike, he continued. "And where'd you get that friggin' in-line fuel filter?"

Al and I had been looking for filters for months.

"Name's Paul," the sixty-seven-year-old glanced upward from his phone. "From Ferndale, Washington."

Ferndale was ten miles from where Alex and I had hatched the original plan for our grand motorcycle adventure two years prior in Bellingham, and we explained the connection immediately while pointing to our Washington State license plates. Paul smiled and surveyed the other bikes.

"Looks like you guys have been on the road for some time," he said, nodding toward our various zip ties and tape jobs.

"My house is about thirty miles from here, on the way to Bocas. My garage there has spare filters, all the tools, and a six-pack in the fridge. You boys are welcome to stop by today."

"Enough said, man," Patrick replied plainly as we all put on our helmets.

Half an hour later, Paul's three-acre plot delivered a panoramic view stretching southerly from the Pacific to the Caribbean from atop a rolling green prairie. The afternoon sun shimmered magnificently across both oceans, with the Darien Gap distantly in between. Panama's isthmus at the bottom of Central America had seemed so far away back in Bellingham, and here I was, now almost 10,000 overland miles from home with its landscape image in front of me on the property of a man born in the same place that the whole dream had started.

Shaded by oak trees, Paul's barn-like garage was big enough to park a Peterbilt. Inside awaited a full assortment of professional-grade tools kitted specifically for motorcycle maintenance. Charlie, Andy, Patrick, Alex, and I followed in amazement as Paul gave us a walking tour of the shop. Then we cracked beers for some serious guy time. Paul's dry floors and full-sized equipment turned the usual dread of maintenance to an outright thrill, and his aftermarket inventory was equally impressive. Every one of us, including Paul, had improved his bike's condition dramatically by dinner time. We stared excitedly at our bikes and thanked him for his generosity.

"You're a hell of a man, Paul, but unfortunately the beer's run out, so it's time for us to go," Charlie joked.

"Don't mention it," Paul smiled. "It was my pleasure. You Washington boys have a ride in the North Cascades for me when you get home, you hear? Now go on and enjoy Bocas."

I got my first glimpse of the Bocas del Toro Archipelago upon arrival at the Almirante port. A nine-island paradise positioned just offshore of Panama's mainland coast, Bocas del Toro featured golden sand beaches overflowing with lush palms. The tropical paradise was also in the rain shadow of the mountains we'd just crossed, offering a much-needed reprieve from the recent torrents. Almirante's water ferry only carried passengers, though. We were forced to cross onto the main island like a pack of mundane international backpackers, after parking our bikes in a guarded lot.

The next several days of Bocas proved to be just as Paul had promised: hot, picturesque, and overrun by partiers. That atmosphere may not have been Paul's cup of tea, but jumping off nightclub dance floors with bikini-clad women into moonlit Caribbean waters suited me just fine for the rest of the week. As my old buddy, Mike, had once so vehemently declared:

"These are your roaring twenties Tom—you got to live like it!"

FINAL BOARDING CALL

Panama City, Panama
Saturday, July 24th, 2011

As romantic of an idea as adventure motorcycling ever sounded, there was no part that was easy. That was evidenced emphatically by continued tropical downpour and major engine malfunction during my final week in Central America.

Patrick fired up his stallion first, after readying his luggage back in the Almirante lot on Friday. Then the others started too, with their cold engines roaring. The herd was preparing to move, so I turned the key, dropped the choke, and hit Thirio's ignition. The familiar crank of her starter motor whined, but for first time in four months, she did not turn over on the third rotation. Instead, the starter continued to drone while I paced through several different variations of choke and throttle. I looked perplexedly up at Charlie, Andy, Patrick, and Alex as it started to drizzle overhead.

"Was your fuel petcock open all weekend? Maybe your carb flooded," Alex proposed.

I ripped out Thirio's heart and disassembled it to find the carburetor clean, with neither detritus nor deterioration. I checked the air filter—there was some dirt but no signs of disorder. I pulled spark plugs—they were charred but clean; I replaced them anyway. An hour later, Thirio still wouldn't start, and her headlight was fading dimmer with the battery on every attempt.

"I don't know, man; let's check the plugs for actual spark," Patrick reckoned. "Just hold them to the engine block and hit the ignition."

The test revealed immediately that Thirio had no current. Given that our posse's collective understanding of motorcycle mechanics was weak in electronics, Patrick had, in fact, clarified the issue and confounded it at the same time. Rudimentarily, we WD-40'd every connection, checked every fuse, and even swapped Thirio's ignition coil for Alex's. Thirio still wouldn't start. It was clear that we needed a professional, as the puddles formed into streams around our scattered tools in the mud.

"I'll stay and help Tom, but you guys should get moving. Panama City is a full day's ride. We'll catch up when we get this pile to turn over," Alex directed as the others mounted.

"Don't dawdle," Charlie replied. "Our *Stahlratte* voyage sets sail for Colombia next week, and I expect you Yanks to be on it. Worst-case you can ship your bike broken to South America, but I reckon the grace of Central America will have you running before then."

Andy returned from paying his parking fee and pointed back to the billing station.

"Actually, I believe your luck is starting to turn already, mates. Hector, the parking lot owner, just offered to haul you to the nearest Suzuki mechanic. It's four hours across the mountains in a town called David, and he only wants $160. You won't find anything better at this moment's notice."

Hector waved from across the lot, while Charlie, Andy, and Patrick saluted with silent nods. The boys pulled out onto the highway as Hector's short-bed Toyota pulled up to the shoulder.

Alex and I removed Thirio's front tire so that she would fit into the bed, and we rested her frame precariously upon the forks, while Hector gathered several townsmen from the street to help lift. Then as everyone gathered for position, one of the volunteers stumbled drunkenly, and tipped Thirio down into the shoulder's three-foot drainage embankment. Her left pannier had still been open, causing my sleeping bag, sleeping pad, and dry clothes to spill scattered into the water below. I stared at my most cherished belongings floating beside my upside-down motorcycle in a gasoline rainbow of six-inch runoff. Eventually, I wiped my brow and jumped in alongside to retrieve them.

"Alright, amigos, you will have to ride together behind me. I have too many tools in the front," Hector explained after he stepped down from the bed twenty minutes later with Thirio's forks tied safely into the corner.

I threw on my riding gear, high-kicked onto Al's seat, and straddled him over the mountains and through the rain for the next five hours. I never heard Al's opinion of that experience (didn't care to either), but suffice to say, I was ready to get off his bike by the time we arrived at David. I knew we were there when Hector pulled into a backyard marine mechanic several miles out of town. Classic of Central America, the "friend" recommendation had brought us to a hole-in-the-wall homie hookup. I lowered my expectations initially as we parked beside a rat's nest of rusted cars, boats, and other assorted small engines.

Tato, the mechanic, was already in the bed of Hector's pickup examining Thirio on his knees before Alex and I even removed our helmets. He jumped down after preliminary inspection and asked everything we had tried. Listening methodically with subtle nodding and pensive breathing, his eyes raced with attention as we explained our earlier troubleshooting. He went straight for his multimeter while we unloaded Thirio from the bed. Returning with the tool and a six-pack, Tato developed a worried look on his face halfway into his first beer.

"The connections that are failing can mean only two things," he said with a swig.

He unscrewed Thirio's computer chip and plugged it into Alex's harness. Al's bike fired with its first rotation.

"And since your bike's brain just started his engine with no issue, that means we are dealing with a failed stator pickup."

I didn't know what a stator pickup was, but my concern grew as Tato drained Thirio's oil and removed her left-side engine case. The failed stator was mounted inside the case, and Tato cut right through the factory gasket to get a better look.

"You didn't need that gasket anyway," Tato reassured me, reaching for his second beer.

He pointed to a tiny box inside, which was connected by two wires.

"Here is the culprit. You can't buy these in Panama. They are special order—and $300 too."

Before I could even get a look, Tato snipped it off with a pair of dykes. He squirreled through a nearby bucket of randomly assorted gadgets and pulled out a similarly shaped box to examine it.

"Off of a 1998 marine outboard, but it will work. Too bad the brackets do not match," he commented, with the crack of his third beer. "I can fix that."

Tato hunched over a grinder and a vice to forge a new bracket from his scrap metal bin. At the end of his fourth beer, he finished the replacement and mounted it. Tato dialed its position, soldered the wires back together, and replaced the casing. Finally, he poured in fresh oil and stroked the ignition until one chug, two chugs, and THREE; Thirio screamed back to life. Tato beamed from ear to ear.

"Next beer's on me, Tato!" I exclaimed in excitement.

Tato had just diagnosed the problem and rebuilt the solution with his bare hands in less than three hours. He'd also dropped everything he had been doing from the moment I'd arrived, and he charged only $120.

"Here you go," I said, handing him a Benjamin and a Jackson (since Panama used the US Treasury bills for its own domestic currency). "Do you think I should replace the stator in Colombia?"

"Are you kidding? That's the strongest part on your bike now!" Tato replied.

Alex and I caught up with the gang on Saturday in Panama City, where an unmistakable bike was parked next to Charlie's, Andy's, and Patrick's at the hostel. Last seen by either of us at Zephyrlodge, it was Tim and Jane's DL1000.

"Mom made a full recovery," Tim greeted from the foyer. "She sent us off as soon as she could, and we've been catching up to you since. Perfect timing, right? We're boarding the *Stahlratte* too!"

It was easily the best news I'd heard all week.

"Tom, we just heard from Justine—she's coming too, while Kelly takes a side trip with some new boy toy," Charlie chimed in. "She'll need a ride to port on the back of your bike . . . you lucky dog."

It was, again, the best news I'd heard all week.

After four months on the road, somehow just about everybody I'd met on this trip had funneled down to the same point along Panama's isthmus at the same time, and now we were all boarding the *Stahlratte* together for a four-day cruise of the San Blas Islands. Given the way my week had just unfolded, I was excited for a break from the captain's seat.

FIRST STACK

Carti, Panama
Tuesday, July 26th, 2011

"Who says you're not a romantic, Tom?" Justine beamed stepping off her chicken bus as I unveiled a brand-new DOT-approved passenger helmet to her.

Unlike the rest of my Central American passengers, Justine was in it for a long haul. Unlike the rest of Central America, Panama actually enforced its helmet laws too.

"It's strange to say, but I can't think of a more amorous gesture," she said, while buckling it over her head. "Except I can hardly kiss you with it on. Are you ready to sail to South America together?"

I was, in fact, anticipating the best four days of my life, but I managed to keep my cool with a lingering kiss on her cheek.

"Alright, you two cut that out," Charlie interjected, rolling his eyes. "Before we get to your pleasure cruise, remember we first need to hurry up for the one landmark attraction we've all been awaiting. Panama Canal viewing hours open in less than an hour. Let's get moving."

There were neither passing tankers, nor changing sea levels, nor even an interesting museum at the Miraflores Locks when we arrived. From its observation deck, there wasn't actually anything happening at all along the critical shipping lane. Even the hard-hatted employees appeared bored to be on their unceremonious smoke break at the east end, while Charlie, Andy, Patrick, Alex, Tim, Jane, Justine, and I posed for photos. However, the true splendor in the end was the symbolism that the Panama Canal represented, which became evident after we took pictures. I gazed across the channel at its two connected oceans. For once, I felt like we'd had made it somewhere, rather than always being on the way.

"I sure wish I were joining you all on the *Stahlratte*, but my Central American expedition ends here," Patrick lamented solemnly in the Miraflores parking lot afterward.

As had been planned from the beginning, Patrick would be flying home to his girlfriend in San Francisco on Friday, to our group's dismay.

"I'll be reading the blogs, though," he winked. "I know you'll keep it interesting."

With a heartfelt wave, Patrick fired up and rode back toward Panama City with the rest of us watching.

"Well, on that note, we'd best get moving," Andy muttered eventually. "GPS shows eighty miles to the *Stahlratte*'s port in Carti, and we're in for one hell of a ride."

He held the screen for all to see. A fitting farewell from Central American infrastructure, the GPS's blue line was a continuous squiggle from start to finish. Justine saddled up behind me.

The torturous jungle rollercoaster ahead proved to be my most difficult ride ever. I was late for a boat in 90F heat atop an overloaded motorcycle with an equally sweaty girl around my waste, but I weaved it confidently for seventy miles. Then just when I was getting comfortable, I snaked into the steepest incline that I had ever ascended—and Thirio stalled in second gear.

Downshifting to first, I popped the clutch hastily, pitching Justine and me instantly into an instant wheelie, until my foot found the brake lever just in time to avoid a backflip. Thirio's front wheel slammed back to Earth at an angle toward the right-hand shoulder for a momentary stop, until all of our seven hundred pounds started rolling backward down the hill. Thirio's front tire skidded despite my full compression of the front hand lever. Her rear rolled freely, as I walked us backward for several steps, unable to apply rear brake. Eventually, I lost control of the hastening crawl completely.

"Shit!"

I was sideways to the pitch in the opposite lane when I tried to heave Thirio uphill in a last-ditch effort, but she high-sided downward, bouncing Justine and me off the tarmac by our helmets as we crashed. The hill was so steep that Thirio began to slide down overtop us across her slick aluminum panniers.

Taking up the rear of our posse, Andy had rounded into the hill moments prior to my initial stall and he'd leaned nimbly to pass right where I'd ultimately dropped Thirio. He stopped right below as Thirio's handlebars collide against his front end. Andy fought hard to keep his bike upright, but the hill's angle made it impossible. His forks dropped sideways across my helmet in a loud jarring crunch, as my neck strained from the motion of being yanked by the head from Thirio's saddle. When the screeching finally stopped, I wriggled my toes. I was immobilized by the spine underneath a motorcycle, but otherwise unperturbed.

"Are we all good?!" Andy screamed over the silence afterward.

"I'm OK!" Justine yelled back.

She hopped to her feet with blood dripping from her elbow, and Andy rose hurriedly from underneath his bike. Together they lifted his handlebars enough to free my neck. All three of us stood up in a triangle with our helmets still on, too dazed to make reason of what had just happened, until I pointed in horror at the scratches across Justine's arm.

"It's already stopped bleeding," she dismissed with a smile. "Good decision buying my helmet. How about you and Andy?"

Andy was fine too, despite some scrapes on his Teneré.

"Piss off mate, this is an adventure! She's supposed to get roughed up!" he encouraged at my loss for words.

Everyone was okay physically, but I was still rattled emotionally, having just lived my two worst nightmares in compromising Andy's adventure and endangering Justine's life. Scuffed hand guards and a punched pannier were the extent of Thirio's visible damage, but she refused to start when I finally found the courage to sit back atop her.

"You lost several liters of gas when you were tits up," Andy reasoned, after several ignition attempts.

Sure enough, Thirio's tank was bone dry. Without further discussion, I reached into my tool kit for the spare fuel hose and an empty bottle, while Andy unscrewed his gas cap. I dropped in the hose, brought the other end below the tank, and took a mouthful of 89-octane petrol exuberantly to the teeth. The burst burned like—well, like gasoline—but I managed to siphon two liters.

Finally, with my face on fire, and to the cheers of my mates, Justine and I pulled exhaustedly onto the dock two miles later. The *Stahlratte* bobbed handsomely offshore in turquoise Caribbean water. I slumped over Thirio's handlebars in ultimate relief there on the dock, with Central America in my rear-view mirror. From my house in Lake Stevens to the loading dock in Carti, I'd covered 10,009 miles and lost ten pounds of muscle, but I'd survived in one piece.

I'M ON A BOAT!

San Blas Islands, Panama
Friday, July 29th, 2011

The hundred-year-old, hundred-foot-long, and two-hundred-ton *Stahlratte* threw an historic wake as she motored toward us to the Carti dock on Tuesday. Dating back to her Dutch maiden voyage in 1903, the *Stahlratte* had debuted as one of the first steel-hulled schooners to ever set sail, before being dry-docked during the Great Depression. She'd rotted in a junkyard for several decades, until a band of hippies purchased her remains and refurbished her with a pilothouse and a propeller for their communal voyage around the world. Funded through various jobs along the way (including a brief commissioning for Greenpeace), the *Stahlratte*'s eccentric new crew had explored far-reaching corners of the globe for nearly a decade before becoming dysfunctional in the end. They'd disbanded ultimately in the Caribbean, where the *Stahlratte* now operated tourist routes between Cuba, Panama, and Colombia under the leadership of its lone remaining hippie: Captain Ludwig.

"We set out seeking a world with neither rules nor responsibilities," Ludwig explained through his thick

189

German accent as he guided the *Stahlratte* alongside us. "But eventually it took so many rules and responsibilities to keep the *Stahlratte* on course that we'd become the same society we'd so resented."

Standing potbellied at the helm in his stained tightie-whities, Ludwig's smile filled the deck entirely, exhibiting unmistakable synergy with his century-old home. After tying up to the dock, his mangy crew of three looped ropes around each bike's frame and hoisted them one at a time to the deck under a man-powered boom winch.

"Welcome aboard, sailors!" Ludwig continued. "As you know, we harbor here tonight in Carti. Then tomorrow we'll pick up our foot passengers and set sail for the San Blas. Dinner tonight is buffet-style Caribbean lobster simmered in rich curry sauce over basmati rice. In the meantime—grab a bunk, get used to your sea legs, and make yourselves at home."

There were a lot of reasons I was enamored with Justine, but most of all, on that Tuesday, it was because she had boarded first while the rest of us were hoisting our bikes—and she'd snagged the only private room on the *Stahlratte*. Directly above the ship's engine bay, down a tiny manhole ladder, our dark fusty cabin was deafeningly loud and scorchingly hot, but at least it was ours. We stowed away early that night after dinner and awakened in a wet tangled mess on Wednesday. I resurfaced to the deck at 8AM for hydration to find Charlie waiting patiently.

"Cheers mate," he said, holding out a beer. "These are only a dollar, so even you cheapskate Yanks can't complain."

He was into his second already.

"Oh, and be careful . . . Flor de Cana rum is only ten bucks a bottle."

I opened my beer, took a sip, and had never cared less.

Ludwig loaded eleven extra backpackers onto the *Stahlratte* that morning. Then he headed thirty miles south under power and dropped anchor next to a pair of uninhabited palm islands and a partially submerged shipwreck. Justine and I snorkeled in warm Caribbean waters that afternoon around the wreck. We reenacted *The Little Mermaid* underwater through the barnacled portholes, and we gazed upon the Islas San Blas' endless archipelago of deserted isles from the rusted bow.

I gorged drunkenly that evening over a lackadaisical campfire dinner of jerk chicken on the nearest island while the stars shimmered off the glassy horizon, marred only by distant unoccupied atolls. Meanwhile, Andy serenaded us with his skillful guitar. The Islas San Blas were home only to sand beaches, palm trees, and the native Kunu. I was physically as far away from a stressful thought as I'd ever been in my life that night, with a beer in one hand and Justine in the other.

Ludwig continued fifty miles further south to another cluster of islands on Thursday, where Charlie, Andy, Tim, Jane, Alex, Justine, and I became better acquainted with the *Stahlratte*'s foot passengers. With an average onboard age of twenty-six and only rum remaining in the coolers, our dinner unfolded into a booze-fueled tribute to the original hippie crew, complete with singing, dancing, peeing off the deck, and even brief public nudity. Everyone, including the crew, partied throughout that night while Ludwig napped. Then at 3AM, Ludwig pulled anchor for our final leg of our cruise—a thirty-hour non-stop power to Cartagena.

"Get ready for swell," Ludwig cautioned, grabbing the wheel as we scurried for our beds.

Justine and I staggered down our cabin ladder just in time for the *Stahlratte*'s engine to fire underneath our pillows, and our hangovers kicked in as the chop intensified into squally international waters. The lot of us were the walking dead on Friday, sprawled in muted silence across the *Stahlratte*'s deck under gray skies and high winds. I'd never felt worse, but still I smiled sincerely while puking throughout the day at the stern. The opportunity to sit back, relax, and let someone else do the piloting had been exactly what I'd needed to recharge for the new continent ahead.

THE NEW WORLD

Cartagena, Colombia
Monday, August 1st, 2011

"Your land legs will return by Monday, which is when Customs opens," Ludwig explained from his Zodiac ferry as Justine, Alex, Charlie, Andy, Tim, Jane, and I all struggled to walk straight on the dock after five days at sea.

"Monday we'll also unload the bikes here and import them. Until then, enjoy Cartagena!" he concluded with a salute.

The rest of us turned to face South America from her shores for the very first time, as Ludwig motored back to the Stahlratte.

Castillo San Felipe de Barajas towered ahead over Cartagena's blue harbor. As the city's most prominent structure, the colossal fort captivated our focus from every angle while we walked through town to our hotel, and therefore, it was our first attraction that afternoon after check-in. The five-dollar entry fee allowed self-guided access inside the castle's sloping walls, wherein a labyrinth of dimly lit armories, dungeons, and catacombs unfolded toward its surface. On the wall walks awaited an arsenal of decommissioned artillery cannons pointing north, east, and west to sea. Castillo San

Felipe's *Pirates of the Caribbean* glory days were undoubtedly in the past, but the monument still commanded undoubted historical respect. Embodying the region's immense colonial past, it was the ideal introduction for our first day in South America.

Justine and I found that same colonial past still flourishing in the streets that night while we wandered oldtown at the base of the castle, holding hands and laughing together. An unavoidable separation loomed ominously ahead for us, though, as our first weekend in South America would also be our last together. Justine and Kelly were reuniting to fly for the Galapagos Islands on Monday, and they would be continuing to Peru at an unmatchable pace afterward. Sunday night's dinner was actually goodbye.

"This trip has a way of bringing people together, doesn't it?" Justine smiled solemnly from across the table, as the final hours approached.

I'd always known the moment would come, but still I was caught off guard.

"We'll cross paths again," I winked back. "I can feel it."

Our farewell back at the hotel proved fleeting that night. On Monday morning there was no time for sendoffs—just a peck on my cheek as Justine slipped out the door for her 6AM chicken bus.

SPIC AND SPAN

Cartagena, Colombia
Tuesday, August 2nd, 2011

Ludwig's 8AM bike swap at the docks allowed little time for me to grieve over Justine's departure, when I arrived to find the *Stahlratte* still anchored distantly in the harbor on Monday. I'd expected to find Ludwig moored and ready with the winch. Therefore, my jaded heart changed focus quickly to Thirio's retrieval as its most immediate concern.

"What the hell is he doing out there?" Alex and I wondered aloud as we peered out at the sea for an explanation.

Unexpectedly, Ludwig and his Zodiac then steered around from behind the *Stahlratte* toward us with Thirio upright in the hull between Floyd's legs. I didn't know the Zodiac's GVWR, but they were certainly pushing it. Suddenly there was a lot more than romance at stake!

"You two hold the lines and keep us tight against the uprights," Ludwig motioned to Andy and Alex as he killed the engine against our mooring. "The rest of you grab the bike. We lift on three."

With Ludwig and Floyd pushing from below, Charlie, Tim, Jane, and I hoisted Thirio by hand two feet up over open water onto the dock.

"You almost said goodbye to both your girls this morning, mate!" Charlie exhaled, as I knelt in relief beside Thirio.

Charlie's Teneré was unloaded next, and the others in succession, until all bikes were ashore, with only one dislodged turn signal in collateral damage.

"Thank you for choosing the *Stahlratte*. It was truly an honor to be your captain," Ludwig concluded with a final salute. "My associate, Manfred, awaits you at Customs. Go there now and find him, but don't get pulled over, because your bikes are still illegal. Warm winds!"

Monday continued to unfold in similar chaotic fashion at Customs, where even with Manfred's assistance, we faced documentation discrepancies, a two-hour Internet outage, and downright lazy immigration agents.

"What say you, Yanks, we head inland toward Medellín tomorrow?" Charlie proposed over a hard-earned dinner that evening. Tim and Jane nodded in agreement.

"Yes, today was certainly enough of Cartagena for me. Plus it's too damn humid and sticky to hang around this coast," Andy confirmed.

Alex and I declined, because we had scheduled appointments for new drive trains, Pirelli MT60 tire mounts, and full-service inspections at Cartagena's flagship Suzuki dealership the next day.

"We'll meet you guys in Medellín—right on your tail," Al assured them. "Trust me, I'm in the biggest hurry to move south out of all of us."

Alex, for once, was not exaggerating, because that same afternoon his girlfriend Kristi had booked a flight to Bogotá for August 23rd. As had been planned since our accelerated departure in April, Kristi would be riding two-up for four weeks through Colombia, Ecuador, and Peru with Alex. Over the phone she'd celebrated excitedly while buying the tickets. I'd cheered along too, because Kristi was bringing me American-priced brake pads, cables, spark plugs, and earplugs. Alex had been most excited, for obvious reasons.

"Right then, cheers," Andy replied glumly before raising his glass at dinner's end. "We'll know where to find you in three weeks' time."

"Bogotá or bust," Tim gestured the same.

"We'll be hitting the road early gentlemen, so this is the last we'll see of each other here," Charlie motioned. "Just don't let Tom get bogged down with Colombian women."

Jane laughed and frowned all at the same time, and then we all finished our drinks and said goodnight.

Thirio shimmered next to Al's bike in the dealership display when he and I retrieved them the next afternoon. Having been fixated with maintenance since the beginning of Costa Rica, I was ultimately relieved at the sight.

"This is like C-3PO getting an oil bath– 'thank the maker!'" I joked as we approached.

The $460 bill was tough to swallow, but I had no regrets in having the bikes tuned precisely in a garage by a professional, rather than amateurishly in the street by trial and error. Initial visual inspection revealed impressive quality of work too— at least until we saddled up to find our gas tanks on empty. The licensed Suzuki mechanic watched, with our money in his pocket and a stupid look on his face, while Alex and I examined our fuel levels. He knew we knew he'd siphoned our gas; he knew we knew he knew too; but in the end, we didn't have the energy to start arguing (he'd, of course, known that from the start). In quiet submission, Al and I pulled out of the lot onto a new continent with fully serviced motorcycles.

Blindsided

Barranquilla, Colombia
Thursday, August 6th, 2011

Like an aging face, you don't notice a motorcycle's minute deteriorations from day to day, but they develop over time. That was never more evident than on the highway outside of Cartagena, where Thirio pivoted effortlessly on fully rounded tires and accelerated precisely across the power band. She was throatier from the freshly cleaned air filter. Best of all, her new fifteen-tooth front sprocket allowed effortless seventy-five mile per hour cruising across northern Colombia's wide-open tidal landscape.

There had been two roads leading from Cartagena to our destination at Pablo Escobar's famed cocaine capitol, Medellín. There was the long way east through the mountains and the short way south through the lowlands. Alex and I weren't on either of those paths on Wednesday. Instead, we'd departed northeast for Barranquilla on the only highway out of town that hadn't been gridlocked with traffic.

"Looks like we can connect with the mountain route if we bear south at this next city," Alex reckoned from the shoulder as we pulled over outside Barranquilla to review our map. "Let's gas up there. We probably added a couple hours taking this route, but we'll still make Medellín by tomorrow. Who knows how long that lowland traffic would have lasted anyway."

I nodded and followed.

Our highway narrowed to two lanes as we passed under Barranquilla's "Bienvenidos!" banner on the industrial outskirts of town twenty minutes later. Alex was in the lead when the first gas station came into view up ahead on the left. He arched across the oncoming lane to pull over when a white wall of cold rolling steel whooshed past my left handlebar. A box truck was passing illegally from behind us.

Al disappeared from my sight behind the truck as the streets rang out with squealing rubber, a metallic pop, and the grinding of steel from the T-bone impact. Brake lights illuminated as Al and his bike panned back into view on the opposite side in a low-side skid, ricocheting toward the curb from the force of the collision. His motorcycle flipped upright, barrel rolled in air, and crashed back to Earth, throwing grass into the sky when it hit the curb. Alex lay discarded and motionless on the pavement when the truck finally stopped with its suspension heaving from front to back. Dismounted on the shoulder, I shoved past a stranger and sprinted toward Al. I noticed blood on his boots as I knelt over him. Al groaned and looked up at me. He moved his extremities and reached for his left foot in pain.

"It's messed up man . . . got to be broken," he grimaced deliriously.

Eyeing the blood, Alex pointed to the stranger beside us, the skinny seventeen-year-old pedestrian whom I'd just pushed aside.

"I chopped him down with my undercarriage just before the curb. He was just walking down the street," Alex winced.

Clutching his arm under a bloodstained shirt, the kid was shaking from the shock. I gestured for him to lie down while Alex checked his own vitals (Eagle Scouts). Scores of spectators surrounded us, tugging at my sleeves and murmuring deafeningly. I pushed back against the crowd, knocking the onlookers into each other until there was enough space to wave in the one woman holding a first aid kit.

"He's alright," she confirmed, looking up from over Al with her stethoscope. "Except for his leg. He pinched it under the motorcycle. The boy is OK too. He just needs stitches."

Alex sat upright in a daze and looked around. His biggest concern now was his bike, which lay ten yards away slumped on its side in the grass with the left signal dislodged and still blinking. Every piece of his luggage had ejected except for his panniers, which were now warped badly. His tank bag dangled by one buckle, and the pizza delivery box was crumpled completely. I lifted the wreckage to its wheels as Al rose to his feet and hobbled over. He hit the ignition and smiled when it started without hesitation. Alex posed for a photo in relief and sat back down with his valuables as emergency sirens approached.

The first cops on the scene had taken me aside for questioning by the time the ambulance arrived. Alex's confident thumbs-up was all the communication he and I had as the EMTs lifted his gurney into the ambulance and closed the doors between us from across the lot. He and I both knew the plan—just like in Baja, someone would have to deal with ground zero, and it wasn't going to be him.

The police wanted to document their investigation after the ambulance left, and I struggled with their Spanish immediately. Colombians enunciated less and spoke under their breath with an entirely different vocabulary than Central Americans. They also formed backward sentences and emphasized opposite syllables. Trying to communicate with a panel of cops in the gas station parking lot proved an awkward inquisition over the next hour without a wingman. I got it across that Alex and I were travelers from the United States and that we had neither local address, or phone, or family—and really no clue where we even were, for that matter. Finally,

I looked at the chief and said I wouldn't go anywhere without Al's bike.

"OK, Americano, we'll take your friend's bike to impound with the truck, and then we'll find him at the hospital," Lieutenant Juan Carlos decided after deliberation.

The rest of his officers tossed on their helmets (without latching them) and saddled up their bikes at his command. Meanwhile, Juan Carlos turned toward Al's bike and mounted it coolly. With a big gleaming smile, the lieutenant pulled down his aviators, rolled on the throttle, and screamed away on a wheelie. Weaving through the traffic ahead, blowing stop signs, and yes—even passing in the oncoming lane—the cops and I followed Juan Carlos' lead as he revved Al's DR all across town to the impound lot.

"This thing runs better than my Yamaha 400! Like a dream!" he exclaimed there as we parked.

Juan Carlos locked Al's bike inside the fence beside the box truck, which had punctures, dents, and fried tire marks across its front bumper from Al's impact. He and I found Alex in the emergency room with severe swelling and discoloration in his ankle. The seventeen-year-old sat next to him sporting three new stitches. All the while, the box truck driver and his insurance lawyer argued a bullshit depiction that Al had cut him off. As the only present witness who had not been involved in the accident (and as Alex's standing family by default), I became an intensely hot commodity to the nurses, doctors, and officers in the ER.

"When was he born? Does he have auto insurance? When did he last eat?"

My Spanish continued to deteriorate under the onslaught of questions. Dehydrated, hungry, and still in full riding gear, my responses resorted ultimately to drawings, hand signals, and charades.

"The gringo can't speak Spanish. His testimony is worthless," the insurance lawyer contested to Juan Carlos as I depicted the events again.

He'd assumed I wouldn't understand, but I glared back and pointed to my ear revealingly.

"My Spanish is still effective enough to shut you up," I replied.

"Alex, you have a fractured ankle, and there are two options: surgery or cast," the doctor explained that evening after another two hours.

"Surgery allows me to screw a plate onto your fibula for a three-week recovery period," he proposed enthusiastically. "The cast requires six weeks of immobilization and subsequent physical therapy. If you want to reach your girlfriend in Bogotá this month, then I recommend surgery."

Al was understandably apprehensive about submitting to a Third World operating table at a moment's notice, but he had no other option with Kristi's deadline looming. After a surreal discussion about how badly he wanted to walk for the next two months, he accepted the doctor's proposal to go under the Colombian knife.

"Safe to say Medellín is an afterthought," Al waved to me as they wheeled him away. "We'll be back on the road in no time, I promise."

"You're making the right decision," I confirmed. "If it makes you feel any better, I can guarantee that your twin brother Andy would have done the exact same thing—or maybe he'd have tried to perform the operation on himself just for the excitement."

"Come back tomorrow to pick him up," the doctor directed me, at which point it was 9PM, and I hadn't eaten a meal since breakfast.

I was exhausted, drenched in sweat, and unable to process another word of Spanish. I turned to Juan Carlos and pointed at my watch to signal bedtime.

"Put the gringo up across the street," the insurance lawyer insisted, fearing that my accommodations would be billed to his client.

"Nonsense, this neighborhood is too dangerous," Juan Carlos cut him off. "I'll take you to Hotel Caribbean Gold. It is safer, and I can point out my favorite strip clubs along the way."

Half an hour later, Juan Carlos booked my room in the Hotel Caribbean Gold lobby. He carried my luggage upstairs, and gave me his personal cell number, with instructions to call in the morning when I was ready to retrieve Al.

"I'll escort you back to the hospital tomorrow when you ring."

I thanked the lieutenant and told him we'd go to the nightclub someday. Alone at last, I cranked the air conditioning and ordered room service. The only English broadcast available during dinner was VH1's *I Love the '90s*, which I absorbed completely over a burger in my underwear before passing out.

"Your friend's operation went fine, but he is still napping in recovery," the nurse told us confidently when Juan Carlos and I arrived in post-op that morning.

I asked her if he would wake soon, and she swallowed wearily.

"I don't know . . . he's finally stopped talking."

It was safe to say, Al's personality was intact. He awoke two hours afterward with plenty to say.

"Dude, it was epic. They gave me an epidural spinal tap that made me numb from the junk down. The doctor kept asking me to move my toes, until finally they didn't move at all. He pricked the arch of my foot with a needle just to be sure. Then he cut along the incision line, peeled the skin back, cauterized all the shit, packed me with gauze, scraped the bone clean, drilled holes in it, measured their depths, and drove eight screws into my leg before stitching me up. The whole time I felt nothing, except for the torque on my body while he leaned into the screwdriver, but I watched the entire operation in the reflection of overhead equipment. Insane!"

Al was discharged from the hospital shortly thereafter, having never received an invoice.

"We have national health care," Juan Carlos declared proudly as he helped me shove Alex and his wheelchair into a cab outside. "You won't pay a cent. Now follow me back to Hotel Caribbean Gold."

Juan Carlos again carried our luggage and reminded us to call him if we needed further assistance before he left. Then after two days of chaos, Alex and I finally found ourselves categorically idle. Lying in our beds that evening and watching the Colombian *Price is Right*, we were clearly without a plan for this newfound abundance of time to kill. Luckily, Hotel Caribbean Gold had air conditioning, in-house dinner, and lightning-fast Wi-Fi.

"Throw in your painkillers, and this really won't be so bad," I lamented out the window that dreary afternoon.

WEARING THIN

Taganga, Colombia
Friday, August 12th, 2011

Stabilized and off his painkillers, Alex had extra gauze, unlimited hydrogen peroxide, and brand-new crutches (which had been special-ordered for his 6′5″ frame) by Monday. His only remaining prescription was more time on his ass for the week ahead, and he could tell that the past four days of surgical aftermath had left me antsy to get out of Hotel Caribbean Gold as I stared out the hotel room window after breakfast

"Take the week off, man," Alex reasoned. "I'm mobile now that I have crutches. Plus, I got Antonio downstairs in case of emergency."

Over the weekend our bellhop, Antonio, had supported us immensely with advice on where to eat and find supplies. Additionally, he had recommended a small Caribbean fishing village called Taganga to the east, which he praised for its cool mountain breeze and clear Caribbean water (as opposed to Barranquilla's smoky piss smog and toxic sludge port). Antonio was a jovial local, always wearing his maroon and blue uniform and always available at our call.

"There's no point in having you wait for me to heal here. Go check out Taganga for the both of us," Al continued.

I looked up and stepped back from the window. Then before Alex could even blink, I was packed for the road.

"Alright, don't go anywhere, you hear Al?" I waved on my way out.

Ninety miles later, I arrived at Taganga's valley beachhead to a literal breath of fresh air. Looking out over a sandy palm shore between coastal cliffs and sloping green foothills, that afternoon I knew that I was exactly where I needed to be while swaying in my hammock with sunglasses drawn and a beer at my side on the hotel rooftop. Over the next few days I didn't take pictures or write notes; I didn't explore past the nearby beaches; I didn't even once look at a map.

Far from my normal behavior of leveraging as many once-in-a-lifetime memories as possible into every setting, my sedentariness in Taganga was a result of recent revelations about the Third World, which had worn me too thin to care. The great chasm between the conditions that I'd always known at home and those that I experienced daily throughout Colombia had unsettled me in a way that I'd never anticipated. My frustration even boiled over in the hotel bar on Saturday, when three Irish girls rolled their eyes toward me at the end of their three-week trip from Buenos Aires.

"Argentina paled against Peru and Bolivia," they chided dramatically, going on and on. "It was just too modern. It lacked the authenticity and quaintness of its northern counterparts."

I explained that those same rugged, dilapidated qualities were starting to gnaw at me after four months on the road.

"Well, you just don't appreciate foreign culture enough," one of the girls quipped back.

I replied that my 10,000-mile motorcycle ride had already exposed more culture than her bus rides and bar tabs ever could. I slammed my beer and walked out. In the end, I looked like an elitist American pig, and the girls revealed themselves as rubbernecking tourists. More importantly, the conversation got me thinking when I returned to the rooftop that night.

Despite its glowing reviews from other travelers, I had some concerns about Colombia. I could tolerate the constant barrage of cocaine dealers, who all introduced themselves as Tony Montana everywhere. I was used to the cacophonous noise levels at night and the smell of sewage in the streets too. What truly scared me was the "neighbors be damned" sentiment permeating everywhere. Even the freeways were overtly unruly, as I'd learned Monday when two side-by-side semis had forced me onto an overgrown shoulder in a sixty mile per hour game of chicken.

"Remember, it's Friday," Antonio had warned back in Barranquilla. "Half the drivers are drunk."

The words had rung through my head there on the shoulder and now still on the roof.

As a foreigner looking in, I knew that there would be cultural differences that I'd struggle to comprehend. I also knew that I was just anxious after being trapped on the same stretch of coast for the past two weeks straight. Plus, having witnessed Alex's obliteration by an out-of-control box truck at the city limits, it was no wonder that I'd been irritated with Barranquilla from the start.

Finally, after four days of dwelling upon my concerns from that rooftop, it became clear that I really just needed to start making progress again (preferably on a four-lane freeway with neither bicycles, nor pedestrians, nor livestock sharing the road). Alex agreed when I returned to Caribbean Gold on Friday.

"I still can't walk without crutches, but my leg feels good enough to shift gears. That means the last major hurdle is getting my bike out of impound on Tuesday, when I sign a document for the box truck's lawyer stipulating that I won't return in the future for reparations."

"Trust me," I confirmed with a certain nod. "Neither of us will be returning to Barranquilla any time soon."

GUNPOINT

Barranquilla, Colombia
Tuesday, August 16th, 2011

Alex and I had developed a warped sleeping schedule at the Hotel Caribbean Gold after weeks on end with abundant free time. So, nothing was out of the ordinary on Tuesday night when I walked into the lobby to buy water at 1AM—except for the trio of strangers standing across from our bellhop, Antonio. The tallest of them in the middle was a man wearing jeans, a purple button-up, and a cowboy hat. With a scrubby male and female counterpart to each side, the purple shirt faced Antonio against the vending machines as I descended the final set of stairs. They all fell silent when I arrived.

"No water for sale right now," Antonio responded hesitantly as I signaled toward the fridge with a $10,000 peso bill.

I could see fresh bottles behind him, though. Having spent the past fourteen hours engrossed in downloaded media upstairs, I was missing Antonio's non-verbal cue to leave. Instead, I walked casually to the candy desk to wait for him, thinking that I'd misunderstood his dialect.

The trio murmured hurriedly back and forth as I debated internally between Snickers and M&Ms with my back to them. Steps approached from behind me, which I assumed were Antonio's. Suddenly, I felt cold steel push forcefully into my rib cage. I turned to find the purple shirt holding my arm in one hand and a revolver in the other. He clenched me firmly, staring angrily into my eyes and turning his weapon upward for my appreciation. I swallowed, gave him a silent nod, and stepped instinctively for the staircase to leave, but his grip tightened.

"No," the purple shirt muttered. "You and I are going outside."

Barefoot, in a pair of athletic shorts and a V-neck tee, I didn't want to go outside, let alone anywhere with the purple shirt and his friends. I looked for guidance toward Antonio, who stood petrified in terror.

Comprehending Antonio's cues finally, I bolted in alarm toward the staircase, but the purple shirt checked me into the floor and waved in his reinforcements. The other two grabbed my arms and lifted me forcibly as I dragged my feet into the slick tile to resist. I heaved frantically toward the stairway, shuffling us into a dog pile against the wall. The gunman stepped back and brandished the pistol clearly for me to see as his two goons wrestled me to my knees.

"Do not play with me gringo," he yelled as he drove his cowboy boot into my gut.

I withstood the forthcoming rib shots in a daze, like a boxer against the ropes. The purple shirt raised his gun high and pistol-whipped the crown of my head, ringing panic through my psyche as I crumpled in shock against the wall. The second man pinned me down as the purple shirt handed the gun to the woman and drew a roll of clear packing tape. He lowered to a knee and leaned in to muzzle me, but I freed an arm and batted the ribbon away. I looked to Antonio again, who remained crouched in the corner with his hands over his mouth. Antonio may have been too horrified to react, but I started screaming bloody murder in every language I knew.

"Shut your mouth or I'll shoot right through it!" the woman screamed back, wielding the firearm frantically like a sword.

As the purple shirt reached back for more tape, I flipped onto my stomach and kicked his counterpart in the chest to free my legs. I pushed to my feet and squared up as both men tackled me into the wall so hard that the picture frames crashed around us. With an attacker on each shoulder, I leveraged myself back against the wall to reach between them until my arm finally caught the stairway bannister. I could tell by their tightening grips that the men were spooked as I found an anchor. I twisted sideways and pulled free from their slipping grasps in one final surge.

My shirt ripped right off as I bounded backward into the staircase. After one stuttering stride, I caught my footing to face the assailants from higher ground. The woman held the gun at her side in disbelief and the men stared blankly upward, each clutching one end of my shirt. We acknowledged each other benignly for a moment before I turned upstairs and ran like the wind. Bare-chested, with blood pouring from my brow, I blasted frantically into the hotel room in an adrenaline-induced blur. I locked the door, collapsed to the floor, and held my hands over my face to confirm I'd survived.

"What the hell happened to you?" Alex exclaimed as he removed his headphones and sprang from the bed with a towel.

My frenzied recount was full of conspiracy as I explained it feverishly. I had Antonio in on it, plus our next-door neighbor, Nicolas, and possibly even the entire hotel staff. Holding the towel to my head, I felt framed, targeted, and hated. Half of me was ready to run downstairs to point fingers, while simultaneously I was too shattered to even breathe. Those emotions were sidelined quickly when a commotion started outside. The voices of screaming men started ascending the stairs toward us. Alex hobbled to his rucksack and retrieved his knife as both of us found defensive positions at the door.

"Policia!" they pounded loudly at the top of the stairs.

I opened the door cautiously to two officers with Antonio between them. Antonio crumpled into my embrace in a sobbing mess of tears and a sputtering series of apologies. The cops pulled him back, confirmed that Alex and I were safe, and hurried back downstairs with Antonio in tow to continue investigating. Our neighbor, Nicolas, peeked out from his room and ordered me to go back inside and lock my door for the night. The police never did return, and from there Alex and I began to process my unexplained brush with death.

It took us until 5AM to deduce that Antonio had owed money to my attackers and that I'd interrupted their late-night shakedown.

"Right place, wrong time," Alex remarked when I walked him through it. "Andy would be proud of this one, if he was alive to hear the story—I think he'd even be jealous!"

Still on my mind was the manner in which I'd reacted to the incident. Mom and Dad had always told me not to follow strangers as a kid, but the instantaneous fight and flight response surprised even me as it unfolded. In retrospect, I acknowledged several underlying cues that had guided my forceful resistance.

First, I'd never sensed that the attackers were playing cutthroat. Don't get me wrong—they'd beat the shit out of me, but they hadn't bashed my head through a wall or broken an arm. Rather, their pushing and pulling had seemed more insistent than commanding the whole time. Second was the gun, which neither the woman nor the purple shirt had aimed at my face directly. They'd waved it around a lot and dragged its crosshairs over my body, but they'd never held it steady at point blank. Third, the amateur thugs had picked the worst tape in the history of kidnappings. Everyone knows that finding the end on a roll of clear packing tape takes time, and I'd made damn sure of that by kicking, screaming, and bleeding throughout the lobby.

There were only three unresolved issues when I finally closed my laptop at 7AM on Wednesday morning as the adrenaline wore off. I wanted my shirt back (I'd only had three); I wanted justice (and I knew I wouldn't get it); and I wanted the hell out of Barranquilla (as fast as possible). I settled for my life and drifted to sleep in the end.

"My leg is good to ride now, dude," Alex assured me from across the room when I woke up that afternoon. "Today we release my bike. Tomorrow at sunrise we leave this shithole."

LONG HAULIN'

Barbosa, Colombia
Saturday, August 20th, 2011

"It's a numbers game," Andy had told me in Panama regarding our trip's inherent risks. "You can't know when the odds will pay out. All you can control is your reaction, which will determine your ultimate success."

I'd been displeased with Barranquilla since the moment we'd arrived, but I made a point to take Andy's advice and put the last several weeks behind me on Thursday. Like Alex, I'd taken my lick of bad luck and come out mostly on top. So, with manufactured faith for the rest of Colombia, I cleared my mind as we departed that morning.

The ride went well as Alex and I tore across half of the six hundred and fifty miles to Bogotá uneventfully, with his crutches strapped to his panniers like a pair of lightning rods. That night's trucker hotel was crawling with long-haulers, whom we impressed with our Alaskan ice road stories over dinner.

"You boys are in for a treat. Ahead you will pass the beautiful city of Bucaramanga, the Guanentá-Alto Río Fonce National Park, and many elaborate mountain ranges enroute to Bogotá!"

one particularly excited trucker named Wilson rejoiced. "I recommend the park foremost. If you take the southern entrance and run out the ridgeline, there are 360-degree views as far as the eye can see ... or you can take the northern entrance first ... or a mile later there is a side road ... "

Wilson continued on and on, but Alex and I both struggled to keep up with his enthusiasm. Too exhausted from our ride to hold a conversation, we entertained Wilson for only a few minutes longer before heading to bed. Al and I hit the road at 7AM for another big run on Friday, only to find ourselves on the shoulder an hour later with unexpected mechanical issues.

"My son of a bitch engine just shut off at freeway speed for no reason!" Alex stammered as I pulled up beside him along an empty stretch of Colombian jungle that morning. "I can't get it to start again."

We stripped his bike and changed the spark plugs instinctively. They were due, but still the engine refused. Alex held his new plugs against the block to deduce that there was no spark—just like when Thirio's stator had failed in Panama. We were debating whether to swap computers when a Colombian motorcyclist pulled up next to us. He was the first sign of humanity we'd seen yet on the shoulder.

"This is guerilla territory. You need to get moving. Two broken-down gringos are easy targets on this highway," he warned sternly before continuing north.

My renewed faith in Colombia waned bleakly as Alex and I looked at each other. With heightened skittishness, we agreed that I would tow Al to the next town using our line of webbing to keep moving. Alex and I were still tightening knots and finalizing hand signals when a drab green flatbed truck rolled slowly past us ten minutes later. We both turned apprehensively as the truck pulled over and shifted into reverse. I feared the worst when the driver's dark black boots kicked open the door after he parked in front of us. Then I smiled joyously to see who it was.

"Hello boys, looks like you could use a lift!" Wilson exclaimed with a smile, stepping down from the cab to our excitement.

He reached back and pulled out four tie straps.

"Remember I said I was heading your direction? Aguachica is the closest mechanic, eighty kilometers south. Let's get you out of here."

"So much for blowing this guy off!" Alex whispered as we loaded his bike into the bed.

I still hadn't eaten since breakfast by the time I pulled up behind Wilson at Aguachica's licensed Suzuki shop to unveil Al's bike to the mechanics. I trudged to the adjacent restaurant to order lunch while they consulted in the garage. Al's muffler blasted to life from down the street before my meal even arrived. Wilson sat down at the table, quipping fault to a loose wire connection in the harness. Alex arrived later after paying the mechanic.

"Go figure—it was the spark plug all along, but some wires got disconnected when we removed the gas tank. I would have figured it out if we hadn't been spooked on the shoulder," Alex proclaimed as he sat down with us. "Wilson, is it true about the guerillas, man?"

Wilson looked down at his food disconcertingly.

"There is no need for you to worry during the day," he replied shortly. "Nighttime is a different story."

I didn't want to know details. To change the topic, I laid out our map and asked Wilson to mark the rest of his route to Bogotá (since neither Alex or I could recall the conversation that we'd cut short the night prior). Wilson circled the major cities and told us to follow the highways. He added a stern warning about a confusing fork thirty miles south.

"The signs for Bogotá will point to the right, but you should bear left. That takes you to the mountains that I described. It is a much better ride."

Wilson wouldn't accept a peso for his service when we finished lunch. Instead, he reckoned that the opportunity to help would be payment enough. Alex snuck to the cashier to pay for lunch anyway, and Wilson blushed upon seeing the tab. He cautioned about the fork again and departed with a nod.

I was still nervous that we'd miss our turn as we approached it an hour later, until exactly thirty miles into the ride, when we spotted Wilson standing next to his truck in the divider signaling us left to ensure our success. Alex and I buzzed by with jubilant waves and excited goodbyes as Wilson saluted. My faith in Colombia was renewed.

Wilson's route lived up to the hype as Alex and I ascended out of the forest into mountainous Guanentá-Alto Río Fonce National Park to find vertical rock gullies and brown shale flats on Sunday. The new terrain was akin to the surface of the moon after five months of lush green jungle. Lack of pollution in the park was a shock too, but best of all was the balmy 66F degree air temperature. Alex and I had to close our armored jackets' vents for the first time that we could remember at the top, where we stopped for our final view of the Caribbean. Gazing across its magnificent waters one last time there, we were officially on to a new chapter.

"My leg is still too weak to support Kristi two-up. I think I'm going to have to park the bike in Bogotá and ride a chicken bus with her to Cusco," Alex admitted in Barbosa that night. Bogotá was just a day's ride away. "It's just too risky. So unless you want to follow our bus, you're going to need your own plan for the next 4,000 miles, man."

Neither Alex or I had ever imagined such a crossroads, as the reality of an open-ended separation sank in. It was certainly not how we had planned it. Luckily, I did not have to fret for long about where I would end up, because Charlie proposed a solution on Monday over Skype.

"Alex and Kristi are setting off on their own adventure, and you need to do the same, mate," Charlie reasoned. "Tim and Jane are ahead of us already, but Andy and I are still here in

Medellín, and we're heading to Cali tomorrow. Why don't you meet us there on Wednesday after Kristi arrives?"

Alex nodded from his bed.

"I'll have seen the rest of Colombia and Ecuador already with Kristi, so I'll be able to catch up with you right away after she flies home," he confirmed. "Just don't haul too much ass with those guys in Peru!"

"Scout's honor—I'll do my best . . . " I replied as I closed my laptop.

CROSSROADS

Bogotá, Colombia
Monday, August 22nd, 2011

Bogotá's climate was cool and crisp when Alex and I arrived on Monday. For the first time in months I was ready for jeans, shoes, and a flannel, like a true Washingtonian. The capitol city reminded me of the Pacific Northwest in other ways than just climate, with its outlying farms and coniferous trees. The 8,600-foot elevation still made me feel further from home than ever, at least until Alex and I found a sense of community in the company of two other bikers at the Cranky Croc hostel.

Riding the KLR650 was Brian, a thirty-year-old Eagle Scout from Colorado, who had worked his way down through Panama a year prior and was now returning home after covering South America.

"You'll love it down south, boys," he smiled wryly, as if trying not to remember. "I'd do it all over again in a heartbeat if I still had the money. Unfortunately, I got bills to pay."

Brian wasn't going back to your typical nine-to-five though—he was a wine importer in Vail.

"Back to the grind," he joked in the hostel foyer while Alex and I checked in.

Next we met Adam, the Israeli Special Forces veteran on an outrageous BMW HP2. Adam had been on the road for two and a half years to-date, covering Africa, Asia, Europe, the Middle East, and South America, with another year and a half slated for North America and Australia. Adam had adventure down to a stoic science. Therefore, I was surprised when his quiet demeanor lit up at the mention of Charlie and Andy. He'd met them in Medellín already.

"Those two are wild—even for Aussies!" Adam exclaimed over lunch. "Tell the boys I say hi. You'll be in good hands riding with them."

"You'll have no problem riding to Cali on your own," Brian and Adam both assured me before their separate departures the following morning.

So, with the reassurance of a ski sommelier and an ex-commando, I was feeling confident that afternoon when Al and I arrived at airport passenger pickup. Kristi's American beauty lit up the entire terminal as Alex lifted her off her feet at first sight. On account of his ankle, he lowered her quickly back to eye level, where they remained beaming with excitement in a dream-like stare.

"And hello to you too, Tom!" Kristi exclaimed, turning to me with a bear hug finally. "Thanks for taking care of this big lug."

Kristi's embrace proved a heartwarming reminder that home wasn't actually so far away. The peanut butter and jelly sandwiches that she'd packed sent me swooning too. Kristi had also brought me new underwear, shirts, and pants from home, which she unpacked at the hostel that evening. However, due to an unfortunate miscommunication (for which I blamed Alex), she'd forgotten my spare bike cables, brake pads, and earplugs. I didn't let that get me down, though, because I strutted through the streets of Bogotá like an icon in my fresh new clothes on Tuesday.

"What should we do tonight? Did you guys want to go out?" Kristi asked with a stifled yawn after dinner.

"There will be plenty of time for that, but first you guys need some time alone," I yawned back.

Alex and Kristi nodded excitedly as we retired to our separate quarters for the night.

Ridin' Solo

Alex and Kristi were so in love that they hardly noticed my 6AM reveille on Wednesday, and with little more than a quip, I was equally quick to take my solo jitters to the road. Pre-trip inspection proved eerily silent without Alex's jabbering in the garage, but Thirio's ignition cleared the air when I pulled into the cold morning after saying my prayers.

Taking a tip from Adam and Brian, I'd memorized every turn out of Bogotá by heart before departure (which was a feat, considering Colombian infrastructure). I covered my first hundred and twenty miles without a single wrong turn to the Pan-American. Adam and Brian had described Cali as a full day's ride, but I was nearly halfway there already by 10AM. Either I was a legendarily superior rider to them (I dreamt), or the best was yet to come (I figured). Sure enough, the four-lane highway narrowed to two as it entered the Andean foothills.

Cascading vistas and towering pinnacles unfolded one after another through the Andean ascent ahead, but I didn't dare take my eyes off the road to marvel at the scenery. Instead,

I jockeyed defensively amongst an agonizingly restless parade of congested cars, busses, and trucks to the 3,300-meter pass up top. It wasn't until I arrived at Alto de la Linea Park that I got to relax and take in my surroundings.

I pulled over and ate a PBJ in the mountain air as the sun hit my back and the clouds darkened ahead. The mountainous terrain was amazing, but anxious traffic and harsh weather fostered higher stakes without Alex. I felt exposed without a wingman.

I adjusted Thirio's fuel mixture screw, slipped into my rain gear, and started down the other side determinedly into a torrent. The rain fell so hard that I couldn't see the highway lines for most of the western face, until the Pan-American flattened into a final hundred miles of farmland to Cali.

"Glad you're alive you crazy Yank!" Charlie hollered from the Casa Blanca Hostel courtyard picnic table as I killed the engine and dismounted.

"Git over here—we've got beer waiting for you," Andy barked, pulling a cold one from the ice bucket. "Give us the honor of hearing about your wild ride!"

The honor was all mine. I got right to it and stacked three empties at the table before even stripping my jacket. A weight lifted from my chest as I recounted Alex's accident and the attempted kidnapping, as if I was able to relax and put the experiences behind me for the first time.

"Forget about that. You're in good hands now, mate," Charlie celebrated afterward. "Andy and I are on a bit of a timeline ourselves, so you know. We're meeting Andy's girl, Cass, in Quito on September 1st when she flies in from down under. Come along—you'll keep up just fine."

"And by the way," Andy chirped in. "I hope you didn't stain our sterling reputation with Adam."

"I just can't understand how you two could have behaved reputably in front of him in the first place. Must have been a short visit," I joked back.

I cracked another beer and sank emphatically into my chair.

Wednesday's solo ride had taught me newfound respect for Adam and Brian. They were braver than I'd ever dreamt for having gone so far on their own, and I was grateful to be back in the cover of company after tasting just one day of their adventure.

CALI DREAMING

Cali, Colombia
Friday, August 26th, 2011

Two days in Cali were not cheap for me, and the money trail started bright and early on Thursday with a man named Ashley, who owned a high-end motorcycling boutique down the street from Hostel Casa Blanca. Casa Blanca catered specifically to adventure motorcyclists with its own garage out back, and Ashley was clearly doing his rounds to drum up business when he stumbled upon Charlie and me over our morning coffees.

"My shop is called Eurocasco. Come on down, and you'll like what you see," Ashley offered, as Charlie looked up with interest. "I carry top of the line Arai and Shoei helmets."

"What say we go have a look Tom?" Charlie entertained back. "I'm still in the market for a more permanent replacement for the helmet that was stolen by that little shit stain in México. Come on, you can catch a retail therapy buzz with me."

I was hell-bent to save my money as we followed Ashley. Nevertheless, I was drawn unwittingly to a pair of touring boots in my exact size on the display wall when we arrived. The TCX Infinity boots were reinforced with extra padding and stitching across all major rubbing points (brake, gear shift, engine case). All black and mostly leather, they offered sturdy protection from ankle to calf with a ratcheting strap system that locked my foot firmly into the heel box. Essentially, the TCXs were glorious in fit, form, and function. Having just born witness to the aftermath of Alex's broken ankle, I had to buy them.

Paradoxically, Charlie erred on the side of financial conservation over in the helmet section.

"Sorry mate, but nobody's melon is worth Ashley's markups," he scoffed empty-handed at the counter before eyeing my boots' $350 price tag. "I appreciate your company here. I'm sure you got a good deal."

"So much for catching your buzz," I replied dryly with my debit card in hand. "Instead, I caught your retail therapy disease!"

"Will that be all?" Ashley asked encouragingly. "Peru and Bolivia don't sell the DR650. This could be your last opportunity for spare parts."

The money bleed continued as I threw in a throttle cable, clutch cable, two spark plugs, and two tubes for good measure, paying Ashley's markups and a ninety percent Colombian import tax too.

"One in the pannier was worth two in a warehouse," I reasoned.

I finally had all the spares I'd intended to carry. Thirio already had fresh tires, a tuned engine, a clean air filter, and a new chain assembly. For once, I was keeping the Boy Scout motto—Be Prepared.

Thursday's spending continued that evening at the local English pub when I spotted a tap behind the bar during dinner with Charlie and Andy. Relishing a rare oppotunity for draft beer, I ordered a pint of their dark ale to start things off. The nitrogen-pressured brew went down smoothly, as did the amber right after it, and then the dark again. The boys switched me to Budweiser when I was starting to become a liability, and that was when I met the bartender, Jeniffer.

The rumors were true about Colombian women—they were hot—and getting hotter as we moved inland from the coast. Maybe it was that these were the first local girls in the last 5,000 miles to wear makeup; maybe it was that they actually donned fitted clothes; maybe it was that Cali had the highest number of plastic surgeries per capita in the world. Whatever was in the water, my bartender Jeniffer fit the bill remarkably. Confident and sexy, she epitomized everything that was idealized about Latin women.

Jeniffer was in flight attendant school and working part-time to pay for it. She was grounded with moral conscience and work ethic, even despite her beauty. I could have listened to her experiences forever from that barstool. She seemed plenty into me, too, as she hopped into my lap right after her shift.

"The prospect of Ecuador is looking a bit dimmer, eh mate?" Charlie smiled to me from down the bar with rosy cheeks.

He had his arm wrapped around the shoulder of another girl, Liliana, whom he'd also just met that night.

"Andy, you can get to Quito on your own, right?" he continued to dream.

Reality struck when Charlie and I asked our girls out for the weekend, because both of them had real-life agendas. Jeniffer had Ethics homework, and Liliana was supporting her sisters. These young up and coming Colombian women were not on permanent vacation like we were. They had aspirations and responsibilities beyond the distraction of two Western flyboys. My encounter with Jeniffer would prove a fleeting moment that evening, but with a girl like her, you took what you could get. Our interaction ended up short, sweet, and refreshingly unforgettable. As quickly as it had started, our romance ended at last call with a kiss goodbye.

"Even with an open checkbook on the adventure of a lifetime, you can't have it all," Charlie groaned as he, Andy, and I piled into our cab that night. "Who knows, mate, next time Colombia might have to be a trip of its own."

JOURNEY TO THE
CENTER OF THE EARTH

Quito, Ecuador
Tuesday, August 30th, 2011

Teeming with unprecedented challenges, unexpected humility, and undeniable achievement, Cali to Quito's three-day sprint was adventure at its finest, starting from the get-go with the Pan-American's roughest sections yet in the mountains of southern Colombia. Porous road conditions and steep alpine passes were somehow the least of my worries on Saturday, though, because even more concerning was the oncoming Colombian traffic that kept careening into our lanes to dodge potholes and patches.

"I'll take a Kenworth six inches off my ass like in Central America compared to today's kamikazes," Andy remarked when we arrived at Pasto that afternoon for rest. "How did your new boots handle the test, mate?"

My TCXs had, in fact, dominated without missing a shift or slipping from the pegs or allowing a draft throughout Saturday's two hundred and fifty miles of turbulent terrain. They were broken in even further on Sunday as Thirio's handlebars shuddered viciously against sixty miles of rippled tarmac and high-speed winds. The TCXs proved rock solid through their sturdy soles, but my arms and legs quivered, regardless, from the constant wobble. I was relieved to take a break that afternoon in Ipiales for a tour of the Sanctuary Las Lajas Catholic cathedral.

"Ashley recommended this cathedral while he was helping me with helmets back in Eurocasco," Charlie explained as we approached the site's gates in the canyon ahead. "He reckoned it's not your typical religious monument, rather more of an engineering marvel."

As we passed through the entry to the chasm's ledge, I understood exactly what Ashley had meant. Sanctuary Las Lajas emerged ahead in the spray churning up from the Rio Quebrada's rapids below it. Built into a stone bridge spanning the river's bedrock gulch, the structure appeared to hover in midair before us. Up close, Las Lajas revealed intricate and opulent craftsmanship during our self-guided tour in the mists over the river. Ornate white trim and innumerable elaborate steeples peppered the exterior, but the cave-like altar inside proved most extraordinary.

With only three man-made walls, Sanctuary Las Lajas's foundation butted against the canyon's northern face for its fourth partition atop the bridge. From the pews, the jagged shadows of unfinished earth contrasted strikingly against the church's extravagant gold-plated arches. That backdrop to Jesus' crucifix was the most powerful I'd ever witnessed as I stood at the entrance while the priest blessed the hosts for Sunday mass. I hadn't attended Catholic service in years, although I'd been saying my prayers the whole way since Seattle. I was transfixed by Sunday's sermon completely, at least until Charlie whispered urgently from behind.

"Hey, mate, I need a pit stop before we return to the bikes . . . I think this sanctuary is releasing my demons."

Outside, Andy and I watched as Charlie waddled directly to the nearest men's room entrance. We laughed aloud as he paid the nominal twenty-five cent fee to the attendant and was allotted only four sheets of toilet paper in return. Paying for restroom access was customary in Colombia, but usually the toilet paper was buffet-style inside. Charlie grimaced calculatingly at his measly four squares.

"Eh, más por favor," he reasoned back, shaking his head hurriedly.

The attendant nodded and handed him four more.

"No, I need . . . necesito más," Charlie reiterated to yet another four.

Charlie pressed his dozen squares between his fingers, thought briefly about his odds, and then pulled five dollars from his pocket.

"It's your lucky day, mate," he signaled hurriedly.

Then he bought the entire roll and strutted triumphantly into the stall as Andy and I applauded.

The three of us were impressed by Ecuador's streamlined customs process south of Ipiales. Our Ecuadorian first impressions glowed even brighter that evening at our hotel in Ibarra, where sixteen dollars bought us personal rooms with hot water, Wi-Fi, and complimentary shampoo. On Sunday night, I slept like an American, with drawn shades, icy air conditioning, and my computer downloading non-stop. Seventy more Pan-American miles signaled the end of our three-day push on Monday, when Quito's metropolis spilled into a grand basin on our horizon.

Centered in between four predominant peaks, at 2,400 meters in elevation, Ecuador's capitol city was surrounded by shantytowns funneling from the foothills to downtown. Charlie, Andy, and I rode under an overhead funicular, through a variety of neighborhoods, and past endless restaurants on our way to the Secret Garden Hostel in the central district that afternoon. However, the hotel bar was the first attraction on our agenda after our grueling ride through the Colombian Andes. It was several drinks later, each, before we even realized that we'd crossed the equator.

"Welcome to our side of the world, mate!" Andy cheered excitedly as he poured the fourth round to celebrate. "That ride certainly made you work for it."

Turistas

Quito, Ecuador
Thursday, September 1st, 2011

Quito was filled with tourists on Tuesday. They were fresh off their long flights and overnight buses, which had allowed them to check out mentally for hours and arrive bright-eyed, bushy-tailed, and ready to explore *Lonely Planet* highlights. Charlie, Andy, and I could hardly identify with them after 12,000 miles on our motorcycles. We battled unsigned roads, combative weather, and maniac drivers for days to reach the same destination on our motorcycles, and we'd been doing it going on five months straight.

Adventuring in real-time via detours and opportunities, our metrics were no longer based in guidebooks or checklists, but rather our hearts and odometers. We weren't interested in snapping cultural photos or reading interpretive murals anymore. Instead, we were inclined to surveying outlying geography and studying upcoming byways. Charlie, Andy, and I had slated just one attraction for our stay in Quito— the equator—and for that we awaited the company of a true tourist to make the experience worthwhile.

"Cass, welcome to Quito!" Charlie waved as she and Andy sat down for breakfast on Thursday after her arrival. "I'd best warn you that common practice in this city is for thieves to throw human feces onto tourists from the rooftops. Afterward, their co-assailants on the street below pretend to clean your garments while they clean your pockets instead. So keep your jet-lagged eyes to the sky!"

Charlie's salutation was true, despite its cheekiness.

"Good to see you too, Charlie," Cass replied with a smile. "I'll watch out. You must be Tom? I've been reading your blog. Thanks for keeping these two in line!"

Cass and I shook hands amicably. Toned and tanned, she was clearly full of adventure.

"Well darling, we've been saving Quito's biggest tourist attraction for your arrival," Andy explained over breakfast. "Get ready for an exciting first day in South America."

Charlie, Andy, Cass, and I arrived at Mitad del Mundo National Monument at noon and passed an army of chintzy vendors through the entry gate. At the site's main plaza we found a tower with a metal globe on its top and the letters *NWSE* around its sides. A metallic line ran from east to west underneath it to designate the equator. Inside, there was an informational display. We took our obligatory photos, stood a few minutes longer, and were ultimately underwhelmed.

"Typical tourist gimmick. This Mitad del Mundo hosts more souvenirs than substance," Charlie, Andy, and I stewed as rubberneckers gawked all around us.

We nodded back toward the entrance to hail a cab back to Quito.

"Calm down, boys. I may be fresh off the plane, but you guys are just jaded," Cass interjected to silence our complaining. "I just spoke to a gentleman with a guidebook, and he reckoned there's an unofficial attraction a hundred yards down the road called Museo Intinan. He says it is heaps better than this joint. What say we have a look?"

Despite our skepticism, Charlie, Andy, and I agreed to test Cass's tourist viewpoint. We crossed the street to Museo Intinan and signed up for the next novelty tour.

"The metallic line at Mitad del Mundo is not even the real equator," our tour guide, Miguel, opened with surprising intrigue.

"The line you saw at Mitad del Mundo was placed incorrectly back in the 1700s, but now military GPS proves that the real equator line runs seventy yards north right here through Museo Intinan. We'll discuss that more in the second part of this tour, but first let's observe the shrunken head exhibit. Deep in the Ecuadorian Amazon, this ancient craft still exists today," he continued.

The boys and I had been discussing a side trip to the Amazon out from Quito, but those desires vanished as Miguel pulled a sheet from over the glass counter beside him to reveal three fist-sized faces, complete with stitched lips and eyelids, on display. Undeniably authentic with their well-groomed hairlines and expressionless outlooks, the remains were a face-to-face peek into an Amazonian nightmare. Miguel described their grisly final moments in gruesome detail, adding vivid emphasis to the step where the skulls were separated from their scalps.

"I know you like your Indiana Jones imagery, mate, but I'm suddenly not so keen on the Ecuadorian rainforests," Charlie whispered.

"Right mate. The Amazon is clearly out of scope for this trip," Andy agreed.

We followed Miguel to the real equator line for the second part of the tour, where he set an elevated basin of water five feet into the northern hemisphere (which he called summer). Miguel set a bucket underneath the basin and sprinkled several leaves to float on top. He pulled a plug out from the bottom and the leaves funneled into the bucket clockwise, like I'd always known. Miguel repeated those steps in the southern hemisphere (winter) to demonstrate the Coriolis

Effect, whereupon the opposite spin was interesting, but predictable. It wasn't until he moved the experiment directly overtop the equator that I became truly astonished, because there the leaves hovered directly above the spout until they were sucked straight downward one by one, unlike anything I'd seen before.

"You see, gravity pulls toward the equator at all other latitudes, but the rules are different on the equator. Here it pulls directly without hemispherical disturbance," Miguel explained to our now consummate attention.

"OK. Last trick," Miguel concluded finally. "In either hemisphere our bodies are reliant upon that magnetic draw from the equator as a personal compass. Let's see you walk without it."

At Miguel's direction, Charlie, Andy, Cass, and I each took turns walking one foot in front of the other down the equator line blindfolded, stumbling like drunks failing sobriety tests the whole way, until we were too worn out to continue. Bewildered, my imagination ran wild the rest of Thursday as I processed the Museo Intinan phenomenon. It had been since my first experience with bioluminescence that I'd found myself so provoked. I had enjoyed being a tourist, at least for one day.

NEW HEIGHTS

Cotopaxi National Park, Ecuador
Sunday, September 4th, 2011

Friday marked nine days since I'd crossed above 2,000-meter's elevation and five days since I'd crossed into winter at the equator. Even though we were marching toward spring every day now, my future in Ecuador looked brisk. Jeans and jackets replaced the stalwart shorts and tees at top of my stuff sacks as we packed to leave Quito.

"If you're cold now, just wait until Cotopaxi tonight," Andy warned me when we saddled up to ride. "Our next stop is the world's highest active volcano. This is low elevation in comparison!"

The clouded 5,900-meter pinnacle shimmered into view as we approached along its northern arm. Cotopaxi National Park's pristine, alpine landscape featured green meadows that sloped upward into rock hills at the mountain's base. Shepherds' ranches dotted lowland fields, with their crops swaying in glacial winds and their sheep grazing atop craggy acres. Enchanting and expansive, all that imagery was lost on Charlie and me entirely during our approach, though, because we spent the whole morning with our rear ends sliding wildly out from underneath us on muddy roads. Our Pirelli MT60s from Cartagena had performed well on tarmac up to that point, but on Friday, they proved loose over gravel and downright dangerous in dirt.

"Tom, you and I both are buying Continental TKC-80 tires in Lima," Charlie remarked as Andy led with Cass on his Dunlop 606s. "Adam from Israel said we won't survive Peru and Bolivia without them."

We grinded the rest of the way until arriving eventually under the shadow of Cotopaxi at Secret Garden II, which was the sister hostel to our Quito lodging—but with an eco-friendly marketing scheme to justify its significantly higher prices.

"A compost toilet and a birdseed menu . . . they certainly use 'green' as a euphemism here," Charlie exclaimed at check-in. "Since when do sustainability and comfort have to be mutually exclusive?"

A two-hour drive across highland grass, alpine forest, and scattered boulders delivered Charlie, Cass and me to the clouded treeline of Cotopaxi on Sunday, where patches of snow and fifteen mile per hour winds awaited at our trailhead. Andy had stayed back to rest.

"Bundle up," our guide, Carlos, instructed as we parked. "We will be hiking much higher."

As soon as everyone was situated, he walked us over to the volcano's shale gradient and pointed directly upward to the outline of a distant building fading in and out of the fog.

"That mountaineer's shelter is our goal. We will climb 1,000 feet vertical in one kilometer. Now, up we go."

There were neither stairs, nor switchbacks, nor cairns between us and the refuge, just one foot in front of the other behind 5'8" Carlos, whose tree trunk legs powered like a machine into the incredible grade. I'd hiked relentlessly in Scouts at lower altitudes, but Cotopaxi's elevation had me gasping by the quarter pole. Charlie was winded too, although Cass became pale and breathless.

"You must descend now. You are experiencing altitude sickness," Carlos instructed to Cass when he checked her at break. "You have just come too high too fast from sea level in the past week. Can you make it back from here?"

Exhausted and hunched over, Cass nodded back understandingly and took the keys. She stood up strong and waved to Charlie and me.

"I'm fine, mates, really. You two should keep going. Take a picture for me at the top, and I'll see it when you come down."

Charlie and I plodded the remainder of the climb in a silent, steady trance as we monitored ourselves for similar symptoms. An hour later, we crested the outcropped ledge up top on a snow plateau. The mountaineering lodge offered refuge ahead, but inside we found neither the fireplace nor hot chocolate that we'd hoped would warm us up. Single pane windows and non-insulated walls made the shelter nothing more than dirt floor hut filled with the leftover remains of expeditions past.

"Cotopaxi draws mountaineers from all around the world," Carlos explained as we caught our breath and looked out at the snowfields. "The summit is still 1,000 meters above us, but we will not be ascending further. We'll turn back here at 4,810-meter elevation to keep you two from getting altitude sickness too."

Neither Charlie nor I had any argument with that. Cotopaxi's -7°F snowfields were the coldest that Charlie had experienced ever. Of course they were mere T-shirt weather for me after my winter in Fairbanks, but we both needed more oxygen. After a brief Snickers break, we followed Carlos back into the cold.

"So that's an icicle, eh?" Charlie smiled as he looked up at the awning on the way out.

Carlos and I had a rollicking laugh at the subsequent realization that Charlie had never seen snow. The three of us bounded down the soft gravel pitch like moonwalking astronauts in just minutes on the way back.

"Welcome back, mountaineers! How was it?" Cass saluted back at the Mazda.

Cass was fully recovered; Carlos was ready to run an Ironman; Charlie and I were wasted. I missed most of the return trip vistas, as I slept the entire ride back to Secret Garden II, but I awoke just in time to see the clouds lift off Cotopaxi at dusk for our first unhindered view of the massive, snowcapped peak. Rumored to be one of the most perfectly formed volcanoes, Cotopaxi filled the entire skyline and peaked thousands of feet overhead at one flawless point. I'd stood proudly on her side and relished her disregard. What I loved about mountaineering was what I loved about motorcycling too—every experience was new unto itself and preparedness was consequently paramount.

CRUISIN' PERU

Barranca, Peru
Friday, September 9th, 2011

A thousand miles in five days brought swift change in scenery after Cotopaxi, beginning along Ecuador's gravelly, red, southern ranges on Monday, day one, and then lowland banana orchards on Tuesday, day two. Southern Ecuador and northern Peru proved worlds apart when we crossed South America's westernmost border. Peru's waterless landscape paled harshly against Ecuador's agricultural prowess. Charlie, Andy, Cass, and I rode several hours of arid Peruvian coastline, all the way to beachside Máncora, where Tim, Jane, Alex, and Kristi were waiting at Loki Hostel.

"We thought you'd never make it!" Alex saluted as he cannonballed into the pool during check-in.

Bursting up from the water, he smiled.

"We're lucky we were able to coordinate this reunion over Skype last night on short notice, because our paths are not crossing for long. Kristi and I are chicken bussing to Lima tomorrow. So hurry and drink up—tonight we celebrate!"

With its bar on the left, swimming pool in the middle, and three stories of dorms opposite, Loki had a reputation for partying, and our crew put that to the test with such rigor that no one achieved more than four hours of sleep that night. Consequently, Alex and Kristi looked uneasy when their bus arrived on Wednesday, day three.

"I think I overdid it last night," Alex admitted that morning while boarding for their eight-hour ride to Lima. "Kristi and I will be heading south to Cusco before you guys get to Lima, so I won't see you for at least a month, until I catch up on my bike. I guess this is the last you'll see of her too."

"Hasta pronto, everyone. It was really wonderful to meet all of you," Kristi replied, with hugs all around. "Now please, Alex, no more talking today. My head hurts too much."

Their bus pulled away with a honk as Tim and Jane saddled up too.

"It's a shame we keep pushing just a day or two ahead of you guys," Tim squinted through his own lack of sleep.

Charlie, Andy, Cass, and I nodded back from our Bloody Mary's over the Loki bar.

"I understand, though. Jane and I needed a day of rest too by the time we got here. Unfortunately, I don't know that we recovered at all, given the way this place parties. It's a little less fun when you're trying to get some sleep. So good luck tonight; you're going to need it."

"Hope to see you guys in Lima—we'll be there for a couple days!" Jane waved as they left.

When the couple was out of sight, the rest of us turned back toward the pool and continued drinking.

Charlie, Andy, Cass, and I would have benefited from heeding closer attention to Tim's advice, in hindsight, because we were all desperate for a restful sleep after partying the rest of the day. Instead, the beat of Loki's infamous nightlife kept everyone awake until 4AM, without reprieve. Tim's words echoed emptily through my psyche as I packed on Thursday, day four, with no energy. Maybe I'd have been more receptive to consecutive nights of such merriment back in Guatemala, but that was 10,000 miles in the past already. I was in adventure mode now—not keg stand—and so, despite Thursday's fatigue, I mounted determinedly atop Thirio to make way at 9AM.

"I don't know what I ate, mates, but my guts are crook," Andy winced as he eased cautiously into his saddle beside me, with Cass wrapped around him. "This could get ugly."

"Well, another night here at Loki won't help, mate. Lima is two days away. Let's see how close you can get before your system shits out completely, eh?" Charlie replied, firing his engine.

Andy and Cass nodded in agreement as we all lifted our kickstands. Andy turned for the worse an hour later, when Thirio fouled a plug and pulled us to the shoulder.

"Mates, I'm clearly on borrowed time. I reckon it's only a matter of minutes before dysentery strikes," he grimaced, changing from pale to green and back as Charlie and I worked to access Thirio's engine on the side of the empty highway.

Andy scanned the horizon and saw no signs of humanity in either direction.

"I'm going to run ahead with Cass and find the nearest restroom. Keep your eyes out—I'll try to park my bike visibly. If I lose you, we'll meet in Lima."

"Feel better, Andy. We'll catch up soon," Charlie agreed as we removed Thirio's seat.

He turned back to me when Andy and Cass sped away.

"Good thing you bought these replacements at Eurocasco, or I'd be ditching you too right now, mate!"

Charlie and I returned to the road just thirty minutes later, but we never did find Andy or Cass throughout the day's pursuit. Rather, we encountered four hundred miles of empty dunes and crosswinds, which stung sand at our necks all afternoon. Missing mates and pockmarked skin proved the least of our worries overall, though, because the Peruvian desert's supreme menace was actually the southbound semitrucks.

The prospect of passing a lumbering semi on an empty straightaway of flat, featureless highway would have been an afterthought with a 650cc motorcycle on most days, but that was not the case on Thursday, due to westerly onshore winds that forced Charlie and me to ride angled toward the shoulder just to keep from being blown into oncoming traffic. Consequently, the wind shadow on each trailer's leeward side required us to straighten our handlebars in a nerve-wracking test of will every time we passed. Otherwise, we'd tangle with the rear axles.

An unfortunate abundance of these trucks delayed us so drastically that Charlie and I were still forty miles from the nearest city by dusk. Watching forlornly from the shoulder as the sun dipped into the Pacific horizon during our final roadside break, we resigned ourselves in silence to breaking adventure motorcycling's golden rule to never ride in the dark.

"Remember mate," Charlie reminded me as we set off into the brief twilight. "There's a reason every rider we've met has likened night riding to a death wish. Stay alert and don't push your luck."

The desert's relentless winds gave way to inundating fog when darkness enveloped the highway after sunset. Visibility dropped to barely ten feet as the cold ocean mist seeped through our layers. Charlie and I clung to the faded white line the rest of the way, crawling thirty miles further through the murky night until we reached Trujillo.

"No word from Andy or Cass," Charlie remarked from his computer that night as we lay exhaustedly in our hotel beds to warm up. "I suppose we stick to the plan then and meet them ahead in Lima. Let's hope tomorrow brings better riding conditions, eh?"

Friday, day five, did deliver more merciful highways in our continued push for Lima. The winds were gone completely, and the scenery improved, with rolling dunes. Our only real hassle that afternoon was Officer Rodriguez, who caught Charlie passing on a double yellow. Charlie and I pulled over a hundred yards past the patrolman from where he waved us down. We planned our evasion strategy as he approached from behind.

"Keep smiling, speak only English, and always divert the conversation," we agreed on the shoulder.

In Central America we'd learned that it was better to play dumb than to try to defend yourself against corrupt cops. If the police knew that you understood them, then they expected coercion; but if you treated them like tour guides, they would grow bored and lose interest.

Officer Rodriguez was short of breath and frustrated already when he finally finished walking up to us. He began explaining Charlie's infraction in an authoritative demeanor with his ticket book open. Charlie and I nodded along attentively as Rodriguez explained the tiered system of fines in detail.

We pointed to our maps and asked the distance to Lima when he finished.

"Listen again," he dismissed, reiterating his threat in a harsher tone. "Do you understand me?"

Charlie and I looked at each other aloofly in response.

"Is it always this cold here?" we inquired back, rubbing our hands across our cores.

We dismounted from our bikes and pointed at the distant Andes.

"What is that mountain there?"

Officer Rodriguez confiscated Charlie's license and stowed it in his book.

"You will not be able to retrieve this until tomorrow morning at the bank in Barranca, unless you pay me now," he warned sternly.

Feigning as translator, I asked Rodriguez to repeat himself several times, before relaying the message to Charlie in emphatic English. Charlie listened extemporaneously, widening his eyes for dramatic effect.

"That's no problem, mate! You see, we're tired anyway, and I've got little cash on me. Go ahead and write the infraction, please. We'll stay the night in Barranca, and then I'll pay it tomorrow morning," Charlie gestured a pen and paper demonstratively with his hands.

What Rodriguez didn't know was that Charlie had actually surrendered his expired license, which he'd packed for this specific scenario, so that he would never need to recover it. Officer Rodriguez retold the bank scenario several more times to Charlie's continued encouragement. Finally losing patience, he changed his tactic on the fourth iteration.

"I have solution," Rodriguez announced, pocketing his infraction book.

He relinquished Charlie's backup license, shook his hand, and requested a small act of kindness, so he could take his wife on a date.

"Cheers mate!" Charlie replied excitedly, handing over five dollars as Rodriguez's demeanor changed entirely.

Officer Rodriguez smiled joyously and asked about our bikes, and the adventure afterward. He even grabbed our map and marked several local attractions. My Spanish improved remarkably too as the conversation shifted its focus, and five minutes later we were basically the three amigos there on the shoulder.

"You will never make it to Lima before nightfall. Let me escort you to Barranca. I won't make you go to the bank," Rodriguez suggested eventually. "Instead, I'll take you to my favorite hotel. It's just a few miles away, and I can keep the other police off you the rest of the way."

"Amazing the difference between bribery and charity," Charlie grinned to me as we readied to follow.

DIPLOMATIC POWER

Lima, Peru
Monday, September 12th, 2011

Peru's northern capitol didn't deliver a promising first impression on Saturday when Charlie and I approached its windswept outskirts. The first ten miles were a sandscape underbelly of rampant litter, congested thoroughfares, and sugarcane huts until Charlie's GPS diverted us off the Pan-American. Our surroundings improved, with well-planned boulevards and industrial warehouses, as we crossed town diagonally toward Lima's KTM dealership.

"This is where Israeli Special Forces Adam told me we could buy TKC-80s," Charlie confirmed to me as we parked outside the dealership garage upon arrival. "He reckoned back in Medellín that our Pirelli slicks would be no match for the Andes—and that there's not another dealership between here and Santiago that will sell Continentals."

Continental TKC-80s were the highest-rated adventure tires on the market, and any advice from Adam had my attention. We each had a front and rear pair mounted, and we purchased an extra set of rears, since the TKC-80s were known to wear quickly.

"Tying these spares down every morning for the next several thousand miles is going to be laborious," Charlie bemoaned in the lot as we lashed them to our luggage. "But we'll appreciate it in Bolivia when the first one is run to shit."

The service door behind us opened for a 990 Adventure R and its silver-haired rider to exit as we finished our knots. He parked several yards away to check his phone and fasten his gloves before looking up and nodding in our direction.

I complimented his bike in timid Spanish, to which he replied quickly in English.

"She is beautiful, no? I just purchased her. Yours seem more broken-in," he gestured toward our bikes. "You two are clearly far from home. My name is Nacho. What brings you to Lima?"

The odds of finding an English-speaking KTM owner who knew Lima and understood adventure motorcycling had to have been close to one in the total population of eight million—and here he was standing right in front of us. Charlie and I latched instantly onto him in a series of questions, which Nacho, in turn, handled like a professional civic host with acute awareness of what a foreigner would and wouldn't know about the area. Eventually, I asked him his profession in Lima.

"I am a Spanish diplomat for the European Union," Nacho answered forthrightly. "This is my third year on assignment in Peru."

My jaw dropped . . . an English-speaking KTM owner who knew Lima and understood adventure motorcycling diplomat!

"Come across town, and let's keep talking. I think we can find a lot to offer each other," Nacho invited as Charlie and I saddled up.

That evening, Nacho took us out in his upscale Miraflores neighborhood for a round of Peru's famous Pisco Sour citrus drinks (which were delicious, but off topic). Nacho's commanding demeanor and collected prose continued to impress as we conversed, and so did the revelation that he'd motorcycled across much of South America already. However, he declined to offer any detailed advice on Peruvian adventure routes when Charlie and I pressed him.

"There is a man named Ivan who can better advise you," Nacho tendered back, ordering a second round. "He is Peru's foremost adventure motorcycling expert, and I've invited him to join us tonight."

Ivan sat down graciously at our table with a wide smile and a hefty girth. Wearing a XXL full BMW suit, Ivan introduced himself humbly and enquired about our journey, nodding knowingly without interruption as we recounted the good, bad, and ugly. He had seen it all before, I could tell, but he wanted to know what Charlie and I were made of—he wanted to understand where we stood mentally on adventure. When we finished our story, Ivan asked for our map. He plotted a route from Huaraz to Cusco via the Andes, which he promised would deliver our most adventurous terrain yet. His advice was both realistic and dramatic, and it resonated exactly as the type of riding that Charlie and I sought.

"Perfect conditions for your new TKC-80s," Ivan winked. "You two are ready."

I asked Ivan how far south he had ridden in his life. He opened his wallet and produced a picture of himself at the bottom of Cape Horn in Ushuaia. Beside him, wearing red bifocals in the image, was a figure I recognized instantly as Hubert Kriegel, the man who had inspired Alex's interest in the sport of adventure motorcycling from the start. Since the day Al had concocted our trip back in Bellingham, he'd never stopped talking about Hubert's Timeless Ride blog, which chronicled his nine-year ongoing journey around the world. Alex had been so enthused that he'd read Hubert's blog posts aloud in our hotel room in Juneau to help solidify our own trip's foundation. Later, when I worked alone in Fairbanks, Al had even emailed me photos of Hubert and his Ural Sidecar in all corners of the globe.

I'd never followed Hubert myself, but ultimately, those iconic red glasses had been the catalyst for this very moment in Peru, where I stared mystified at a picture of them next to the man sitting across from me. God only knew where in the world Hubert was at that moment, but the planet got smaller as our lives crossed paths. Saturday night taught me that you really could accomplish anything if you put your mind to it. Nacho and Ivan were living proof.

"Happy trails, gentlemen!" they saluted when we disbanded. "Don't get caught up in the details along the way."

With over 150,000 miles of Latin American adventure riding between us, the respect was palpable between both parties as we waved goodbye. Nacho and Ivan admired our youth, while Charlie and I coveted their wisdom.

"Let's grow up and be like them someday," we both agreed back at the hostel before bed.

All he and I could talk about was Nacho and Ivan's route when we reunited with Andy, Cass, Tim, and Jane on Sunday. Our enthusiasm fell flat, though, because they were all packing for the Pan-American instead.

"I'm sure the views will be great, but I can't risk the roads getting any worse than the Pan-American riding two-up on a 1000," Tim reasoned. "We have to push south today, anyway since our Machu Picchu tickets are already booked."

"Can we meet you in Cusco?" Jane offered.

Charlie and I agreed to try, even though they'd be at least a week ahead.

Andy and Cass were leaving too, as they were slated to fly home to Australia together out of Chile in less than a month.

"Sorry mates, I knew this day would come. There's just no time left for extra mileage," Andy explained.

"I've had enough of the Third World, anyway, after that last bout of the shits, ye hear? I want our final weeks of this trip to be over Argentinean steaks and Malbec wines. I was afraid I wouldn't see you again on this continent when I couldn't get Wi-Fi until yesterday," Andy continued. "You're a good bloke, Tom. Don't let Charlie rub off on you too much."

"He's your responsibility now, Tom!" Cass chirped with a hug while Charlie masked his emotions.

Tim, Jane, Andy, and Cass pulled southbound onto the highway with one final wave.

Alex was a thousand miles ahead, Nacho and Ivan were already away on business, and I hadn't heard from Justine in weeks. All of them would be lifelong connections, and yet I didn't know when I'd see any of them again. Five months of goodbyes had taught me to just be grateful for having known them at all. Anyway, Charlie clarified what we were really there for as the posse disappeared out of sight.

"Well Tom, if I'm stuck with anyone on this continent, I suppose it's best with you," he said, holding up the map and Ivan's scribbled route. "Now come on, mate, let's show them a real adventure."

IN THE ANDES NOW

Huaraz, Peru
Thursday, September 15th, 2011

Dreaming about South America in my hotel room back in Alaska, I'd always imagined high revs under a snowcapped backdrop with clouds forming in the distance. I'd envisioned climbing into the untouched splendor as high as Thirio would ride, and then ditching her on the fringes to push further on foot. A truly raw experience was what I'd craved, and two hundred miles north of Lima, my dreams manifested in Peru.

Temperatures dropped and sprinkles turned to rain as Charlie and I peeled inland off the Pan-American into red rock bluffs at the start of Ivan's Cusco route. We ascended switchbacks through an intensifying squall to the 4,000-meter pass above, where Peru's interior horizon panned into view under a howling gale. Towering ahead was the Cordillera Blanca, a jagged range of glaciated peaks that tapped instantly into my imaginations from those sunless days in Fairbanks. Charlie and I both smiled from atop our motorcycles, shielding our eyes against the wind. Such imagery was exactly what had drawn us so far into South America.

"That must be Huaraz, as Ivan described," Charlie yelled, pointing down to a distant collection of lights shimmering up through the shadowy air.

As the world's highest mountain range outside the Himalayas, the Cordillera Blanca was a hotbed of mountaineering, and Huaraz was its basecamp for adventure. Our hostel teemed with veteran climbers pouring stoically over topographic maps and meteorological reports. Dissecting ridgelines and interpreting readings, these weren't run-of-the-mill backpackers. They were hard, weathered adventurers— living, breathing replicas of my childhood heroes, whose first-ascent posters still hung on my bedroom wall of legends. Charlie and I blended in surprisingly well with the mountaineers, trading our stories over coffee with reciprocal admiration the next morning. When we asked how to best sink our tires into Huaraz, the consensus was clear from all.

"Go to The Way Inn. It will provide backdoor access to Cordillera Blanca's Huascaran National Park, and you can only get there via fifteen kilometers of rutted staircase gravel," the mountaineers agreed.

On Wednesday, Charlie and I let loose our TKC-80s to devour the ruts and bumps effortlessly into the Cordillera Blanca's highland prairies. Up top we found The Way Inn perched on a green rolling bluff overlooking Huaraz. We toured the magnificent main lodge, which appeared straight from Disney's *Heidi*, with its old growth beams and river stone hearth. We followed our host to the cave-like dormitory next, which was straight from *The Flintstones*, with slab rock bunks and faint candle lighting.

"Eh, what else you got?" Charlie asked bluntly with one look at the archaic dorm.

Given that his desire for creature comforts did not diminish off the grid, he was far better suited for the couple's suite, which featured a queen size bed, a Jacuzzi, and a fireplace.

"That's more like it. We'll take a cot in here too," Charlie requested as he paid the night's charge with one look. "Tom, I know you're too cheap to split this fare, so give me the cost of a bunk and you're square to board with me."

Like I'd done with cigarettes, booze, and God only knew what else along the way since Los Angeles, I accepted Charlie's handout with a shameless nod.

I needed to focus on motorcycle maintenance before getting too comfortable in the couple's suite. The altitude had been getting to Thirio on the way in that morning. She'd struggled to hold higher gears on the straightaways. Outside, I swapped her fifteen-tooth front sprocket for my fourteen-tooth spare to increase torque.

"She won't stride at eighty miles per hour at sea level anymore, but I've got no plans of descending soon anyway," I explained proudly to Charlie that evening as we traded turns in the fireside Jacuzzi.

"Good on ya, mate," he replied. "Now explain to me again how I ended up in this room tonight with you, instead of a girl?"

After a good laugh, we both got to bed for an early rise.

With her gear ratio optimized, her panniers removed, and her fuel-mixture screw dialed, Thirio was ready to thrash the Cordillera Blanca when Charlie and I left at dawn to explore. Chunky roads followed bright blue streams into alpine valleys to the Huascaran National Park border, where we negotiated our park entry fee down to half a sandwich and three cigarettes with the on-duty park ranger. Thirio handled like a banshee along single-track terrain toward the snow-covered mountains above, carving aggressively and chugging wildly as the TKC-80s attacked the Earth to the end of the road.

Charlie and I parked on the shoulder and scrambled onward via goat track to where our path dead-ended at the crux of a glaciated gully. Cresting the trail's final knoll atop the ravine, we came upon a turquoise glass lake with the perfect mirror reflection of our overhead panorama. The two massive peaks that we'd chased all morning loomed dramatically above, with a vertical saddle between them advancing glaciers into the water from the far shore.

"Beats the Outback, no doubt," Charlie mused as we sat down.

We unwrapped our lunches and basked in the high-altitude sun. Shifting, cracking, and reverberating throughout the valley as they fell into the water ahead, icebergs floated otherwise silently before us. High clouds moved fast overhead, birds darted for insects through the trees, and a cool breeze ran down from the mountains as we ate.

"You won't be able to capture this one in your blog mate . . . no offense," Charlie cracked, removing his shoes for an afternoon nap.

"What blog?" I replied back eventually and closed my eyes.

ADVENTURELAND

Yungay, Peru
Friday, September 16th, 2011

Leading up to Peru, every northbound adventure motorcyclist I'd encountered had recommended the same stretch of highway north of Huaraz. Known as Canyon del Pato, the seventeen kilometers were an uncommon commonality for a community of international trailblazers all bent on seeking individual paths. Therefore the route was clearly a must-see.

The accounts all varied in direction, description, and demonstration of course, but paramount in every rider's tale were thirty-six magnificent tunnels. With that in mind, Charlie and I were getting jittery when the rolling hills and green fields around us turned to steepening sidewalls and reddening crags along the Rio Santa. We knew we'd arrived when the river disappeared downward into a bedrock chasm around the next corner.

Measuring three hundred meters deep and fifty across, Canyon del Pato was staggeringly steep from that initial vantage (and all those that would follow as well). Even more dizzying was our highway's barely perceptible continuation through its narrow center ahead. Before my eyes, our road turned to dirt at Canyon del Pato's entrance and etched precariously into the vertical western wall toward an ominous one-lane tunnel at the bend. Charlie and I approached the shaft cautiously, watching our tires kick gravel over the edge, with neither guardrail or shoulder as protection from the churning river below. Passing under the dark opening of Tunnel #1, we entered the mountainside into disorienting, muted blackness.

Several minutes passed as Charlie and I navigated blindly in the dust while keeping our handlebars equidistant from their peripheries along washboard ruts toward a distant pinhole of light. Finally, at the tunnel's opposite end we blasted into daylight and stopped in our new surroundings. Deep within the canyon now, I could no longer see over the walls or out either end, but the high noon sun illuminated every outcrop and crevasse from directly overhead. Rope ladders hung from walls, fortified by lashings like an *Indiana Jones* set. Loose boulders teetered precariously, with only rusted bolts holding them in place. Best of all were the domino entrances of our next three tunnels ahead.

Over and over again, Charlie and I charged into the darkness and then burst back to light as we continued. Always in the distance were the outlines of more to come as our highway serpentined deeper. Ranging from ten meters in length to over five hundred along the next seventeen kilometers, Canyon del Pato's tunnels made for a magical ride by the time we passed through the thirty-sixth into Huallanca that afternoon. Luckily, the adventure was still only half over from there.

"Ivan's route continues from Yungay tomorrow, which means that you and I have to backtrack thirty miles south now," Charlie reminded me with a grin as we tipped our server after lunch.

I was prone to deplore retreads as a waste of time in most cases, but those tunnels were equally exciting from the opposite angle on the way back.

"The pictures will never do Canyon del Pato justice," Charlie and I both agreed in Yungay that night. "But all the other riders captured it best with the same five words anyway—'coolest road in the world.'"

SHIT THE BED

Huari, Peru
Sunday, September 18th, 2011

The motorcycles performed admirably as Charlie and I pushed deeper across the Cordillera Blanca into rural Andean Peru on Saturday, starting right outside of Yungay, as Ivan's unmaintained highway snaked between alpine lakes, free-range livestock, and mountain prairies to the base of Yanarahu Pass. A trio of glaciated peaks overhead was our single point of reference as we pushed into a misty switchback ascent. After an hour of slippery scree slopes, our roadway carved defiantly through the final hundred feet of the cordillera's rigid spine. There at 5,100 meters (the highest elevation ever in our lives again), Charlie and I pulled over in a flurry of accumulating snowflakes to look back on the preceding thirty miles, which unfolded like an EKG monitor below through breaks in the clouds.

Panting and shivering in the thin mountain air, we soon clawed down the opposite side for oxygen to find abundant potholes, washouts, and stream crossings along the single lane of dirt on the cordillera's eastern face. South along the range's base, we barely encountered another soul until Huari.

Even after all that, Saturday's ride paled in intensity compared to what lay ahead for me in Huari, because that evening, I awoke at 1AM with rumbling guts after a chicken dinner. I countered the indigestion sheepishly with Imodium until an hour later, when I awoke again to sharp stomach cramps and a discouragingly soft bowel movement. Then, all hell broke loose Sunday at 6:30AM when I opened my eyes to a warm, grainy sensation dribbling down my butt cheek. Rising in a panic, I sprinted to the bathroom with brown trail in my wake.

"Good God, mate! What did you eat?" Charlie woke to the clamor as I slammed the door behind me.

"The same chicken you did!" I yelped back in agony from my hands and knees.

I took turns deciding which way to face the toilet, with seldom a flush in between for the next three hours. Between bouts I crawled into the shower to rinse before staggering out to collect my sheets and wipe the walkway.

"Thank God the beds were plastic and the floors linoleum," Charlie jabbed with delight when he returned from the pharmacy at 10AM, at which point I was finally back in bed, but still wide-awake from the trauma. "You won't be putting this part in the blog, will you mate?"

Charlie administered a cocktail of Tinidazol antibiotics and Norfloxacin antidiuretics—the strongest pills he'd been able to buy for me. By 2PM I'd stabilized and started hydrating, but it wasn't until 9PM that I finally let my guard down enough to sleep again. Only then had I recovered from the trauma of literally shitting the bed.

HIGH TIMES

Huancayo, Peru
Tuesday, September 20th, 2011

Thirio's saddle had always forced me upright to tiptoes since Seattle. She'd also always bobbed once and then settled over speed bumps. However, I knew something was wrong on Monday when I stood flat-footed overtop of her after a particularly bouncy section of Peruvian highway.

"Blown rear shock mate, probably the result of a pressure leak from the mountain pass," Charlie diagnosed. "Your spring will still carry you for now, but I reckon you're in for a bumpy ride until we can find a mechanic to fix it."

I hung my head in response. I'd known since time began that the stock DR650 shock was a liability, but that $1,000 upgrade had seemed too expensive for a "non-essential" modification back in Seattle. Now that same cash that I'd saved was essentially worthless in the Peruvian Andes, and a functioning suspension was suddenly priceless.

"So I'm riding a pogo stick up shit creek from here, on account of my own frugality," I muttered.

Conditions compounded at the Cordillera Blanca's southern toe, when Ivan's route peeled east toward desert foothills and thickening clouds. Monday's two-hundred-mile route had appeared elementary on the map before departure, but it proved quite contrary with rain slapping at my brow atop a shot shock that afternoon. With Thirio bucking around every corner along wet and hellish roads, it wasn't until after 8PM that our dark and dreary day ended fittingly with a nighttime descent to Huánuco. Charlie and I both regretted having had to break the golden rule again as we surrendered to bed in our hotel, but there had been nowhere else to stop along the way. Plus, we'd needed to keep to Ivan's schedule if we wanted to have a chance at seeing our mates again in Cusco.

"Remember," Charlie and I agreed wearily as we closed our eyes to sleep that night. "This is what we asked for."

As promised, Ivan's path delivered another sixteen hours of interior wilderness the next day, during which indigenous Peruvians wearing colorful throws and pinned-on hats looked on with muted reception as Charlie and I leaned our five-hundred-pound dirt bikes disruptively through their old-world communities. Scenic highlights included the billowing mines of Tajo Abierto, the oasis-like serenity of Lago Chinchaycocha, and the endless herds of wild llama. I was too preoccupied to appreciate any breathtaking splendor or cultural revelation, though, because my singed asshole was still not getting along with Thirio's unpredictable suspension. Consequently, I was desperate for a break when we arrived in Huancayo on Tuesday.

"That Ivan is one hell of a rider, eh?" Charlie exhaled on the outskirts of town as we contemplated our plan for lodging. "I'm beginning to feel like livestock on a cattle drive trying to keep up with his pace. This Huancayo seems big enough to lift my spirits."

I nodded exhaustedly and flagged the first taxi in sight.

"Lead us to the finest hotel in town," I directed, at Charlie's delight.

That night, I was not too cheap for the finer things in life. Hotel Presidente was expensive at eighty dollars a night, but I was content to spare no indulgence with lotion, Q-tips, and a bathrobe for the first time in months. Ivan's route was calling ambitiously for another five hundred miles in the next two days. With that looming on the horizon, I settled gratefully between my pillow-top mattress and goose down comforter to recharge.

UNTITLED II

Huancayo, Peru
Thursday, September 22nd, 2011

"Shit," Charlie groaned as we packed in the Hotel Presidente lot on Wednesday before checkout.

Pointing to two broken welds on his pannier rack, he continued.

"These are load-bearing points. They must have broken yesterday. My luggage will fall right off without them." Charlie stepped back with a look of defeat. "Sorry mate, but what do you say to we book another night here and find a blacksmith to take a look today? Perhaps we could even get your shock fixed too."

Charlie had expected me to be disappointed with the prospect of another costly night at the finest hotel in town, but I nodded excitedly. I didn't need to be talked into another twenty-four hours of presidential treatment. In fact, I was so content that Charlie had to drag me forcibly from the room out to Honda of Huancayo that afternoon.

Honda's 5'1" head mechanic, José, jumped up immediately from under a 125cc scooter at the sight of Charlie's Teneré when we arrived.

"I can fix the welds," José assured us, without inspection. "But I'll need a test ride to be sure."

Charlie knew that rack welding had nothing to do with riding performance, but he yielded and handed the keys over in cautious good faith. José jumped atop Charlie's bike and eased it upright off the kickstand with his ass slung all the way off the seat hanging by a knee. He juiced the throttle, dropped the clutch, and vanished in a cloud of burning rubber. Charlie's Teneré faded back into view briefly through the smoke with its rear tire flaring out of control as José wheelied onto the highway and out of sight. Having just witnessed his bike being treated like a toy by a man the size of an action figure, Charlie boiled in silent rage beside me until José's eventual return.

"Actually, my welding machine is broken right now," José confessed shamelessly as he dismounted. "I just had to ride this machine. But my friend, Tato, down the street will weld these racks. He'll fix the Suzuki shock too. I stopped and confirmed with him during the test ride—just sixty dollars each."

Charlie and I looked at each other with furrowed eyebrows. Neither of us trusted José further than we could throw him (which would have actually been quite far). We proceeded to Tato's anyway, with lack of a better option.

"I'll take care of it. They will both be ready by 10AM tomorrow," Tato confirmed confidently when we dropped the bikes with him.

After another night at Hotel Presidente, we returned optimistically to find satisfactory results upon initial inspection. Charlie's welds looked strong and Thirio's suspension sat stiffer.

"The racks are like-new and that shock is good for at least another 1,000 kilometers with the nitrogen I put in it," Tato proclaimed.

Charlie and I paid quickly and sped back to the hotel with newfound excitement to hit the road, but a raw deal proved evident as soon as we started packing.

"Bullocks! Assuming these porous misaligned seals hold, my aluminum boxes are never coming off again," Charlie muttered disgustedly as he hammered his panniers back onto Tato's misplaced welds.

In the same breath, Thirio sagged back to her lowest position ever as I saddled her luggage.

"We could have gotten a suite at Hotel Presidente for the same price of this shit work!" we both fumed as we left town.

In the next nine hours, Charlie and I encountered only dust, mud, and gravel reminiscent of a post-apocalyptic scorched moon along Ivan's route. Three dilapidated communities of dirt-floor-tin-roof buildings were the only signs of humanity throughout a hundred and fifty miles of rutted track. They faded forlornly onto the horizon and then silently into my mirrors, with neither name nor recognition. I'd seen such living conditions as far back as Guatemala. However, those had been tropical paradises, with Latin hip-hop in the air and mangos falling from trees, not Andean highlands, with desert side winds and overhead vultures. Back in Central America the children had come running, but on Thursday the streets were barren. No one greeted Charlie or me with smiles or admiration. Rather, the rare onlookers appeared startled and confused by our approach.

The sun hung low at the last of the communes when Charlie and I pulled over next to three women to ask directions for Ayacucho.

"This road goes nowhere," the first one hissed, shooing us away.

"You shouldn't be here," the next warned.

"Turn back and go now," snarled the last. "You missed your turn thirty minutes ago."

Charlie and I were invasive by our nature, and the women were unimpressed with our carefree charisma. We returned promptly to our saddles as more residents came to their doorways and stared coldly against our audacity for adventure. As we doubled back, I noticed a young man my age on the corner wearing tattered clothes and a hopeless demeanor. He had a frantic look in his eyes and a rock in his hand, which he arched back to throw as I passed him. I gassed Thirio as hard as I could to send preventative fire from her slipping rear tire in my escape. I never looked back until the turnoff for Ayacucho, at which point the kid was long in the dust—never to be seen by the likes of me again. In the end, I didn't know whether he had thrown his rock, but he'd certainly thrown my conscience.

Charlie and I stopped short of Ayacucho in a township called Churcampa, where residents poured jubilantly out of local businesses to ask questions, offer advice, and even negotiate with the town priest to organize overnight parking at the Catholic church. The people in Churcampa were a heartwarming signal that civilization was on the horizon. More importantly, they helped to revalidate the self-image that I'd come to expect. Still, I was haunted by the experiences from earlier.

My rock-wielding counterpart had clearly understood the chasm between us. He'd known that we money-clad westerners were off-course in his crumbling community. He'd known, moreover, that we would take our otherworldly prosperity and leave as soon as we figured it out. There was Tato too, who had been adamantly proud of his work that morning when we'd left. Not knowing any service better than absolute cut rate, he was destined to deliver it for the rest of his unwitting career.

The fact that neither Tato nor that kid would ever see a realistic chance at my First World opportunities gnawed profoundly at my self-confidence that night as I readied for bed. They had both been forgotten by modernity for no reason other than fate. Therefore, everything that I had always been so proud of seemed suddenly less of an accomplishment, and conversely, more of an entitlement.

"Amazing what you can do in a lifetime if you're at least born with a chance," Charlie reasoned that night as we debriefed.

"I guess not everyone gets to live the American dream," I replied. "I'll be hitting that priest's collection box tomorrow morning."

DIRT

Cusco, Peru
Saturday, September 24th, 2011

On the seventh day of dirt, Charlie and I did not rest. Instead, we departed Churcampa at 6AM for our final leg. Ivan had plotted Ayacucho to Cusco as a one-day ride, but Ayacucho was still two hours away from Churcampa that morning. I knew that the odds of finishing were slim, given our new normal of high elevation, inclement weather, and mechanical failure. Nevertheless, I was desperate for it to end as we gassed up at the onset.

"You can reach Cusco in twelve hours," the attendant reckoned at the station.

"My cousin did it overnight once," an old man recalled from the next pump over.

"Two days, more or less," the cashier argued.

"These varying transit times to the nearest major city are ridiculous," I muttered to Charlie in frustration.

"Mate, consider this—there's no pavement for a hundred miles in any direction from here," Charlie reminded me. "You just rode 14,000 miles from Seattle for sport. A journey to Cusco is likely a faded memory for most of these people, more folklore than fact, if even at all."

"I don't even care anymore. I just want to get back on some asphalt," I groaned, closing Thirio's gas cap forcefully.

What followed was eight consecutive hours of additional washboard dirt, during which Charlie and I fell further behind schedule with each passing mile. Thirio's pannier racks loosened over every bump in an increasingly shrill metallic scraping against her frame. With her condition deteriorating around each bend, I went from resenting her, to pitying her, to praying for her. My back was sore, my guts were off again, and the piercing sum of constant clutch and throttle adjustments knotted a dime-sized point in my shoulder.

Determined to keep pace, Charlie and I still cornered aggressively for lost time, which was why I found myself leaned fully into a single-lane turn that afternoon when two oncoming semis rounded ahead into view. I snaked past the first six axles narrowly on the inside edge with no time to react. The second truck's sharper trajectory cut off my runway just a microsecond later. Leaving the road was my only chance at escaping collision. I dove turbulently into the inside ditch with a muddy halt as the trailer thundered past.

The thrill of adventure got the best of me finally, as tears leaked uncontrollably down my face in the silence left behind. I was tired of endless mud, fed up with my limping motorcycle, and overwhelmed with social inequality. I couldn't even fight the emotions while pinned there to the hillside under Thirio's weight. Instead, I hunched numbly over my handlebars and cried until I had none left.

"Where you been, mate? I'm on my third cigarette waiting!" Charlie clamored when I finally caught up to him at dusk, after a muddy effort to get back onto the road.

Acknowledging the tear tracks running my dust-caked cheeks, he put out his butt and grimaced.

"Never mind. I won't ask."

"If Peruvians can live in this world, then I can ride through it," I resigned.

"Right, the least we can do is finish this trip and remember what we've seen—for everyone's sake," Charlie concluded.

We both buckled our helmets and continued as the sun set.

Cusco was clearly off the table that night, as Ivan's dirt highway descended through granite valleys back below the tree line into the first forests since Huaraz. A skittish forty-mile descent of loose-graveled cliff edges capped the dirt march, appropriately in the dark, until Abancay, where we booked a hotel and passed out promptly.

Charlie and I rolled tall and proud across a hundred miles of pristine new pavement from Abancay to Cusco on Saturday morning. We checked into Hotel Casa Grande at the recommendation of Tim, Jane, Andy, and Cass, who had just left on Friday. We'd missed our mates by only two days, but that was an afterthought by now. More importantly, the ten-day dirt battle was over. I certainly hadn't won, but somehow I'd survived.

ADVrescue

Cusco, Peru
Monday, September 25th, 2011

First on my agenda on Saturday was to send an SOS out to the tight-knit legion of adventure riding "inmates" at ADVrider.com for advice on Thirio's suspension. Less than an hour after check-in, I got a reply from inmate Pat, who offered to sell me his like-new original equipment shock for only $150. Pat had been following my blog since Seattle, and he'd offered a lot of good tips along the way. I trusted Pat's integrity in the proposed sale, but there was still one problem, which was explained to me that evening when I met with Ivan's associate named Powers at the Norton Rat's Tavern.

"You're basically up shit creek here in Cusco," Powers described from behind his desk in the back of his bar. "Because if Peruvian customs agents discover that you're shipping aftermarket parts, they'll make you come to Lima to pick them up anyway. Then they'll charge you twice the value in import taxes and take three weeks to process it too!"

Powers was Cusco's foremost expert on adventure riding, according to my notes from Ivan. He was American, and he owned the bar. I listened closely.

"Ivan is a good friend, and I'd help you if I could here, but honestly, Cusco doesn't have the network of mechanics or distributors that you need for repair. Your best option is to ride back to Lima. At least there you'll have an easier time with import, if you can't get it repaired. Or you can tough it out through Bolivia, all the way to Chile, where they sell the DR, but I wouldn't recommend that. I mean, Ivan sent you through the ringer already," Powers concluded as he led me back to the bar from his office.

"There's no good option. Have a drink on me . . . and good luck with your decision."

Powers' words echoed through my head as I mulled over my options while watching Monday Night Football, and it was his final statement that resonated loudest when the Packers ultimately won. The last thing I wanted was to backtrack all the way to Lima after two and a half weeks of Ivan's Third World reality tour. So, that evening back in Casa Grande, I borrowed a flathead and a hammer to tighten Thirio's spring preload discs.

"I figured that if the shock is there to steady the spring's rebound, then tightening the discs should reduce the travel," I explained to Charlie that night when he returned from a guinea pig dinner down the street.

Thirio did sit noticeably taller.

"I really think it's stiff enough to get me through Bolivia now."

"Well, that is a valiant effort, mate," Charlie admitted, running his hands through his hair.

He turned to his bike and grimaced.

"Unfortunately, I think I've tipped the scales toward Lima nonetheless. You see, I discovered a rather serious oil leak on my forks today while you were meeting with Powers. The forks are certainly not fit for Bolivia, which means KTM is my only option for replacement WP seals at the moment. What do you say we head back there via the Pan-American? Andy and Tim made the opposite journey once already . . . how bad could it really be?"

With both of us now facing suspension issues, Charlie and I finally resigned ourselves to the seven-hundred-mile one-way trip back north that evening. We packed our bags in quiet contemplation until just before bed, when I remembered that Kristi had flown home on Sunday.

"What about Alex?" I asked, rising from my pillow in a stir. "Isn't he landing in Bogotá today and then hitting the road tomorrow?"

Charlie queued the familiar Skype ringtone from his laptop with a responsive grin, and Al answered exuberantly.

"You'd better believe it!" Alex exclaimed after we'd explained our plan to him. "I just landed. I already saw plenty of Ecuador with Kristi, so I'll haul ass straight to you. See you in five days, max."

I looked over at Charlie as he closed his computer at the end of the call.

"We just cranked up the adventure, mate," we both smiled, warming suddenly to the prospect of heading north. "Hold on to your butts!"

ICE ROADS

Lima, Peru
Tuesday, September 26th, 2011

Charlie and I had been obsessing a lot over our weight until Tuesday. No, we weren't getting pudgy—we were just carrying too much shit everywhere. So, he and I stowed our side panniers at Casa Grande for our 1,400-mile Pan-American round-trip to Lima, and we hit the road with only our tools, spares, and essentials bungeed in dry bags to our tails. Thirio's compromised suspension handled more responsively under the lightened load as we backtracked to Abancay to start the day, and her tightened spring bobbed less through the aggressive corners. There would be no settlements for another two hundred and fifty uncharted miles from Abancey until Huallhua, according to our non-topographical map, but Charlie and I showed little concern as we gassed up. This was the Pan-American after all, and we assumed a cakewalk, compared to Ivan's route.

Unbeknownst to us was that a stormy Andean high plain traverse waited ahead between us and the Pacific. Rains started in the foothills outside Abancay and intensified through every bend along the increasingly rapid Rio Pachachaca for several hours. Charlie and I pulled over in a puddle of slush to reassess our situation when the squall turned to sleet at 4PM. We had managed to stay dry by wearing our rubber outers from the first sign of sprinkles, but the 4,000-meter air was still bitingly cold.

"Huallhua is one hundred miles away, so it would be longer to retreat than to push onward from here. Visibility is deteriorating behind us, so the storm must be passing," Charlie and I agreed on the shoulder before forging ahead into the flurries. "Plus, weather hasn't stopped us yet."

Our optimism faded as the storm continued to strengthen. Charlie and I were soon slowed to a crawl when the ascent leveled into a blizzard plateau an hour later. Thirio's handlebars and headlights accumulated inch-thick blocks of ice from the increasing onslaught of snow. My armor caked over, cooling my arms and legs into distant memories, as the last remaining sunlight faded to a black horizon at 6PM.

Breathing deliberately through my nose and cursing angrily through chattering teeth, I couldn't believe that I'd left my tent, sleeping bag, and heavy clothes back in Cusco to save weight. I'd used that gear twice in the past 15,000 miles, and now on the first day without it, I was in desperate need of emergency bivouac.

Charlie and I would have been forced to pull off if the road had turned to ice, and God only knows how we would have survived from there. Luckily, the pavement remained miraculously wet through Tuesday's frigid climax. At what seemed like the night's darkest hour, we crested the 4,600-meter pass. I had never been happier or colder in my life as chunks of ice flew from our bikes and our bodies during the descent back into welcoming rain on the western face. Thirty miles later, we reached Huallhula with gratitude to be out of the death zone.

"Let's say we check the weather, and we attempt that pass before 4PM on our way back, eh?" Charlie managed to joke finally when our shivering stopped in our beds. "And maybe all future routes as well?"

A grunt was all I could muster back, but my affirmation was clear.

HOLD ON TIGHT

Lima, Peru
Wednesday, September 27th, 2011

"We stock your fork seals. I can have them installed by tomorrow," the KTM mechanic replied from behind the parts counter to Charlie and me in Lima after 400 miles of flat, dry, tarmac on Thursday. "But the Suzuki shock is more difficult. We'll take it to a specialist named Tato. If anyone can fix your shock on this continent, it's him."

I nodded anxiously, handed him Thirio's keys, and started drinking back at the hostel that afternoon. Mounting maintenance expenses and mechanical uncertainty had been taking an increasingly burdensome toll on me of late. I contemplated Thirio's jeopardized future in South America should Tato fail to deliver. My concern grew after my second beer, when I hopped online to realize that my bank account was down to four figures—because even leaving Thirio behind was an expensive proposition in Peru.

Unlike some backpacker, I couldn't just hop a bus or book a flight out of Peru on a whim with my last couple hundred bucks. As an adventure motorcyclist, I was attached to Thirio via passport documentation—and ineligible to leave without a documented explanation of her whereabouts. Selling Thirio to a local was almost impossible, due to overbearing Peruvian import laws and taxes. My best choices would be to pay LTL freight to ship Thirio home or to find another traveler to buy her. Both of those options would come with their own hassles and expenses too.

I became increasingly worried as my empty beer bottles continued to stack, until eventually I muttered something to Charlie about cutting my losses, scrapping Thirio with Tato, and flying home with my remaining cash from Lima. As I cracked my fifth beer and started prophesying my next adventure (I had Alaska in mind), Charlie rolled his eyes and stopped what he was doing.

"Riding north seven hundred miles can mess up your mood, mate, but don't lose sight of what you've accomplished," he explained, taking the drink from my hand.

He jotted several keystrokes and held his computer in front of my face. I winced to clear the double vision until a pole-to-pole map of the Western Hemisphere came into focus.

"Argentina is not a finish line, mate. It's a new horizon—and it's just around the corner. You are, after all, age twenty-four hurtling toward Tierra del Fuego on an intrepid DR650 at the moment, and there is no sum of money or planning that could ever replicate this opportunity right here in front of you."

After a stupefied moment of awe, I realized that Charlie was right. In just three days, October 1st would mark a full year on the road for me, during which I'd experienced four months of Alaskan trucking, two months of trip preparation, and six months of motorcycling through Central and South America. In truth, I'd been living in the moment for so long that I'd lost touch with how far we'd come in the past twelve months. I'd enjoyed such a wide range of experiences that I was clearly stalling on where to push next. Just because Alex and I had only ever talked about getting to Argentina didn't mean that the dream was almost over. Rather, Argentina's open-ended expanse represented the pinnacle of all that planning.

Tracing the map with my eyes from Fairbanks all the way to Lima, I became suddenly determined to finish victorious as I processed Charlie's words. I didn't care if I had to crawl home shirtless. I was going to ride until my last silver dollar with the wind feathering my face and Thirio's engine screaming beneath me! I rose to my feet excitedly and high-fived Charlie with newfound vigor. Stumbling backward into empty bottles, I sat back down to focus my energy into some writing. My emotions were still running high that night when I started reading my blog's recent feedback. The following post caught my attention quickly:

" . . . you've devoted an inordinate amount of press to things that displease you. We get it. Point made. We know shit exists; now get past it. Leave the smelly Third World if it's so irritating. Find your dream job at a surf shop or in the mountains, but please STOP BITCHING. It's a dreadful habit."

Now, there may have been some truth to that, but my response was equally clear:

"These are not bedtime stories. If reading the rough spots from this journey is getting you down, then try riding them. Pick up a *Lonely Planet* if my realities are too harsh, because this is an adventure. Now hold on tight!"

BACK IN THE GAME

Lima, Peru
Thursday, September 28th, 2011

"The DR650 shock? Yes, it is fixed," Tato greeted casually in his specialty suspension yard on Thursday.

I followed him past several other encouraging Japanese and European bikes to the garage, where Thirio's shock sat in a vice. Tato compressed the rod with his hand and released it to demonstrate the rebound.

"See, it remained down until I fixed the bladder leak and replaced the nitrogen. That's a common failure for stock shocks at high elevation," he explained. "It was like riding a pogo stick, right? I recommend you replace it when you get to Argentina. This rebuild won't last forever, especially if you're going to Bolivia."

Some of the conversation was lost between Tato's broken English and my mechanical shortcomings, but one thing was clear—his $150 job was far more professional than what I'd paid for in Ayacucho. I beamed with optimism at Thirio's freshly tuned suspension that afternoon enroute back the hostel.

The only Third World country remaining between Argentina and me was Bolivia, perhaps the most dilapidated of them all, but I was ready to validate all the hard work, obnoxious claims, and shameless machismo that had gone into my Seattle-to-Buenos Aires planning. In fact, I was still so pumped up from Charlie's pep talk the day prior that I could have departed and ridden straight to the bottom of the world right then, if Alex hadn't still been two days north.

"I'm hauling ass!" Al confirmed that evening in an email update.

With the edge of the world at my fingertips, I waited excitedly with Charlie.

A Different Trip

Sunday, on our six-month anniversary since leaving Seattle, a sixty-year-old drunk stumbled off the sidewalk into a fifty mile per hour head-on collision with Alex in Azogues, Ecuador. Al escaped with a fractured collarbone, and the Ecuadorian was in a coma. The old man was on life support with critical injuries, according to Al from his hospital bed via Skype on Monday.

"He is expected to live. I'm still processing everything, but what matters to you is that my new lawyer says it will be at least three weeks before I'm allowed to leave here," Al lamented. "It'll take that long for me to straighten out my bike and my riding gear, anyway, since the cops stole half my shit while I was in the ambulance."

Al ran his hand through his hair.

"Keep your head up, Alex. For once it wasn't your fault," Charlie broke the ice.

"Unfortunately mate, we're not going to be able to wait up for you any longer," he continued regretfully. "You see, Tom and I both committed to firm timelines down south just this morning."

The poignancy of the news' timing set in as Charlie explained further.

"My brother, my mate, and Tom's mother all booked flights to meet us in Santiago for November 15th. We were excited to invite you along when you got here."

"Don't worry about me, guys," Al replied, forcing an exhausted smile. "Although, I might just ditch the bike at this point."

Alex was trying to stay positive, but I could hear in his voice that he'd been shaken to his core. I disclosed to him that I'd shared similar sentiment just days earlier and advised him to let the dust settle first before making a decision.

"I'll be on your ass again one way or another when I get out of this mess. In the meantime, just pray for the Ecuadorian guy," Alex concluded our debriefing with a determined nod.

Charlie and I hung up and shook our heads at each other with disappointment. Mom's booking was still the greatest news I'd heard in months. Meanwhile, Charlie's brother, Andrew, and his mate, Greg, were sure to invigorate the adventure. Regardless, the enthusiasm in our hotel room was suddenly muted, now that Alex was out of the picture and an innocent man was on life support. Like many elements of our adventure, this was not how we had planned it.

MACHU PICCHU

Aguas Calientes, Peru
Monday, October 10th, 2011

The return trip between Peru's two capitols proved dry and nondescript as Charlie and I hit the plateau pass on Wednesday to blue skies on our repaired suspensions. We arrived in Cusco with our minds set squarely on what had long been our distant beacon of adventure in South America.

Machu Picchu could only be reached via a three-hour train ride or a three-day trek of the Inca Trail from Cusco. Every backpacker ever had insisted that the hike was essential in experiencing the park's true splendor. Charlie and I argued that we'd already experienced plenty in just getting to Cusco over the past 15,000 miles. Therefore, we ignored the backpacking hype and kicked up our feet to let Peru Rail do the conducting. On Saturday at dawn, we passed through Machu Picchu's park entrance into one of the most recognizable sights in the world.

Immediately inside the gates, Machu Picchu's terraced mountainsides rose from the fog out of the Sacred Valley before us. Daybreak sunshine painted shadows across the entire city as roofless neighborhoods sparkled in morning dew. Charlie and I stopped in disbelief at our first glimpse of the monumental vista in its full glory. Eventually, the queue of visitors nudged us forward, and we bounded eagerly into ancient history behind the lines of others ahead. Unlike the parks in other Latin American countries, Machu Picchu did not offer free range of its grounds. The site instead offered 360 degrees of surrounding cliff lines, along which its 2,500 daily tourists who would surely kill themselves if left to wander. The park could only be navigated via crowded pathways, which showcased the city's ancient splendor from start to finish.

Every wall, walkway, and window throughout Machu Picchu's ageless layout had been compiled astonishingly from smoothed boulders that jig sawed tight without mortar or gaps. Ranging from the magnitude of a Miata to the parvitude of a pinky, the stones followed neither pattern or convention. They appeared as if cobbled together at random with whichever was within closest reach. Machu Picchu's development sprawled across every scalable degree of hillside throughout the park. Charlie and I hiked through intermittent mist to Huayna Picchu's egg-shaped peak for the most memorable view of the day, looking back from opposite the entrance.

The tourists around us complained of the surrounding clouds, but I was silently pleased with the inclement conditions up top. We had all seen Machu Picchu's unobstructed magnificence on cubicle screensavers long before arriving at the park's prominence. However, piecing the city together through the fog, rainbows, and breakthroughs proved far more engaging to me. The fact that Machu Picchu still stood so long after its sixteenth century abandonment was impressive enough, regardless of the view. Perched perilously amongst the clouds on a saddle between two mountains and teetering thousands of feet over the Sacred Valley in the middle of the Peruvian Andes, Machu Picchu deserved its recognition as one of Seven Wonders of the World.

SMILE FOR THE CAMERA

Puno, Peru
Wednesday, October 12th, 2011

Thirio's lightweight performance to Lima and back had been so enlightening that I decided to streamline her luggage permanently before departing Cusco. Having nearly frozen to death during that same enlightenment, though, I was never going anywhere again without my tent and sleeping gear. So, I paid three dollars to a local welder to fix her squeaking pannier racks. I reinstalled the aluminum side boxes and fired my Pelican case into the dumpster. Then, to make up for the lost capacity, I gathered all the items that I hadn't used in months and routed them to Mom and Dad via the Peruvian post office.

In all, I'd shed twenty-five pounds total by the time Charlie and I departed for Bolivia. Thirio responded jubilantly by sustaining fifth gear for five straight hours along Southern Peru's vast Altiplano plains, all the way to 3,812-meter Lake Titicaca on Wednesday. The ride was graciously blank and uneventful, aside from long-distant mountains and the occasional gas station. Our only snag was when two officers asked for proof of insurance at the last checkpoint before Puno.

Neither Charlie nor I had insurance, because, by law, we didn't need it; and after an entire month of Peruvian corruption, we were ready to go toe-to-toe over it on our last day before the border. We argued defiantly that we were legal motorists. Voices were raised, and fingers were pointed. The dialogue climaxed when Charlie turned on his camera and snapped mug shots of each officer. Looking up, he read their names aloud from the image display in his palm.

"Garcia and Diaz, eh?" Charlie questioned curiously as the officers' body language retracted.

The argument ended there.

"Maybe it's allowed in your country, but here in Peru you do not take pictures of police officers!" the commander stammered as he relinquished our expired licenses.

"Well, that's because in my country the police aren't corrupt," Charlie replied.

OUT OF THE FRYING PAN, INTO THE FIRE

La Paz, Bolivia
Friday, October 14th, 2011

The Lake Titicaca border crossing started excitingly as Charlie and I stamped out of Peru, but our jubilation was stifled immediately with a whole new level of Third World bureaucracy on the other side.

"Proof of insurance," our Bolivian customs agent demanded.

"This again? We didn't have insurance in Peru. It wasn't required, and it wouldn't have covered us here anyway," we argued. "Where can we buy Bolivian coverage?"

"In La Paz. One of you will have to take the bus, buy the policies, and return tomorrow with proof. The other can stay here with the motorcycles," the agent replied.

That solution wasn't going to work for me, because I had a long-awaited date cooking up ahead in La Paz that night. After two and a half months since Cartagena, Justine and I were finally intersecting again in the capitol city on Thursday. Justine was scheduled to be checking into Hotel Leon at that very moment. I pressed the agent further in pent up excitement, but he held his ground.

"You cannot pass without insurance! Now leave, or I will have you escorted away by the two policemen out front!"

Charlie and I turned and stepped outside to reformulate our plan. The two officers out front approached as we lit a pair of cigarettes on the sidewalk.

"Is insurance really required in Bolivia?" Charlie asked them brazenly, holding out his pack.

The officers nodded and lit up. They grinned on exhale.

"Yes, Bolivia requires insurance," the senior replied. "But don't listen to that asshole inside. Just get your stamps and buy it in La Paz. We're not looking."

So, with the closest thing to the law on our side, Charlie and I walked calmly back into customs and harassed the agent for another half hour until he realized that he'd been bought by a pair of smokes.

"Welcome to Bolivia," he grunted, opening his inkpad.

"Looks like we're out of the frying pan and into the fire," Charlie scoffed as we walked out.

Panoramic views of glimmering Andean ranges unfolded ahead as Charlie and I navigated along a barren yellow peninsula out into Lake Titicaca. Eventually, we rolled onto a wooden skid ferry to cross world's highest navigable lake. We stayed on our bikes for balance as the Third World contrivance creaked and twisted through subsequent chop under its outboard Evinrude across the Straight of Tiquina.

"Alright mate, don't forget that I exist over the next several days after you find your girl," Charlie warned me at disembarkation.

My guts had been cramping all morning, so I made no promises to wait up. I set the land speed record to La Paz for a much-needed toilet and a long-overdue date—in that order—as soon as the ramp lowered. Anticipating immediate gastric release, I parked and hurried into the Hotel Leon lobby, where Justine was waiting at the main bar with cold beer on ice.

"Hey stranger!" she welcomed me.

I stifled my indigestion and approached like nothing was wrong.

"I'm glad we were able to reunite here. Kelly headed to London last week for a new job, and I'm taking a six-week Spanish immersion course in Cochabamba next week," she continued as we hugged hello.

Justine handed me a beer and motioned us to her table. I sat down using my arms to keep from exploding. The beer's carbonation alleviated my cramping, mercifully, after the first sip. My outlook continued to improve as I finished the drink and my guts settled further. Charlie retired to our room after another round, leaving Justine and me finally alone for the night.

"Too bad about the timing with your mom, or I'd tell you to come stay with me in Cochabamba!" Justine teased.

I smiled back, imagining the possibilities as we leaned in to kiss.

"I might head to London for work after my course. So who knows . . . this could be our last weekend together," she concluded.

With that, we both rose from our chairs, heading to her private room upstairs, when my guts gurgled loudly.

"It's nothing," I insisted.

The indigestion intensified, though, forcing me to cut my losses and run after I released an awful fart in the elevator.

"I can't believe I'm saying this, but I've got to call it a night," I gasped hurriedly, punching the close button and hanging back when we got to her floor. "Now!"

The doors closed between us, and that was goodnight.

"Talk about romance!" Charlie snickered the next morning as I trembled from wailing all night into the toilet.

My misery continued on Friday too, as I hardly left bed. It wasn't until Saturday that I finally gathered the fortitude to venture further than waddling distance from my toilet.

A major commotion echoing through the streets got me out of bed ultimately. Charlie, Justine, and I gathered at the hotel room window as the strengthening chorus of chants and explosions began that morning. A short walk later, we found the epicenter of civic upheaval downtown, as thousands of miners marched chaotically along La Paz's central boulevard.

Screaming in unison and pumping their fists, they were protesting wages and working conditions in their raggedy stained coveralls and soot-covered helmets. To make sure they were heard, they were clearing hundred-foot-radius circles at every intersection and lighting sticks of dynamite in the streets. Shockwaves reverberated thunderously as I watched the explosions from the curb. I knew nothing of Bolivia's mining industry, but the emotions in the air were clear. We watched until the demonstrations passed.

On the walk back home we detoured to San Pedro prison. San Pedro had been exposed in the book, *Marching Powder*, as an institution where inmates acted as citizens and the guards acted blind. According to Charlie, who had read the international bestseller, San Pedro was a fully functioning society, where prisoners bought their cells like real estate and furnished them with entertainment centers, wet bars, and even family members. Inmates managed businesses amongst each other, trading everything from household amenities to gourmet food to professional services. Craziest of all was the prison's economic lifeblood—its decades-long production of Bolivia's purest cocaine, which proliferated throughout La Paz.

"Remember, all of these stories came from a book," Charlie reminded us as we stared at San Pedro's entrance from across the street. "They could all be outrageous embellishments."

That was when we met inmate Dave from New York, who confirmed everything with vivid detail. Smelly, strung out, and yet surprisingly amiable, Dave was on work release for the afternoon, with only two weeks remaining on his twelve-year sentence for a botched Miami drug run. His stories validated San Pedro's notoriety as a truly unique experience, and he even pitched the famous prison tour to us with his authentic Brooklyn accent.

"You see, as a foreigner on work release, I'm ineligible for real employment at these nearby businesses," Dave explained. "So San Pedro's prisoners and guards pay me to recruit gringos for the tour every day before they let me back in."

The authors of *Marching Powder* had met on a tour, one as a tourist and the other as the inmate guide. Popularity from the book's ensuing proliferation had caused authorities to crack down on prisons of late. There were many stories of tourist deportations after getting caught inside San Pedro. Eyeing the cops at every corner, we declined Dave's offer, despite his insistence that the police were already bought. Dave was entertainment enough anyway.

"Your loss," he concluded, before leaving us there with a final thought. "Man, the thing that gets me is that they caught me in Miami with three kilos of the finest yay you'd ever seen, and as punishment they locked me away right here where we make the shit!"

It struck me that Bolivia was unlike any country I'd ever experienced as Dave scurried over to the next group of gringos. Cops could be bought with cigarettes, rioters blew up dynamite in the streets, and prisoners manufactured cocaine openly. I'd thought that Peru's dilapidation and poverty had been extreme, but at least it had seemed stable. Bolivia, on the other hand, appeared teetering on the edge—just like my bowels from the moment I'd arrived.

DEATH ROAD

Potosí, Bolivia
Sunday, October 16th, 2011

Back in April, I'd left Seattle with the ultimate aspiration of finding a girl just like Justine. When I met her in Guatemala, she'd blown me away with her foreign, athletic, and adventurous attributes. She proved to be potentially the highest caliber woman I had ever courted as our adventures intertwined throughout Central and South America. Just like ten weeks prior in Cartagena, though, there was still no amount of attraction that was going to distract her or me from our own ambitions on Sunday.

Determination and self-reliance was what had brought the two of us together under Guatemala's untethered backdrop of limitlessness in the first place, and that same individuality had only since solidified after six more months on the road. Neither of us worried about when we'd meet again during our heartfelt goodbye in La Paz. We were, instead, happy to have shared the moment—and excited for whatever came next.

"I had a great time. The world gets smaller every day," Justine winked as she stepped onto her chicken bus for Cochabamba in the morning. "Enjoy the rest of your adventure and don't take Death Road too literally today."

Charlie and I waved back from the parking lot from atop our idling motorcycles as the bus closed its door.

"Something tells me that five years from now you might not have let that one walk away, mate," Charlie remarked over the engine when the bus pulled away.

"Maybe," I replied. "But I wasn't ready to let her stop me today. I'm taking my chances with the road."

We lifted our kickstands and pulled out in the opposite direction.

Already fully armored and packed for what Justine had alluded to, Charlie and I were headed straight to Bolivia's notorious Death Road, which had built up a dramatic reputation leading up to La Paz. Backpackers had described forty kilometers of single lane mud along a continuous ledge of vertical cliffs leading down to a city called Coroico. They'd rumored that overhead waterfalls, hairpin curves, and uncontrollable slides had taken tens of thousands of lives to its valley floor below.

"Seriously, you might not survive . . . " the backpackers had trembled.

Charlie and I were prepared for the worst when we arrived at Death Road's nondescript turnoff, north of La Paz. We pulled over to tighten our gloves and say our prayers there at the ominously misted entrance. Rather than an apocalyptic drop into an empty Andean abyss, we instead encountered half a dozen tour vans unloading gringos and mountain bikes.

"You see, in 2006 the Bolivian government built a new highway to Coroico, complete with steel guardrails and opposite lanes. Now we attract vacationers to ride bicycles down Death Road, and we drive them back up via the new road," one of the guides explained to me at the top.

Death Road's true hazard proved to be reckless rubbernecking bicyclists, among which Charlie and I snaked casually from top to bottom that afternoon along terrain far gentler than we'd ridden in Peru.

"Where did you rent those?" one of the backpackers asked Charlie and me in Coroico at the bottom.

He pointed to our motorcycles while he snacked on his pre-arranged lunch.

"We brought our own rides mate, and 20,000 kilometers of experience the like," Charlie replied. "We're not on vacation."

He and I turned away and buckled our helmets.

"Somehow, even in Bolivia, the innocence of the backpackers remains unblemished," Charlie smirked to me as we saddled up.

"At least Death Road made for decent distraction from saying goodbye to Justine today," I replied.

We took off on the good road while our inquisitive friend finished his ice cream sandwich.

FOREIGN PLATES

Potosí, Bolivia
Monday, October 17th, 2011

Despite the lighthearted experience on Death Road, my concerns about Bolivia's stability deepened after Coroico, when the five-year-old "good" highway showed severe deterioration the whole way back to La Paz.

"Hard to believe that new route failed to tolerate even half a decade's worth of weather," Charlie remarked in La Paz when we stopped for gas. "Those brand-new retention walls had exposed rebar and gushing runoff coming out of them!"

He and I didn't have time to expound on Bolivian civil engineering for long, because our gas station attendant revealed Bolivian tax policy to be even more inept as we opened our empty tanks.

"I cannot sell petrol to foreign license plates—it's Bolivian law," our attendant balked, shaking his head and denying us. "Gasoline here is subsidized so drastically that our border towns are overrun with neighboring citizens and their thirst for cheap fuel. In January, President Evo Morales responded with a reactionary decree that foreign plates be charged three times the subsidized price."

313

"Whatever, we'll pay the higher cost," I dismissed quickly.

"I wish it were that simple," the attendant replied. "But it's illegal to sell at the higher cost without documentation, and now, even ten months later, the government still hasn't rolled out the paperwork required to permit foreign sales. The law is enforced most heavily within the La Paz city limits. You might have better luck outside of town."

"Forget about the crumbling infrastructure, mate. This is a whole new level of unorganized chaos," Charlie stammered as we took to the streets to search for fuel.

"Let's get the hell out of here before Bolivian incompetence stops us completely," I answered.

We found an old man generous enough to sell us each two gallons for only double the normal price from his milk jug reserves, and we departed in a furious hurry.

I nearly boiled over with frustration during the hours-long traffic jam that was our ensuing escape from La Paz, until my tensions eased finally when we returned to the empty Pan-American Highway with all 19,974 feet of Huayna Potosi's enigmatic peak glowing orange ahead under the setting sun. The otherworldly Altiplano landscape was a reminder that I had not come to South America seeking United States standards. So, in spite of all the turmoil, I managed to construct a more compromising outlook for Bolivia as Charlie and I charged into the serene desert at dusk. The next morning, as if on queue, our motel owner Francisco announced a true Bolivian windfall.

"Today is Election Day, so all roads are closed," Francisco explained as he retrieved our plates after breakfast. "Even liquor sales are forbidden today."

"Keep the population sober and immobilized for when the results come in, eh?" Charlie snickered. "I guess we aren't getting to Potosí today."

"Actually with foreign plates you two are in luck," Francisco replied with a grin. "You will have the roads to yourselves today."

It took a moment for Charlie and me to process that our license plates' non-sovereignty had become a sudden advantage. Then we jumped excitedly to our feet and made haste to pay the bill.

The most dreamlike ride of our lives ensued as Charlie and I rode without passing a single automobile, aside from an ambulance, all the way to Potosí. As the highest plateau on Earth outside of Tibet, the Bolivian Altiplano would have been surreally devoid of humans, animals, and plants, even on a normal day. Therefore, the blank rubble landscape and distant snowcapped peaks on Election Day were akin to a Martian *Mad Max*. Five hundred kilometers of lichens and dust were all we encountered along Monday's bewildering ride, until finally we were blocked by the last police checkpoint outside Potosí.

"You cannot pass until polls close at 7PM," Comandante Alvaraz decreed there, sentencing Charlie and me to bake in the sun for the next three hours.

Despite the fact that his command didn't align with previous checkpoints, I was impressed that Alvaraz hadn't requested a bribe. Rather than argue for entry, I sat down in Thirio's shadow to wait alongside Charlie without a fuss.

A few minutes later, I was just nodding into a roadside nap when the familiar sound of a motorcycle muffler approached from inside Potosí. Glancing up from my slumber, I identified it instantly as a Honda Africa Twin. The rider and his passenger pulled up to Alvarez's checkpoint and stopped briefly on the other side. With just a handshake, they passed quickly through the gate. Charlie and I both rose to our feet in astonishment as the Swiss rider, Hans, pulled alongside us with his Bolivian girlfriend, Nora.

"My fellow Bolivians . . . you look bored on this Election Day," Hans greeted through his helmet. "We are heading to a hot springs for the afternoon. Care to join? I can see by your bikes that we'll find plenty to discuss."

"Absolutely, but how did you get through the gate?" Charlie and I nodded back eagerly.

"Easy—I just slipped the commander five dollars for permission," Hans replied.

Alvaraz waved to us from the guardhouse as I looked in his direction.

"Again, at least he didn't ask outright," I shook my head.

Hans, Nora, Charlie, and I soaked in supple mineral water, trading stories and advice for the rest of the afternoon. Hans was on a 'round the world trip, but he'd hung around Bolivia for the last several months, on account of meeting Nora in Potosí. Together they knew the area well and had lots of good information.

"Are you here in Potosí for Cerro Rico? The mine tour is an adventure of unmatched scale," Hans inquired over dinner that evening.

Cerro Rico was the silver-rich mound of rock outside our window that cast its shadow across the city. Known as "the mountain that eats men", Cerro Rico's mineshafts were rumored to have taken the lives of over eight million souls since their slavery beginnings in the 1600s. Charlie and I had, in fact, come to tour it on Tuesday. We were ready, more than ever, for whatever Bolivia could throw at us.

CERRO RICO

Potosí, Bolivia
Tuesday, October 18th, 2011

Standing in yellow jumpers, rubber boots, and single cell facemasks on the side of Cerro Rico, Charlie and I peered cautiously into the mineshaft ahead at a pair of ancient steel rail tracks fading to blackness through a smoke-filled entrance. Our tour guide, Tata, strapped hard hats over our heads and explained the mine's dangers through her mouthful of coca leaves.

"There are over 16,000 miners in Potosí, and their average lifespan is ten years after starting," Tata detailed. "Most of the deaths are from black lung disease, but accidents are also common. You can turn around if you get scared while we're inside, but I'll be continuing the tour for everyone else. So it is important to remember the way, since this is one of five hundred tunnel entrances in Cerro Rico."

Tata turned on our lamps and waved us one by one into the first several hundred yards of the increasingly dark mine. The brick walls, which crested into a 5'6" arch overhead, had been constructed under Spanish command by Bolivian slaves four hundred years prior, according to Tata.

"The conquistadors would force their slaves at Cerro Rico to work for six months at a time without surfacing, often working them literally to death," she revealed as we continued to where the rails submerged into six inches of murky piss-reeking water. "Here begins the section where the Bolivians were freed and continued to mine on their own."

My rubber tour boots leaked instantly as the ceiling lowered toward the sludge. The sturdy brick walls were abandoned for splintered wood braces and sheet metal reinforcements in the steps ahead. The next quarter-mile was strafed with overhead piping, which hissed air from tiny leaks as we crouched on hands and knees through thickening smog and increasing temperatures. Eventually, Tata stopped us at a cramped 80F degree enclosure.

"Here is where we transport the ore out of Cerro Rico."

Two shirtless miners rested opposite of us on the ground with shovels beside them as the headlamps of three others approached from behind a cart further down the mine. Navigating the broken rails, the distant trio slammed and strained their bodies all the way to our clearing. They rocked the cart to its side to topple their one-ton load of tailings onto the floor upon arrival. Then, they re-erected the cart and pushed it back into the loud darkness as the shovelers rose to load the debris into a bin.

The eventual pull of a draw cord signaled to the surface that the bin was full, whereupon it was pulled up by rope to the sluice boxes on top. Not once did the miners try to entertain our company, even despite our whispered murmurs and camera flashes throughout the ordeal. Instead, with their limited breaks, they just sat back down, filled their mouths with coca leaves, and stared in exhaustion at the floor that they'd just cleared.

Tata led us twenty minutes deeper to an agonizingly hot 95F degree dead-end with four more miners huddled ahead.

"And here is where we extract the ore from the mountain," Tata screamed over the roar of generators and gas lines behind her. "We can only be here a short time without getting in the way of the carts, so take your pictures quickly."

There at a half-mile's total depth, the final four miners chipped away at a silver vein above us with pickaxes at the end of the tunnel. Hunched over and covered in soot, they slammed their axes into the mantle and pushed their tailings down a ramp into the carts. They were dripping with sweat, contorting awkwardly, and exerting full force under the deafening roar of surrounding chaos. Petrified, I stared in awe of the vicious labor until Tata ushered me forcefully out of the way of the next cart.

Back on the surface, I removed my facemask to find it blackened at the end of our one-hour tour. The miners hadn't been wearing facemasks, I acknowledged as the sensory intensity subsided. Only then did Cerro Rico's brutality begin to hit me. I turned to Charlie for reassurance from his mining background.

"Are you kidding? They're still using four-hundred-year-old technology following tiny veins, killing themselves for fourteen dollars a day. The First World stopped mining like that two centuries ago. Instead of digging hundreds of little holes, we just move the whole damn hill now! A real mining company would consume that mountain in months, ripping it apart and pulling the good bits later," Charlie exclaimed back tensely.

"Consider yourself lucky to not have known the dangers in there, mate," he continued. "One gas pocket, one earth tremor, or one falling rock would have killed us all. That suffocating workplace and its miners' inevitable demise are inexcusable, given available modern technology. No wonder they were rioting in La Paz!"

Nora elaborated on what we'd seen as I continued to wrap my head around Bolivian labor standards that evening.

"The current government under President Morales does not allow foreign investment. That is why these conditions continue. Bolivia is heading rapidly toward a communist dictatorship, due to Morales's alliances with Castro and Chávez," Nora expounded during our goodbye dinner with her and Hans.

As an outsider, I couldn't speak to Morales's leadership, but one look at the Cerro Rico mines had confirmed that Bolivia had a problem.

"Worst of all is that Cerro Rico is a co-op by name, but the oligarchs up top still collect the real money," Nora concluded. "Someday the injustice will be curbed, but in the meantime, a lot more Bolivians are going to die."

FOUR WHEEL DRIVE

Uyuni, Bolivia
Thursday, October 20th, 2011

Charlie and I were ready for a change in scenery after Cerro Rico. So, we were excited on Tuesday when Bolivia transformed into burgundy rock ledges and yellow sand deposits enroute to Uyuni. Dotted with intermittent cacti and tumbleweed, the landscape was a stark contrast to the brown, barren blend of the recent Altiplano. In fact, Tuesday was the actual set of a Wild West classic.

"On your way to the Uyuni you will be riding through the exact same canyons where they filmed *Butch Cassidy and the Sundance Kid*," Nora had explained at departure that morning.

Although there were no remnants of Hollywood, the backdrop was remarkable.

Tuesday's most impressive view came on the outskirts of Uyuni that afternoon, where Charlie and I first laid eyes on the world's largest salt flat. Salar de Uyuni was a great white expanse stretching indefinitely into the northwest horizon ahead, and on its opposite "shore" began Bolivia's famous Atacama—the world's driest non-polar desert.

The outpost of Uyuni was the gateway to the boundless exploration of the Salar's harsh and disorienting terrain, which Charlie and I planned to experience first-hand. We knew better than to put our bikes through the Atacama's rigor, though. Our first stop in Uyuni was to sign up for a three-day Land Cruiser tour of the countryside.

Our grizzled guide, Robert, was difficult to comprehend through his seven total teeth and pre-elementary English as he stepped down from behind the wheel to pick us up the next morning, but his opening remarks set a tone for adventure, regardless.

"Hi everybody, I am Robert, like De Niro, and I used to work in the Potosí mines. When I was fourteen, my mine collapsed and killed half of my coworkers at once. The rest of us drank our own urine for eight days until rescue. I'm grateful to be alive and excited to be your guide. This trip is not nearly as dangerous, but do not stray over the next three days, or you could get lost forever."

He tipped his ragged hat and waved us into a late-1990s Land Cruiser.

A 6,000-square-kilometer slab of foot-thick salt atop a mammoth concealed lake, Salar de Uyuni was stark white, perfectly flat, and void of any landmarks as we glided across it to start Robert's tour. The only visible dissonance, apart from the blue horizon and white landscape, was a pattern of residual pentagonal evaporation lines, which formed into one another like the stencil of an endless soccer ball across the surface.

The sensory deprived panorama made our ninety mile per hour cruising speed feel like standing still, as Robert navigated indistinguishable ruts without GPS or even a map to our first stop on Fish Island. After lunch on the small rock atoll, he taught us how to use clever camera perspectives against our infinite backdrop for illusory photos. We snapped Charlie standing inside a cereal bowl, my being crushed by Charlie's boot, and best of all—my smiting a tiny-sized Charlie.

Robert checked us in at a hotel built entirely of salt on the opposite side of the flats that afternoon. Hotel de Sal's walls were constructed of salt bricks and salt mortar, its chairs and tables of stacked salt slates, and its floors of crushed salt. "Pass the salt" jokes were overplayed as Charlie and I acquainted ourselves with the accompanying guests over an expectedly salty soup that evening. Overnight, my salt mound bed frame proved to be a poor insulator in the freezing high desert.

The 12,000-foot Atacama hosted neither vegetation or landmarks, aside from the distant 6,000-meter peaks, as Robert again drove wherever he liked atop sand and gravel rock plains for hours. Our first stop of the day promised plenty of intrigue when a mogul field of dirt domes appeared across the otherwise blank landscape.

"These little mounds are not natural to the Atacama," Robert pointed as he parked alongside them. "They are the remains of a pigmy mummy graveyard. Most of the tombs have already been looted, but you can still see what the pirates left behind."

I stepped down from the Land Cruiser and approached the nearest knoll, which stood five feet high. I pulled off my sunglasses and peered into the hole in its wall at the person inside. Sitting upright in a fetal position, the child-sized mummy was mostly skeleton with intermittent patches of skin and an oblong alien head (the result of ancient infancy ritual). Robbed long ago of all its afterlife treasures, the figure's only remaining artifacts were the leather shoes still laced to its feet.

There were maybe twenty mounds in total, each of which contained its own distinct mummy with its own unique character. I gazed across the graveyard reverently after studying each one. Of all the places to be eternally preserved, the solitary Atacama would have been low on my list. As if we'd never been there at all, we departed without a trace.

The Atacama remained dead numb on the heels of the mummies' glaring mortality until a dark red lagoon emerged on the horizon like a mirage a hundred miles later. The color was so sharp that I thought my eyes were deceiving me until Robert confirmed it.

"Wake up for a phenomenon, everyone! Look at the water—that coloration is caused by phosphorescent Atacama microbactierials."

The ruddy color pervaded bizarrely from shore to shore like nothing I'd seen before. When we parked at its edge, Charlie pointed offshore toward a flock of unmistakable birds wading nonchalantly in the shallows.

"Bloody hell . . . flamingos?"

"Yes—the wild flamingos eat the microbacterials, which is why they turn pink," Robert nodded. "You see, the Atacama is very alive!"

There were several other Land Cruisers parked nearby leading other tours. As everyone else scurried excitedly with their cameras, I sat down on a rock by myself. The sight of such regal animals in the Atacama was too contradictory for me to absorb through a camera's lens. Instead, I stared onward undistracted, burning permanently into memory the images of wind dancing across blood red waters and flamingos flourishing in an empty desert.

The following day, after another frigid slumber, Robert woke us at 4AM for our ten-hour drive back to Uyuni, during which my hands didn't warm up until our first stop at a series of geysers.

"The edges are soft and will collapse if you get too close," Robert warned before letting us out to explore.

The geysers steamed vivaciously ahead.

"Do not fall in, or you will be boiled alive."

Luckily, not all of the spouts were bubbling magma-hot water, because just down the hill was a hot springs for our first cleanse of the tour. In spite of three days of salted, windswept desert, I felt smooth and supple for the rest of the ride back. I was glad to have spared Thirio from the same paint mixer experience when we pulled into Uyuni. Robert's nine hundred kilometers of salt, sand, and stone would have rattled her to bits and rusted what was left. He confirmed it too when I asked how long his Land Cruiser would last.

"About four seasons, even with full underbody sprays after each expedition," Robert replied.

I stared perplexedly as he pulled away after a wave. Only in Bolivia could the salted Earth be eyed as profit. With all judgments still set aside, I was ready to leave the Third World.

DELIVERANCE

La Quiaca, Argentina
Sunday, October 23rd, 2011

Charlie and I were ready for some class after the harshness of Salar de Uyuni, and Saturday we high-tailed the hell out of Bolivia. Escape did not come easy, because the Argentinean border was still two hundred kilometers south, across washboard gravel just as bad as the Atacama. The ruts were so rough that Charlie's triple-tree rattled one of its four primary bolts loose in the first hour. We harvested a replacement from Thirio's engine guard to keep him going safely. Thirio struggled too, initially with her windscreen slapping wildly against my face guard, and ultimately with her shock failing for the third time. Charlie watched as I pulled off my helmet and spewed a blue streak on the shoulder. He patted my back when I finally gasped for air.

"Well, Tato got you close to Argentina with that fix back in Lima. Better than I expected," he reasoned. "At least your mum is bringing a new shock in only a couple weeks, mate. In the meantime, I recommend you kick it into fourth gear the rest of the way today, because at least you'll only hit every third bump at fifty miles per hour."

"Like riding a broken bicycle, you never forget," I replied shortly. "Good thing I have so much practice already without a suspension."

He and I booked a hotel in La Quiaca after stamping through Argentinean Customs that night. The place had a furnace, hot water, water pressure, Wi-Fi, multiple power outlets, locking doors, and a bidet. More importantly, we could finally flush toilet paper. Both of us celebrated by ordering room service steaks, which measured an inch thick and spanned the entire plate. Seared to perfection with two fried eggs on the side, the meal was matched gluttonously with a liter of beer.

I crashed into bed that evening at 8PM, exhausted at the day's milestone accomplishment. Argentina had been my heart's ultimate destination for the past several years of planning and seven months of riding. I marveled at its visa stamp in my tattered passport before I hit the lights. Eventually, I looked closer and realized I had ninety days to get a job or go home.

SIESTA TIME

Cafayate, Argentina
Wednesday, October 26th, 2011

"Hey Mates, we just read your blogs . . . welcome to
Argentina! We're a day's distance south of you in Cafayate
currently. Come on down for some wine to go with those
steaks. It's been too long!—Eddy and Lizzie."

Charlie and I both read the invitation aloud from our
inboxes Sunday morning in La Quiaca before closing our
laptops, jostling our keys, and racing to pack to see our first
familiar faces since Lima (the first time around). Argentina's
four-lane freeways and well-signed arterials delivered an
unprecedented mix of civil traffic and civic maintenance
across painted hills and long pine forests that afternoon. Even
despite our noontime departure, we still made it to Salta by
6PM.

Salta was our last stop before Cafayate, and it was easily
our most developed city in recent memory. Department
stores, parking lots, and stoplights budded in the southern
hemisphere springtime, with vegetation blooming pinks
and purples everywhere. There were neither stray dogs nor
steaming refuse in the street. Motorists drove with respect,

and the pedestrians used crosswalks. Cafés even dotted each corner, permeating the aromas of espressos and croissants that I'd long forgotten. I felt more modern just driving through.

Charlie and I continued from Salta into coniferous valleys at dusk, as the magnificent Andean sunset preceded a clear starry sky. Moonlit vineyards and virgin wilderness proved to be equally comfortable and exhilarating as we glided through the night. Charlie and I hadn't forgotten the golden rule of riding. Instead, we'd thrown out the rulebook entirely for once. Our headlights sliced the darkness, and our engines shattered the silence until Cafayate shimmered finally onto the nocturnal horizon.

"You two couldn't outrun us forever!" Charlie jabbed as we sat down heavily in our riding gear at Eddy and Lizzie's curbside table downtown.

The last time we'd seen either of them had been barely a month into our trip back in Mazatlán—before the accidents (most of them, at least), the breakdowns, and all the other hardships. Interestingly, it had been springtime then too.

"Well you certainly could have dragged your feet less in Peru," Eddy countered. "Lima wasn't enough the first time around?"

It was clear we still got right along together. Eventually, Lizzie acknowledged a more somber update.

"It's crazy that Alex isn't with you. We heard about his incident when it happened. I can't believe he's still stuck in Ecuador with no timetable on when he can leave."

"The good news is that the old man woke up, but the bad news is that he has permanent injuries," I explained.

Al had sent us an email update just that morning, which we'd read prior to meeting Eddy and Lizzie.

"He's staying positive, despite mounting delays, but the Ecuadorian judicial system is still the last place he wants to be. He hopes to be cleared to leave legally within a month."

"Well, on a happier note, Eddy and I are touring wineries tomorrow. Will you join us?" Lizzie invited after a moment of silence.

Charlie and I both grimaced.

"That sounds romantic Lizzie, but we're much more easily entertained," Charlie smirked.

He kicked his feet up and yawned emphatically.

"I don't know about Tom, but these days every mount on the bike is a mental trip into battle for me. Even after a ride as glorious as tonight's, the war drums of the road are still only beginning to fade from the forefront of my psyche," he continued, raising his beer. "A couple more of these, and then a full day's rest is my agenda for tomorrow,"

"Plus, we're still replenishing our red blood cells after the Altiplano," I nodded in agreement.

Charlie was right. I still needed to decompress too. The condition, corruption, and complacency of Peru and Bolivia had shellacked me so hard that life on the road had turned daunting. Luckily, we both found exactly the reprieve we needed the next day from atop our hotel balcony over the town square.

Cafayate teemed below us in antiquated economic vibrancy, with pedestrians, livestock, and autos all cohabiting seamlessly in a daytime buzz. From the farmers and their harvests to the winemakers and their vintages, downtown Cafayate exhibited an earnest pride for life that I had not sensed since México. There were pretty girls, too, whom Charlie and I admired humbly from the shade of our awning during the city's siesta.

Cafayate was paradise, and our two servers reflected its cool and casual attitude perfectly that afternoon. Reminiscent of my friends from back home, the servers wore backwards hats and neon sunglasses as they bobbed their heads to a funky beat from the kitchen radio. They were unshaven and loose, just goofing around and collecting stories, with ambitious futures and the world at their fingertips. I hadn't seen such optimism in ages.

MENDOZA GIRLS

Mendoza, Argentina
Wednesday, November 2nd, 2011

Charlie and I could have unwound for weeks on our hotel balcony in Cafayate, but rumor had it that Mendoza had the same deep-rooted Argentinean culture on a bigger city scale. That meant even prettier girls, according to our servers on Monday. Charlie and I were excited to follow when Eddy and Lizzie booked southbound tickets.

"Check it out," Lizzie announced proudly when their modern coach arrived. "It's not a chicken bus! See you in Catamarca tonight and then Mendoza tomorrow!"

Mendoza was seven hundred miles away, and Charlie and I planned to keep pace with the Aussies' bus over the next two days. Therefore, the war drums were pounding at full bore as we latched our helmets and pulled on our gloves for the undertaking. Meanwhile, Eddy and Lizzie shuddered at the thought of impending captivity as they stowed their luggage and slid into armchairs. Eddy lowered the window from above us as the bus released its brakes.

"Enjoy your all-day siesta," Charlie joked, revving his engine. "Don't worry on our account!"

"I just found out they serve drinks on Argentinean coach lines," Eddie yelled back smugly, rubbing it in. "I'll ask for an extra stiff one on your account!"

Charlie and I flipped him the bird and flipped our helmet visors down. Then we leapfrogged the bus out of Northern Argentina's diminishing foothills into its agricultural lowlands, where the flat and predictable highways proved ideal for Thirio's shit shock the rest of the day. The Andes were a distant sliver along the horizon for the first time that I could remember as the sun set that evening in Catamarca. Our hostel owner, Julio, treated us like royalty as he explained his own fascination with adventure motorcycling over dinner. He described in detail the surrounding countryside, which he'd ridden extensively on his F650.

"It is a shame about your suspension, or else I'd invite you to tour the northern deserts with me here," Julio concluded at checkout the next morning. "But given your shock's current state, I recommend that you head straight to Mendoza as planned. You will enjoy the exquisite girls more anyway."

With the suspense continuing to build, Charlie and I set out into rolling wine country for an audacious five-hundred-mile run, which put us back in the shadow of the Andes already by 5PM.

"Mendoza is still over a hundred miles away. Do we really want to push our luck with another uncharted night ride?" I questioned hesitantly at dusk.

We scanned for hotels on the outskirts of Bermejo and soon encountered an Argentinean BMW rider, who recognized my accent immediately.

"You are American? I spent several years in the United States playing center for the San Antonio Spurs. My name is Fabricio Oberto."

I was no NBA expert. However, at 6'10", with hair down to his shoulders, Fabricio did not have to convince me. That physique made his R1200GS look like a Honda 90.

"Mendoza is not far. If I were going your direction, I'd take you. It's an easy ride, even at night. Trust me—the girls will be worth the distance!"

After having Fabricio sign our maps, Charlie and I pushed onward for Mendoza in even greater excitemen, and we reunited with Eddy and Lizzie the following morning for street-side scones in Argentina's wine capitol. Mendoza's civic bliss proved clean, bright, and colorful over my coffee at first blush. Its idyllic influences of European colonialism, agricultural prowess, and high fashion pushed new trends subtly while still venerating ancient tradition.

Most importantly, and exactly as promised, Mendoza had the most stunning girls I'd seen since Cali. Mendoza's goddesses commanded attention and walked with purpose. Their hair roughed perfectly atop toned shoulders, while their muted designer stitching revealed undeniably Latin curves. They were everything I'd forgotten that I'd missed about home, combined with everything that I'd learned to love about Latin America.

"Lock it up, Tom," Lizzie teased when I spilled Malbec wine down my chin as one of them passed during Tuesday's dinner.

I was on my fourth day of chronic swivel-neck for the local girls by that point, having yet to even talk to one of them, out of sheer adolescent awe.

"Tom, you've barely closed your jaw once here in Mendoza," Charlie laughed while handing me a napkin. "There's skiing not far off in the Andes . . . are you thinking of pulling up stumps?"

"Not yet," I fanned, jerking my head back from gawking. "But I've never wanted to leave less."

CHEE-LAY

Santiago, Chile
Saturday, November 12th, 2011

Mendoza's five-day break was more than just women and culture—it was also a welcome opportunity to recharge from the inherent risks of adventure motorcycling. Charlie and I could have easily stayed longer before wanting to wander again, but our visitors were incoming to the west in just over a week. So, we rallied on Wednesday to follow Eddy and Lizzie into the Argentinean Andes. On the way, we passed South America's highest peak, Aconcagua.

A short walk from our highway's ascent revealed Aconcagua that morning. The 6,900-meter white beast shimmered through thin altitude air like a distant mirage over its neighboring snowcapped ranges. Aconcaqua's megalith was higher than anything I'd yet seen along the entire Andean stretch, which was no small feat. I shivered at the sight from our 2,500-meter vantage and nodded to Charlie's assessment when we turned back toward the bikes.

"Considering our experiences in the Cordillera Blanca, I'll happily keep my distance from that one, mate!"

337

The Argentina-Chile border crossing proved smooth and routine at 3,200-meter Paso Internacional Los Libertadores, where both countries collaborated to create a fluid stamping process through a single uniform building. Afterward, Charlie and I descended serpentine switchbacks down the steep rock slopes of Chile's western Andean face to the coast, where we caught up with Eddy and Lizzie in Valparaíso.

Wednesday night's Cerro Concepción neighborhood was known to be the cultural heart of Valparaíso because of its showcase embrace of vibrant graffiti and lively colors. Both its thoroughfares and alleys permeated with flowers and artwork alike as we explored. Tim had been exactly right several weeks earlier when he'd written during his visit that "Valparaíso would be the perfect place for some pithy writer to waste a year drunk on wine and chain-smoking."

Despite all the character, I never took any pictures or wrote any notes on Valparaíso's distinct soul during our week-long stay there. Somehow, seven days with a cigarette in one hand and a drink in the other, instead, stirred zero inspiration for me to document.

"That's because you're an adventure writer, not some pithy snob," Charlie explained perfectly when we arrived in Santiago on Friday. "Argentina and Chile are blasé in comparison to what you and I experienced in Peru and Bolivia. I don't know that the capitol here will offer much adventure this weekend either, but at least it is the most modern city either you or I have seen in months."

Charlie was right too. Santiago's streets were free from holes, rebar, bums, and garbage. Furthermore, its expansive parks, enigmatic architecture, and energetic development connected seamlessly via subway from our Bellavista hostel. Everything from its culture to its customs to its class would be ideal for our incoming guests.

"This really is a great spot for us all to launch into the next phases of our adventures," Lizzie beamed during dinner on Friday night. "I just wish that it didn't mean goodbye."

"Right—we fly to Europe in two weeks out of Buenos Aires, mates," Eddy continued. "There is plenty that we need to see there, so we're catching a cross-continental bus tomorrow. I'm afraid this is likely the last you will see of us on this adventure, but there will be more opportunities down the road, I'm sure."

"Well, the last several weeks with you two lovebirds were beginning to feel like a lesson in couple's therapy for Tom and myself anyway," Charlie joked back. "At least now Lizzie won't have the two of us bad boys distracting her doting Eddy."

"Although I suspect Charlie and I will learn newfound respect for you two immediately as we try to secure non-motorcyclized transportation this weekend for the first time in almost a year," I agreed.

I needed to book bus tickets to Buenos Aires and back for Mom's two-week stay. Meanwhile, Charlie needed to hire a rental for his upcoming four-week road trip with Andrew and Greg. Neither of us had a clue on where to start.

"For once we could use the expertise of backpackers," Charlie continued to tease. "Anyway, wish us luck!"

Charlie and I waved Eddy and Lizzie off for the last time when dinner ended. Then we lit a pair of cigarettes at the table and ordered a nightcap.

"It's been one hell of a ride, mate," Charlie exhaled as the drinks arrived. "Cheers to the road ahead."

FAMILY REUNION

Santiago, Chile
Thursday, November 17th, 2011

Adventure jammed right back into fifth gear when Mom bounded out of customs to deliver my biggest hug since home.

"I can't believe I'm here!" she exclaimed as Charlie and I picked her up in his Hilux rental.

We headed downtown for an introductory lunch.

"It's great to finally meet you, Lucy. I'd love to pick your brain more about what makes this son of yours tick, but you're undoubtedly exhausted from your flight right now." Charlie suggested after the meal, "How about I drop you two at your condo rental, and then we meet up tomorrow when Greg and Andrew arrive?"

Coming off sixteen hours of continuous airline travel, Mom's enthusiasm was, in fact, short lived. While she napped that afternoon, I took the opportunity to address some long overdue maintenance at Suzuki of Santiago. My principal job for the mechanic was installing inmate Pat's used DR650 shock, which Mom had packed in her luggage.

In addition to the shock installation, I requested that the technician scribe a few other loose ends onto the work order for good measure: clean gas tank, clean carb, clean chain, lubricate cables, lubricate swing arm, lubricate all other moving parts, new fuel filter, new air filter molding, replace leaking hoses, replace horn, and fix anything else broken, missing, or failing. The technician observed Thirio's 25,000-mile odometer and nodded understandingly as I handed over the keys. Then, he gestured toward a rack of brand new DR650s crated behind him, which he'd been assembling when I'd arrived.

"She'll be just like new," he assured me.

I stood and took one last look at Thirio before leaving. The next two weeks were going to be the longest we'd been apart since Alaska, but I knew that she would be in good hands. At ease, I headed back to the condo to find Mom bright-eyed and bushy-tailed from her nap.

That evening as we toured the town, Mom's exuberant passion for adventure left me wondering at what point along the way I'd become so contrastingly jaded. Mom approached every statue and lookout with vigor. She was floored by the sunset atop the San Cristobal Hill funicular rail and engrossed in Santiago's colonial Plaza de Armas.

"Tom, stand over there. OK, smile! You're not smiling . . . OK, great!" Mom directed with her camera on quick draw for the majestic architecture and flourishing markets.

I tried my best to match Mom's gusto as we finished the evening back in Bellavista, at least until her jetlag caught up again and she crashed at 10PM.

Mom and I shared a more equal pace for adventure on Wednesday, when we each bought passes for the local Turistik bus line, which advertised a loop of thirteen stops around the city, with regular interval pickups and drop-offs at each location. What the advertising did not highlight, of course, was that the first seven stops were all within ten minutes' walking distance of each other, and that the other six gems included the mall, the shittier mall, and even the Sheraton Hotel. Mom and I could have walked the entire route with a pair of cab rides for half the cost, but we still managed to enjoy the tour.

We got to know Charlie's brother, Andrew, and his friend, Greg, over a raucous dinner that amassed six empty bottles of wine later that evening. Andrew resembled Charlie, just more mature; Greg resembled Crocodile Dundee, just more polished. Together they triggered a boyish new dynamic to bring the best out in everyone at the table throughout the meal. Despite keeling over in laughter from the first glass to the last, we all sobered quickly for goodbyes.

"Pleasure to meet you both," Andrew and Greg confirmed with smiles when we got outside.

The Aussies were heading south in their rental pickup the following morning. Meanwhile, Mom and I were catching our bus to Buenos Aires. Charlie and I squared up.

"Andrew, Greg, and I are bound for Patagonia, which means we'll be a long way from here when your mom flies out in two weeks. Regardless, I hope we meet again on this continent, Tom," Charlie winked with a firm handshake. "Keep in touch and take care of yourself until then. Oh and Lucy, don't let him get too wild on your watch!"

"What a fantastic friend!" Mom exclaimed as we walked back to the condo afterward. "I'm so glad you and Charlie were able to travel together all this way."

"Yeah, Mom, me too," I replied heavyheartedly.

I'd lost Alex months ago, I'd just waved off Charlie, and on top of that, I'd left Thirio in a garage. Every link of chain from our original posse was broken finally for the first time since Los Angeles. That didn't get me down, because Mom's arrival was filling the gap tremendously—and she was ready for adventure.

GOOD WINDS

Buenos Aires, Argentina
Friday, November 25th, 2011

I couldn't help but feel neutered as I stepped aboard an overland tour bus after nearly eight months of motorcycling. Nevertheless, the cross-continental Andesmar coach line proved surprisingly plush from the moment I sank into my leather recliner. A hot meal and whiskey nightcap helped too as the bus crossed back over the Andes past Mendoza that evening. With the overhead blinds drawn, Mom and I slept for 1,100 kilometers until the scent of the Atlantic woke us on Sunday.

Buenos Aires's unheralded draw unveiled itself immediately as Mom and I stepped off the bus into Plaza de Mayo's morning sea breeze. Magnificent plazas and architectural masterpieces the likes of Paris or Rome stretched hub and spoke in every direction, each outclassing the next with competing columns, arches, balconies, and gargoyles.

On foot throughout our bohemian San Telmo neighborhood, Mom and I discovered the fine arts of Casa Rosada, the magnificent ceilings of the Metropolitan Cathedral, and the grandiose tombs of the National Cemetery that afternoon. We toured the rest of the city via tour bus on Monday, whereupon the scale of Buenos Aires' thirteen-million-soul megalopolis exceeded my wildest expectations as our double decker showcased miles of distinctly diverse districts and boroughs. Our favorite neighborhoods were La Boca, the antique area that was full of sleazy street solicitors, as well as Palermo, the upscale district that was free from tourist commercialism.

Having seen Buenos Aires's highlights by nightfall, Mom and I caught another redeye Andesmar bus back to Mendoza that evening. Tuesday and Wednesday involved wine-touring and window-shopping in Mendoza. On Thursday we escaped to a cottage in the Andean village of Uspallata, where the rustic atmosphere and rustling pines contrasted relaxingly after the past ten days of pinnacle cities. Adventure didn't stop in Uspallata, because Mom and I still managed to stoke adrenaline highs on Friday while rafting the raging Rio Uspallata.

"Well, I certainly learned Spanish for left, right, and forward on the river," Mom exclaimed with a yawn after our 11:30PM dinner (Argentina's normal hour). "How fun! And we still have almost a week to go on Chile's coast."

I nodded and forced a smile, despite my growing concern for the solitude ahead. I'd already received several deflating updates regarding my prospects for camaraderie in the future. The first had been from Alex, who'd emailed me that morning:

"Sorry I wasn't able to connect with you dude, but I got bogged down in Peru and Bolivia with mechanical issues and no Internet after my release from Ecuador three weeks ago. Unfortunately, I'm done here in South America. I've found a traveler in Buenos Aires who is buying my bike this week and then I'm flying home to be with Kristi. She's going to be a part of the rest of my adventures. It was a great ride, dude, and I'm glad you came along. Let's hit the road together back in Lake Stevens on the first clear day that you're home!"

I'd thanked him and told him I would honestly miss his incessant chatter. The next email I'd received was from Tim:

"Good to hear from you, Tom, but Jane and I are wrapping it up now. I proposed to her down here at the bottom of the world, and she said yes in Ushuaia. We're crating the bike up in Buenos Aires this week to head home and start our next chapter. We might even run into Alex there. Good luck, and I hope you can make it to the wedding!"

I'd congratulated them before jumping on Facebook to find a message from Justine:

"Hey there, I took a job offer two weeks ago and called it quits in South America. I'm going to be working in London for the next year. Enjoy the rest of your trip and drop me a line if you're ever in town!"

Meanwhile, I'd still not heard from Charlie since Santiago.

In summary, Alex was on his way out; Tim and Jane were living happily ever after; Eddy and Lizzie were touring Europe; Justine had left the continent; Mom would depart in a week; and Charlie, Andrew, and Greg were off the grid. Thirio and I were shaping up to be the lone survivors within a thousand miles for the foreseeable future.

By Land, By Sea . . .

Santiago, Chile
Wednesday, November 30th, 2011

Mom and I said a teary-eyed goodbye after finishing her trip with a week of surf towns on Chile's Pacific coast. I was sad to see her go.

Thirio puffed right to life on first stroke when I returned to the dealership Tuesday afternoon. It had been over two weeks since she and I had last held each other, and her new shock absorbed my ass luxuriously as I sank into the saddle. All her other creaks and groans were gone too, because of the mechanic's handiwork. Most impressive of all was her new horn, which was chrome with red detailing straight off a Grand Vitara.

After paying the bill, I handed the keys back and asked Tato to leave her parked for two more weeks, because I wasn't going to be riding Thirio just yet. Instead, I'd finally reconnected with Charlie for a spectacular turn of events.

"I don't know that I've got it in me to continue on my own. My only other options are to stay here or go home," I'd explained to him Monday afternoon over a weak Skype connection while Mom packed. "You might be right about pulling up stumps here. Santiago has a windsurfing beach an hour south and a ski hill an hour west, which makes it one of only a handful of places in the world that I could live happily."

"What say we put off any preemptive quitting for at least another two weeks, mate?" Charlie had interrupted.

"I talked to Andrew and Greg. We want you to fly down to Punta Arenas on Thursday, so we can pick you up at the airport. We'll drive to the bottom of the world and turn around for Santiago together," he'd continued with earnest excitement.

"Trust me, you don't want to ride all the way to Patagonia on a motorcycle anyway. The winds and rains were miserable, even in the Hilux. We'd never have made it without heating, air conditioning, radio, windshield wipers, and our locking waterproof cab."

"Go!" Mom had interjected adamantly from her bulging suitcase across the room. "You're lucky to have friends who want to pick you up. Plus, I don't want you riding alone!"

So, with no need for further consensus, I'd purchased a one-way ticket to Tierra del Fuego that evening—and Thursday I would take to the friendly skies.

END OF THE ROAD

Ushuaia, Argentina
Saturday, December 3rd, 2011

Torres del Paine was Patagonia's most recognized range. Images of its peaks had hung on my bedroom walls as the ultimate symbol of adventure throughout my youth, inspiring ambitions to explore the world even before my interest in motorcycling. Located at the southern tip of the Andes, just a day's drive north of Punta Arenas, Torres del Paine had more recently become the ultimate symbol of my overland dream as I'd inched toward it for the past eight months.

Unfortunately, Charlie, Andrew, and Greg had already toured Torres de Paine National Park during the week prior to our reunion. My singular regret as I boarded at Comodoro Arturo Merino Benítez International Airport on Thursday was that I was going to miss the formation entirely. Then, as luck would have it, the skies proved crystal clear to the south from 20,000 feet.

"Ladies and Gentlemen, those of you on the left side of the plane will be able to look out your windows and see the Torres del Paine range for the next several minutes," my LAN pilot announced mid-flight as I slipped open my window.

One by one, the alien peaks moved into view, with each enigmatic spire clawing right up at me from the head of Glacier Grey. The sight was everything I had always imagined from Patagonia's landmark landscape. Charlie, Andrew, and Greg had hiked fifteen miles over the past three days to see those same peaks from the ground, and yet I'd managed to land an over-the-top aerial view by chance. The Aussies had earned a more intimate experience, absolutely, but I was smitten nonetheless, given my previous resignation to missing Torres del Paine altogether. I watched the rest of Patagonia pass slowly beneath me until the Andes petered out for the first time since Colombia. The plane touched down in Punta Arenas, with South America narrowing toward Tierra del Fuego.

"Sounds like you got some bang for your buck on that flight, mate," the Aussies all agreed as I explained the experience to them at baggage claim. "You would have enjoyed the hiking we just did, but you would have hated the prices equally. Patagonia was expensive, and it pissed rain the whole time we were there!"

Charlie, Andrew, Greg, and I piled into the Hilux and found a hotel in Punta Arenas. We plowed through four boxed wines in two hours to kick off a jovial evening that would lead inevitably to a 3AM last call at the local casino. Friday morning was consequently painful as we awoke just hours later to cram back into the Hilux for an early start. Our 7:30AM hangover haste was partly to escape Punta Arena's mandatory tsunami drill that morning, and more importantly, to get Greg to the airport for his pre-planned flight home.

"Well mates, it's been an amazing adventure," Greg squinted as we approached departure drop-off with the tsunami sirens starting. "But I reckon you'll keep making the most of it without me. Have fun out here while I'm back at work. Now hurry and get out of here before the authorities send you to higher ground."

Charlie, Andy, and I waved back and smiled before driving south into worsening headaches for the remainder of the day.

We reached Ushuaia finally at 9PM in broad summer daylight after three hundred kilometers of Tierra del Fuego's remote windswept plains. Tierra del Fuego was so desolate until that point that I'd anticipated Ushuaia to be a hardened port at the end of a windy spit. Waterfalls, rivers, and lakes were a welcome surprise upon arrival.

Tucked in the shadow of the Martial Mountains, Ushuaia's outpost atmosphere triggered the overwhelming sense of a true frontier, just like Alaska. I felt adventurous just waking up there, and I certainly didn't need a map to determine that I was at the end of the Earth. Hosting helicopter flights, penguin tours, and Antarctic excursions, Ushuaia teemed with adventure tourism at every corner, but the opportunity just to gaze out across the convergence of the Pacific and Atlantic Oceans at passing icebergs was enough for me. It was there on the beach that my mood turned melancholy.

Despite having finally reached the bottom of the world after eight months on the road and three and a half hours in the air, I felt like I'd left something unfinished by leaving Thirio behind—as if I'd abandoned the one principle that I'd managed to still hold onto since Seattle. I began to fixate on how many days it would have taken to ride those five thousand Patagonian miles instead of fly them. I started calculating a budget that could have afforded the endeavor, just barely. When I couldn't take it any longer, I even bemoaned the tragedy aloud to Andrew, who in turn, replied pointedly.

"Pole to pole in twelve months is plenty good, regardless of how you did it, mate. Plus, you didn't ride from the tip of Alaska to start this off, either. As I understand it, you flew back to Seattle, rode a dirt bike 20,000 miles to Santiago, and then flew again to Ushuaia in a mirror for both hemispheres," Andrew assured me with wide eyes.

I nodded reluctantly as he continued.

"After a trip like this, you should know better than I that there are compromises in everything. That's what makes adventure interesting. Nothing ever goes according to plan.

You can't fret about what you can't control. You just need to recognize that what you've managed to accomplish here is amazing."

Andrew's words hung in the air as I continued to stare back out to sea from Cape Horn.

"You're right, Andrew," I replied eventually. "I don't know why I'm so hung up on principles at this point anyway. Alex and I planned to ride all the way around the world originally, and that idea was scrapped before we even started. We also expected to ride the whole way together, which didn't happen. In fact, all of my principles have been challenged or broken at one point or another over the past eight months."

I skipped a rock across the ocean in front of me.

"Of course, I'll want to have ridden Thirio everywhere from now on. That's the love for the ride that I never want to lose, but the truth is that there are more important aspects to life than principle—and I'm happy to have ended up here at all, given what it took to learn that."

"Right," Andrew confirmed. "This last-second decision to fly for the sake of camaraderie doesn't sour anything. It's a continuation of your life's grand adventure."

FIN

Santiago, Chile
Thursday, December 22nd, 2011

Salar de Uyuni was where I first started dwelling on home in the same way that I'd use to dream of adventure. Even there in the center of the world's largest salt lake, all I could think about was waxing my skis, reinstating Xbox Live, and tinkering on my Yamaha 550. The novelty of familiar surroundings, clean clothes, and a steady diet beckoned against the reality of living from stuff sacks, smelling like gasoline, and surviving on fast food.

I wasn't ready to quit then, because in my head this had always been a ride from Seattle to Buenos Aires. I still needed to keep moving for the sake of telling the story to American girls (because, face it, Seattle to Potosí just didn't have the same ring to it).

I finally revisited those feelings during the 2,200-kilometer drive to Bariloche from Ushuaia—on my way north for the first time in almost an entire year. There in the midst of two border crossings and one ferry ride, with Tierra del Fuego fading in the rear-view mirror and Patagonia framed ahead in the windshield, I found myself ignoring the local splendor completely. Instead, I was raving to Charlie and Andrew about Yosemite National Park and the Cascade Mountain Range. That trend continued when we arrived at Bariloche in the Argentinean Andes. Again, I contrasted the dense evergreens and placid waterways to Washington's forests and Wisconsin's lakes.

A tourist getaway for Argentinean and Chilean elite, Bariloche blossomed in the rugged Andean summer as we rested at a lakeside cabin rental on the shore of Lago Gutierrez. The erupting volcano, Calbuco, to the northwest, piled ash by the inch the whole time, creating an unforgettable hue across the royal blue shoreline. Bariloche was one of the most beautiful places I'd seen, regardless of the limited visibility and browned snowfields. Still, my appreciation for home had never been higher.

National media back at home had begun to convince me that the United States' best days were in its past before I'd left, but a couple border crossings to the south was all it took to understand the power and draw of the USA from the road. Seattle traffic and partisan politics were inconsequential problems compared to what I'd witnessed in the rest of the world since leaving. Just because we didn't have the rest of the planet by the jugular anymore didn't make the United States any worse of a place to live. The look across every foreigner's face when met by an American was a reminder that the United States still symbolized exceptionality throughout the world. For the first time that I could remember, I wanted to return home rather than escape it.

We continued north to the Chilean ski town of Pucón after Bariloche, and it was there that I realized I had nothing left to prove on the road. Such blissful complacency in the face of unbridled opportunity would have been blasphemous back in March, but all I wanted was to sunbathe, eat, and sleep in Pucón.

Back in March, I'd spent the two past years working my fingers to the bone to reach the precipice of this grand adventure around the world. My conviction in seeking the wildest imaginable escapade had been so unwavering that I'd even thrown myself a "Ready to Die" birthday party during my final days in the Pacific Northwest to prove a point to everyone who was worrying. Having since stared down a gun barrel, watched Alex disappear underneath a truck, and lost Bitsey without saying goodbye, I finally acknowledged in Pucón that I'd pushed the envelope plenty after traveling 20,000 miles unscathed. Nine months later, my focus was on living long and well, rather than constantly by the seat of my pants.

The final leg of our return drive north delivered us back to Santiago in mid-December, where the Chilean rental agency was not thrilled to find that we'd added 9,000 new kilometers to the Hilux's odometer. That night, Andrew readied for his return flight to Australia, while Charlie and I confronted our own futures.

"Mum wanted me to thank you for taking care of my little brother all these months, Tom. Great to meet you, mate. Come visit Perth at any time," Andrew saluted gregariously to me when we dropped him at the airport.

He hugged Charlie next.

"Charles, we miss you at home. Do return in one piece."

Neither Charlie nor I spoke of Andrew's final statement as we tore aggressively into a pack of cigarettes back at the hostel that night. Instead, we did our best to ignore it by contemplating Uruguay and Brazil as our next logical steps. The bikes could handle it without issue, we agreed cautiously. We outlined every element of the journey, including financing, weather, and language barrier. Eventually, the plan was dialed completely.

Then, Charlie and I went unexpectedly reticent. We both continued to stare at the map again, as if burrowing for more information. The silence turned deafening. With nothing more to decode, we looked back up. Staring at each other tiredly through the thickening smoke, a sudden unflinching nod was all it took for each of us to admit in unison that he no longer had the grit to keep riding.

"Well mate, all good things must come to an end," Charlie remarked nostalgically, after a long pause. "I know that I've seen enough of the world to hold me over for a while, and from the look on your face, it seems that you're not going to talk me out of it. What do you say we get the hell out of here?"

I couldn't have agreed more. For the first time since I'd been asked it for the past two years, I finally knew how to answer the incessant question: "What are you going to do when you get back." I had heaps of short-term and long-term objectives to hit the ground running when I got home. The what, where, and how would just be details along the way. Adventure had given me perspective on what I needed to be satisfied. At the same time, it had illuminated countless pathways and expanded limitless parameters. I was determined to never quit wandering with curiosity, but always in forward motion, without ever treading water. The Gonzaga University School of Business was right that globalization was the future of our economies, and my next adventure would be to leverage my international experiences to a sizeable advantage back home.

"I've accomplished my goal to live freely, at least for once. Life is short, but I've got a long future ahead of me too. Let's get off this continent with our health and no regrets. I'm ready to hit the ground running and make the rest of my twenties count for a lot," I smiled back with certainty.

We extinguished our butts to wrap it up.

"What do you say we get the gang back together for Alaska again in coming years?" I asked Charlie as we shook hands before his Tuesday flight home.

The bikes were already crated onto boats for a twelve-week ocean voyage home.

"I'm imagining stronger bikes, smarter routes, and lighter gear—and the opportunity to focus more on riding and less on partying. Next time, I want sunrise starts and legendary mileage."

That wasn't to say I regretted the partying to date. At twenty-four, I was the youngest adventure motorcyclist that I'd encountered along the entire trip, and I'd had an absolute kickass time.

"Right then, cheers! Thanks for coming along, mate. It's been a pleasure. Now don't go home and do something stupid like getting married," Charlie grinned as we hugged at the departures gate.

I remained in Santiago two more nights on my own as the last of my kind before boarding a sixteen-hour flight home that would cover the same distance as my nine-month adventure. I threw my last pack of smokes in the garbage and vowed never to touch them again as I arrived at the airport. Then at takeoff, I dialed the *Indiana Jones* theme song on my iPod and imagined my intrepid red line stretching the boundless globe beneath me.

Also from Road Dog Publications

Those Two Idiots![1 2] *by A. P. Atkinson*
Mayhem, mirth, and adventure follow two riders across two continents. Setting off for Thailand thinking they were prepared, this story if full of mishaps and triumphs. An honest journey with all the highs and lows, wins and losses, wonderful people and low-lifes, and charms and pitfalls of the countries traveled through.

Motorcycles, Life, and . . .[1 2] *by Brent Allen*
Sit down at a table and talk motorcycles, life and . . . (fill in the blank) with award winning riding instructor and creator of the popular "Howzit Done?" video series, Brent "Capt. Crash" Allen. Here are his thoughts about riding and life and how they combine told in a lighthearted tone.

The Elemental Motorcyclist[1 2] *by Brent Allen*
Brent's second book offers more insights into life and riding and how they go together. This volume, while still told in the author's typical easy-going tone, gets down to more specifics about being a better rider.

A Short Ride in the Jungle[1 2] *by Antonia Bolingbroke-Kent*
A young woman tackles the famed Ho Chi Minh Trail alone on a diminutive pink Honda Cub armed only with her love of Southeast Asia, its people, and her wits.

Mini Escapades around the British Isles[1 2] *by Zoë Cano*
As a wonderful compilation of original short stories closer to home, Zoë Cano captures the very essence of Britain's natural beauty with eclectic travels she's taken over the years exploring England, Ireland, Scotland, and Wales.

Bonneville Go or Bust[1 2] *by Zoë Cano*
A true story with a difference. Zoë had no experience for such a mammoth adventure of a lifetime but goes all out to make her dream come true to travel solo across the lesser known roads of the American continent on a classic motorcycle.

I loved reading this book. She has a way of putting you right into the scene. It was like riding on the back seat and experiencing this adventure along with Zoë.—★★★★ Amazon Review

Southern Escapades[1][2] by Zoë Cano

As an encore to her cross country trip, Zoë rides along the tropical Gulf of México and Atlantic Coast in Florida, through the forgotten backroads of Alabama and Georgia. This adventure uncovers the many hidden gems of lesser known places in these beautiful Southern states.

> . . . Zoë has once again interested and entertained me with her American adventures. Her insightful prose is a delight to read and makes me want to visit the same places.—★★★★★ Amazon Review

Chilli, Skulls & Tequila[1][2] by Zoë Cano

Zoe captures the spirit of beautiful Baja California, México, with a solo 3 000 mile adventure encountering a myriad of surprises along the way and unique, out-of-the-way places tucked into Baja's forgotten corners.

> Zoe adds hot chilli and spices to her stories, creating a truly mouth-watering reader's feast!—★★★★ Amazon Review

Hellbent for Paradise[1][2] by Zoë Cano

The inspiring—and often nail-biting—tale of Zoë's exploits roaming the jaw-dropping natural wonders of New Zealand on a mission to find her own paradise.

Mini Escapades around the British Isles[1][2] by Zoë Cano

As a wonderful compilation of original short stories closer to home, Zoë Cano captures the very essence of Britain's natural beauty with eclectic travels she's taken over the years exploring England, Ireland, Scotland, and Wales.

Shiny Side Up[1][2] by Ron Davis

A delightful collection of essays and articles from Ron Davis, Associate Editor and columnist for *BMW Owners News*. This book is filled with tales of the road and recounts the joys and foibles of motorcycle ownership and maintenance. Read it and find out why Ron is a favorite of readers of the *Owners News*!

Rubber Side Down[1 2] by Ron Davis
More great stuff from Ron Davis.

[Ron] shares his experiences with modesty and humor, as one who is learning as he goes along. Which is what we all do in real life. And he does what all the best motorcycle writing does: he makes you wonder why you aren't out there riding your own bike, right now...his work simply helps you stay sane until spring." –Peter Egan, Cycle World *Columnist and author of* Leanings 1, 2, *and* 3, *and* The Best of Peter Egan.

Beads in the Headlight [1] by Isabel Dyson
A British couple tackle riding from Alaska to Tierra del Fuego two-up on a 31 year-old BMW "airhead." Join them on this epic journey across two continents.

A great blend of travel, motorcycling, determination, and humor. —★★★★★ Amazon Review

Chasing America [1 2] by Tracy Farr
Tracy Farr sets off on multiple legs of a motorcycle ride to the four corners of America in search of the essence of the land and its people.

In Search of Greener Grass [1] by Graham Field
With game show winnings and his KLR 650, Graham sets out solo for Mongolia & beyond. Foreword by Ted Simon

Eureka [1] by Graham Field
Graham sets out on a journey to Kazahkstan only to realize his contrived goal is not making him happy. He has a "Eureka!" moment, turns around, and begins to enjoy the ride as the ride itself becomes the destination.

Different Natures [1] by Graham Field
The story of two early journeys Graham made while living in the US, one north to Alaska and the other south through México. Follow along as Graham tells the stories in his own unique way.

Thoughts on the Road [1] [2] by Michael Fitterling
The Editor of *Vintage Japanese Motorcycle Magazine* ponders his experiences with motorcycles and riding and how they've intersected and influenced his life.

Northeast by Northwest [1] [2] by Michael Fitterling
The author finds two motorcycle journeys of immense help staving off depression and the other effects of stress. Along the way, he discovers the beauty of North America and the kindness of its people.

. . . one of the most captivating stories I have read in a long time. Truly a MUST read!!—★★★★★ Amazon Review

Hit the Road, Jac! [1] [2] by Jacqui Furneaux
At 50, Jacqui leaves her home and family, buys a motorcycle in India, and begins a seven-year world-wide journey with no particular plan. Along the way she comes to terms with herself and her family.

Asphalt & Dirt [1] [2] by Aaron Heinrich
A compilation of profiles of both famous figures in the motorcycle industry and relatively unknown people who ride, dispelling the myth of the stereotypical "biker" image.

The Hog, the Dog, and the Iron Horse [1] [2] by Alex Kendall
A Brit crosses the pond in search of real America and real Americans. After a stay in Manhattan, Alex sets out by Greyhound bus (the "Dog") bound for the West Coast and returns by train (the "Iron Horse"), finally traversing north to south on an iconically American motorcycle (the "Hog"). Flavors of Kerouac and Thompson flow through this unique narrative.

Chasing Northern Lights [1] [2] by Miguel Oldenberg
A Venezuelan immigrant sets out to get to know his new country on the motorcycle ride of a lifetime.

A Tale of Two Dusters & Other Stories [1] [2] by Kirk Swanick
In this collection of tales, Kirk Swanick tells of growing up a gearhead behind both the wheels of muscle cars and the handlebars of motorcycles and describes the joys and trials of riding

Man in the Saddle [1] [2] *by Paul van Hoof*
Aboard a 1975 Moto Guzzi V7, Paul starts out from Alaska for Ushuaia. Along the way there are many twists and turns, some which change his life forever. English translation from the original Dutch.

Dis Big Pella Walkabout [1] [2] *by David Woodburn*
A unique tale of travel around the world by an Australian, his Philipina wife, and infant daughter on a BMW sidecar rig. Composed of two "books" in one, it is a mobius strip of sorts, with one book telling of the family's struggles crossing the African continent while the other provides a reflective biography of the author and the background of his subsequent adventures until it catches up with the other story.